James Britton on Education

James Britton's work addresses central educational questions that are as relevant today as they were half a century ago. Britton was the architect of a theory of language and learning which has influenced the thinking and practice of generations of teachers across the anglophone world. This Reader helps teachers and students explore his theories of the relationships between language and thought, between thinking and feeling, the links between unconscious and conscious ways of knowing, and the symbolising nature of language.

This carefully curated collection of Britton's key writings renders his work accessible to today's students, educators and researchers. Fully annotated chapters explore how his work fuses observation and theory in a remarkable synthesis, and demonstrates the continuities between the early use of language and later, more complex achievements in speaking, listening, reading and writing.

All those involved in teacher education and training, including researchers and scholars, will find this a rich and insightful text.

Myra Barrs was Honorary Senior Research Associate at the UCL Institute of Education, UK, and former director of the Centre for Literacy in Primary Education.

Tony Burgess has been a secondary-school teacher, before working in research and teacher education at the UCL Institute of Education, UK.

John Richmond has been an English teacher, an adviser of teachers and an educational broadcaster.

Jenifer Smith has been an English and drama teacher in both primary and secondary schools, before becoming a teacher educator at the University of East Anglia, UK.

John Yandell taught in secondary schools for 20 years before moving to the UCL Institute of Education, UK, where he is Professor of English in Education.

James Britton on Education

An Introductory Reader

Edited by
Myra Barrs, Tony Burgess,
John Richmond, Jenifer Smith
and John Yandell

LONDON AND NEW YORK

Designed cover image: Photograph kindly supplied by Alison Britton

First edition published 2025
by Routledge
4 Park Square, Milton Park, Abingdon, Oxon, OX14 4RN

and by Routledge
605 Third Avenue, New York, NY 10158

Routledge is an imprint of the Taylor & Francis Group, an informa business

© 2025 selection and editorial matter, Myra Barrs, Tony Burgess, John Richmond, Jenifer Smith and John Yandell; James Britton's writings, the James Britton Trust and other copyright holders

The right of Myra Barrs, Tony Burgess, John Richmond, Jenifer Smith and John Yandell to be identified as authors of the editorial material, and of James Britton to be identified as author of his writings, through the James Britton Trust and other copyright holders, has been asserted in accordance with sections 77 and 78 of the Copyright, Designs and Patents Act 1988.

All rights reserved. No part of this book may be reprinted or reproduced or utilised in any form or by any electronic, mechanical, or other means, now known or hereafter invented, including photocopying and recording, or in any information storage or retrieval system, without permission in writing from the publishers.

Trademark notice: Product or corporate names may be trademarks or registered trademarks, and are used only for identification and explanation without intent to infringe.

British Library Cataloguing-in-Publication Data
A catalogue record for this book is available from the British Library

ISBN: 978-1-032-87486-9 (hbk)
ISBN: 978-1-032-87485-2 (pbk)
ISBN: 978-1-003-53287-3 (ebk)

DOI: 10.4324/9781003532873

Typeset in Bembo
by Apex CoVantage, LCC

I pin my hopes to quiet processes and small circles in which I believe I shall see, if I'm still alive at the end, vital and transforming events taking place.

James Britton, quoting Rufus Jones

Contents

List of figures	ix
About the editors	x
Acknowledgements	xii
Note of appreciation	xiii

INTRODUCTION: JAMES BRITTON'S LIFE AND WORK   1

SECTION 1   THE LANGUAGE OF YOUNG CHILDREN   17

     1.1 The development of language: 'Learning to speak'   19

     1.2 Early literacy: 'Young fluent writers'   29

     1.3 Meaning-making, interaction and play: 'The anatomy of human experience – the role of inner speech'   38

SECTION 2   LANGUAGE AND LEARNING AT SCHOOL   51

     2.1 The value of talk: 'Now that you go to school'   54

     2.2 'Language and learning'   65

     2.3 In defence of 'progressive' practice: 'Language in the British primary school'   71

     2.4 The disorderliness of learning: From 'Talking to learn'   83

SECTION 3   WRITING — 113

   3.1 Expressive writing: 'Writing to learn and learning to write' — 116

   3.2 Functions and audiences in the development of writing: From *The development of writing abilities (11–18)* — 135

   3.3 What writers have in common: 'Shaping at the point of utterance' — 143

SECTION 4   TEACHERS AND RESEARCH — 153

   4.1 'A note on teaching, research and "development"' — 155

   4.2 'A quiet form of research' — 159

   4.3 The community of the classroom: 'Vygotsky's contribution to pedagogical theory' — 166

SECTION 5   A CERTAIN IDEA OF ENGLISH — 175

   5.1 The scope of English: 'What is English?' — 178

   5.2 'Literature in its place' — 188

   5.3 Autobiographical coda: From 'English teaching: retrospect and prospect' — 198

   5.4 Today's student teachers reading and discussing Britton — 203

Index — 208

Figures

Figure 3.1.1   125
Figure 3.1.2   126
Figure 3.1.3   127
Figure 3.1.4   129

About the editors

Myra Barrs was the author of many books and other publications on language and learning in education, including *Vygotsky the Teacher: A Companion to his Psychology for Teachers and Other Practitioners* (Routledge, 2022) and (as co-editor with John Richmond) *The Vygotsky Anthology: A Selection from his Key Writings* (Routledge, 2024). She was Honorary Senior Research Associate at the UCL Institute of Education, UK, and former director of the Centre for Literacy in Primary Education. She died in 2023.

After teaching in secondary schools, **Tony Burgess** moved to the UCL Institute of Education, UK in 1970, where he worked in research and teacher education until retiring in 2006. He is co-author of *The Development of Writing Abilities (11–18)* (Macmillan, 1975), with James Britton and other colleagues, and of *The Languages and Dialects of London School Children* (Ward Lock, 1980), with Harold Rosen. His particular interest has been on language and learning in classrooms, and more recently on maintaining historical perspective in English teaching discussions.

John Richmond has been an English teacher, an adviser of teachers and an educational broadcaster. He is the author of *The Resources of Classroom Language* (Edward Arnold, 1982), lead author of *Curriculum and Assessment in English 3–11: A Better Plan* and *Curriculum and Assessment in English 11–19: A Better Plan* (both Routledge, 2017) and co-editor with Myra Barrs of *The Vygotsky Anthology: A Selection from his Key Writings* (Routledge, 2024). He is a former Visiting Professor at the University of Nottingham, UK.

About the editors

Jenifer Smith has been an English and drama teacher in both primary and secondary schools. She was a teacher educator at the University of East Anglia until her retirement in 2016. She is co-author of *Introducing Teachers' Writing Groups: Exploring the Theory and Practice* (Routledge, 2015).

John Yandell taught in inner London secondary schools for 20 years before moving to the UCL Institute of Education, UK, where he has worked since 2003. As a teacher and teacher educator, he has written extensively on policy and pedagogy, curriculum and assessment. He is the editor of the journal *Changing English: Studies in Culture and Education,* and the author of *The Social Construction of Meaning: Reading Literature in Urban English Classrooms* (Routledge, 2013) and *Rethinking Education: Whose Knowledge Is it Anyway?* with Adam Unwin (New Internationalist, 2016).

Acknowledgements

The editors are grateful to the National Council of Teachers of English for permission to republish 'A quiet form of research', and to the National Association for the Teaching of English and the editor of *English in Education* for permission to republish 'Vygotsky's contribution to pedagogical theory'.

Chapter 4 of *A language for life* (the Bullock Report), subject to Crown Copyright, is included in this anthology under the Open Government Licence (www.nationalarchives.gov.uk/doc/open-government-licence/version/3/).

The editors would be glad to hear from the copyright holder of *The development of writing abilities (11–18)*, extracts from Chapter 1 of which are republished here, whom we have been unable to trace.

Copyright in all other pieces rests with the James Britton Trust. The editors gratefully acknowledge permission granted by the trustees, Alison and Celia Britton, James Britton's daughters, for the republication of this work.

Note of appreciation

This collection of James Britton's writings reflects the help of several colleagues who sadly died in the course of the book's preparation.

In March 2016, the London Association for the Teaching of English held a conference on Britton's work. The guiding lights behind the calling of this conference were two familiar figures in the world of English teaching: Morlette Lindsay and Anne Turvey. Their recognition of the continuing relevance of Britton's work in education and the need for a re-presentation of his ideas in contemporary times lit the fuse for the return to Britton's writings offered here.

Once the decision had been taken to move ahead with the project, contact with Gordon Pradl at New York University was an obvious next step. Gordon's long working relationship with Britton had led to *Prospect and retrospect* (1982), an edited collection of Britton's writings, which remains an important resource for approaching his work. Some pieces from this earlier collection reappear in the present work, but now, with the whole corpus of Britton's writings available to us, we have been able to select more widely.

Gordon joined our editing in the early stages of the book, contributing insights and suggestions by email from New York, but sadly did not live to see the work completed. Had he done so, he would certainly have checked how adequately Britton's commitment to the teaching of literature was represented. We hope we would have satisfied him in that respect.

Myra Barrs was a central presence in our team of editors, providing an initial impetus for the work and subsequently keeping us at it. Her lifelong interest in Britton's work continuously illuminated the choices and decisions that we made, and her influence will be detected in much of the accompanying commentary.

Note of appreciation

It was her insistence that we construct an introductory reader for a new generation of teachers and educators, not simply a collection of pieces. This we have sought to do. Her death in the final stages of the book's preparation robbed us of her final imprimatur, but the work we offer here would not exist without the fire that she maintained.

Introduction
James Britton's life and work

James Britton was a teacher and educator who has had a major influence on the development of English as a curriculum subject. As Head of English at London's Institute of Education, and subsequently Professor of Education at Goldsmiths College, he offered an intellectual leadership that was widely acknowledged and respected.

Britton's focus on an operational view of language – on young people's real and active use of language, and on real purposes for their talk and writing, reflecting children's intentions and experience – gave impetus to a quiet revolution in English teaching, both in the UK and in other countries.

This book's editors include former colleagues and former students, whose understandings were shaped by the voice that Britton brought to English teaching. We are seeking to re-present that voice, through a selection of Britton's writings, in a manner that will help a new generation of teachers to engage with the hopes of his project and the insights that he offered.

As inheritors of Britton's legacy, and – some of us – as collaborators with him, we are aware of the extensive commentary on Britton's work in his lifetime and in succeeding years. We have not seen it as our task to engage with this in detail. To seek to do so would have been beyond the scope of what we have attempted in the present undertaking. We have hoped to provide an introduction to Britton's work and an invitation to explore it further.

We have drawn on the entirety of Britton's writings in making our selection. We hope that the selection does justice to Britton's ideas and also catches something of his character as teacher and educator. For Britton is remembered by us not only for his contribution to national and international developments, but also for the quality of insight that he brought to everyday instances of teaching and learning.

The induction into English teaching

We begin with a biography, setting out the main lines of Britton's life and contribution to education. We then come to consider Britton's work in the context of his time, and provide an introductory account of his ideas.

Britton was born in Scarborough, England in 1908. His family moved south, and he spent his childhood and youth in city suburbs, attending schools in Clapham, Brixton and Southend. He subsequently completed a degree in English at University College London, in 1929. Unusually for someone with his qualifications embarking on secondary teaching at that time, he studied for a teaching certificate at London Day College, shortly to become the University of London Institute of Education. This was the beginning of a long association.

At that time, English at the Day College was in the hands of Percival Gurrey, a major figure in education, with interests in poetry and language, and particularly in re-shaping the teaching of grammar. While still a young teacher, Britton prepared his own language and composition course for schools, *English on the anvil* (1934), in part as a tribute to Gurrey's methods – and his first act of 'insurrection'. Britton refers to the syllabus presented to him by his first department head – 'the unbroken chain of exercise numbers in *Morgan's Junior English Grammar*': the tradition in English teaching that both he and Gurrey were seeking to transcend.

Britton taught in schools in the 1930s, principally at Harrow Weald County Grammar School, where he worked with Nancy Martin, who became a lifelong friend and colleague. He left Harrow Weald in 1938 for educational publishing, as Head of the Educational Department at John Murray, and stayed in publishing until 1953, interrupted by his war service, where he was three times mentioned in dispatches.

After the war, looking for a move to teacher training, he left John Murray and worked for a year at Birmingham College of Art, before his appointment as Senior Lecturer and Head of English at the London Institute of Education, in 1954. But he was a presence at the Institute long before his appointment, organising a Friday afternoon programme of poetry, drama and other arts activities, and contributing to English seminars.

Britton was also occupied at this time with the development of the London Association for the Teaching of English (LATE), founded in 1947. LATE originated as an initiative from the Institute department. It was decided to turn an informal group of Gurrey's former students, the 'Institute Old Scholars Association', into the new London Association (Gibbons, 2014, p. 7). Britton was a founder member, and his hand is evident in setting the focus of the Association. This was to be on the 'practical study of problems connected with the teaching of English . . . primarily by means of group investigations' (London Association for the Teaching of English, 1947, cited in Gibbons, 2014, p. 7). As LATE's first secretary of studies, Britton coordinated the pattern of working groups that were characteristic of the new Association's way of working.

By the time Britton joined the Institute as Head of English, work in LATE had begun on developing an alternative 'O'-level paper, a key project of the Association led by Harold Rosen, and Britton had himself chaired a working group on *The meaning and marking of imaginative composition* (London Association for the Teaching of English, 1950), one of the Association's first initiatives. The emphasis on enquiry, so central to the development of English teaching subsequently, owes much to Britton's continuing influence.

Those who knew the Institute in those days will not forget the triumvirate of Britton, Martin and Rosen.

Nancy Martin was there first, appointed initially as part-time English tutor in 1944, and then as a full-time lecturer in 1946. Harold Rosen arrived in 1963, after work at Walworth School, and, in teacher training, at Borough Road College of Education. He had worked with Martin at Harrow Weald prior to his call-up to the American army, and was well known through his contributions to LATE. With Britton's departure for Goldsmiths in 1970, Martin was appointed Head of English until her retirement in 1976, and Rosen went on to lead the department, as Head of English and professor, from 1976 to 1984.

In their work together, Britton, Martin and Rosen made the Institute a stimulating place for English teachers and for educators generally. They used their links in LATE and in teacher training to create a network of teachers, and gained from these connections, breaking new ground in a number of associated schools. They promoted enquiry and research, both through LATE's working groups and through their own investigations. Joined in due course by Margaret Spencer, with her interests in literacy, the department became increasingly a focus for international contacts and visiting scholars.

Britton was Head of English at the London Institute for 16 years. He left to become the Goldsmiths Professor of Education from 1970 to 1975, a period which saw the publication of his *Language and learning* (1970). Then, in a strikingly productive retirement across the next two decades, he worked extensively in Canada, Australia and the US, as well as in the UK, as speaker, visiting professor and consultant.

He continued to write prolifically. Some of his most thoughtful essays were written at this time, together with his marvellous book *Literature in its place* (1993).

He also wrote a memoir of war service in Crete, *Record and recall* (1988), in which he probes the interaction between memory and event. Finally, a collection of his poems, written across the years, *The flight-path of my words*, appeared in 1994, just before his death.

We turn in the following two sections to a more detailed account of Britton's work. First, we set his work within the wider national context; then we offer a brief account of his ideas.

In the context of his time

A first step in representing the scope of Britton's work requires a recognition of the hopes for schooling in the post-war years. Britton re-entered work in education, following his war service, at a time of national change. Butler's 1944 education act had pointed, if imperfectly, towards long-cherished notions of secondary education for all. (Its vision of grammar schools and secondary moderns suited to different abilities – the system was never fully tripartite – also clearly preserved existing divisions.)

Introduced shortly afterwards, the Ordinary and Advanced levels of public examinations replaced the former School Certificates for the 16+ and 18+ age groups. However, since the new school leaving age was set at 15, and not raised to 16 until the 1970s, a large proportion of young people leaving school at 15 were destined to continue their lives without any academic system of accreditation. These were years, then, in which new hopes were emerging, but also with much to do.

For teachers, perhaps as always, two considerations went together: the challenge of engaging with the experience of a new generation entering classrooms, and alongside this a commitment to further, more inclusive, development. Across the next decades, national developments included the spread of a comprehensive system of secondary schools, and the introduction of public examinations for all: the Certificate of Secondary Education (CSE) in 1966 and the General Certificate of Secondary Education (GCSE) in 1987, which combined 'O'-level and CSE. Meanwhile, English teaching practice and the structure of the English curriculum developed in classrooms, largely through professional initiatives, though with different levels of external support. Britton and his colleagues were hugely influential here, working with teachers to develop approaches that were responsive to the experience of young people.

Central to the questions confronting practice was how to modify the best of English teaching developed in pre-war years, predominantly in the grammar schools, to meet the needs of an emerging comprehensive education system. Pre-war initiatives had centred on the teaching of English as a living language. It would be wrong to think of pre-war grammar schools as simply enclaves of tradition. Teachers such as Britton had looked to move beyond a methodology based in the teaching of the classics, in which debates about the teaching of grammar were clearly central. The emergence of a new literary criticism in the universities, led by I.A. Richards and F.R. Leavis, was also influencing the teaching of English in school. Issues were already being raised about the textbooks in use in English classrooms and the place of formal exercises in instruction. The emergence of the new comprehensive schools and the raising of the school leaving age from 15 to 16 brought a new edge to these initiatives and questions.

Interests that Britton had developed in his years at Harrow Weald continued to shape his subsequent work: a commitment to the importance of poetry for young people, advocacy for personal and imaginative writing, a re-thinking of the role of grammar. There is no doubt either that his time as a teacher in schools shaped his commitment to the work of teachers, both as a teacher educator and in his research. The drive of his thinking was always a shuttle between observation of young people and explanation, and from explanation back to classrooms; he sought at the same time a community of English teachers, with a shared interest in practice, and a shared acknowledgement of English teaching's significance. The development of Britton's thinking can be traced as much through his contributions to LATE and to teacher conferences and in-service courses as through his published work.

In his work at the Institute, the central thread of Britton's work lay in his commitment to the development of English teaching's rationale, which he found in a focus on young people's use of language and on the part that language plays in their thinking, learning and human development. His interest in the use of language began, though did not end, with the study of his daughters, whose talk he recorded from earliest childhood and which he draws on memorably in *Language and learning*, the book that remains the fullest exposition of his guidance and ideas. The account developed there was the fruit of exploration over many years, continuously shared with teachers and developed by their contributions.

Representing his work, Britton often cites the transition from a behavioural psychology to the cognitive psychology of learning and language acquisition as key markers of his thinking. In fact, he drew on many influences, and an important aspect of the operational view of language that he developed was its synthesis of contributions from a range of different thinkers and disciplines. He turned above all to the cultural psychology of the Russian psychologists, Alexander Luria and Lev Vygotsky, and to the aesthetics of Susanne Langer. Both sources come together in his emphasis on feeling, on the place of felt experience in the evolution of young people's picture of the world, and, in his own words, on the importance of the poetic as well as the transactional in young people's use of language.

The ideas for which he is well known – the notion of expressive language, the categories of audience and function in the development of written language – took time to develop: the fruit of continuous thinking and re-thinking. His earliest research began with his MA in Psychology (1952) where, for his thesis, he pursued the statistical study of improvement in poetic judgement. Later work in the sixties and seventies was partly shaped by a sense of national requirement, yet drew also on insights about young people's language and learning that Britton had been developing. With the founding of the Schools Council for Curriculum and Examinations (1964) and the development of CSE, he directed a project on the *Multiple marking of English compositions* (The Schools Council, 1966), which established decisively the greater validity of shared judgement over individual marking. A major study of writing, *The development of writing abilities (11–18)* (Britton et al., 1975), was seeded by the work on compositions in this earlier project, and was taken further by Martin's later studies of writing across the curriculum (Martin, 1976).

In the sixties, Britton's advice was instrumental in identifying projects besides his own for funding by the Schools Council, including those on oracy and literacy. He was a member of the Enquiry into Reading and the Teaching of English chaired by Alan Bullock, whose outcome was the Bullock Report (Department of Education and Science, 1975), where his hand is evident, especially in Chapter 4, a classic statement of English teaching's rationale. (It appears as 2.2 below.) Later in the report, there is extended reference to 'language across the curriculum', LATE's concept developed in the 1960s, to which he had contributed, alongside Douglas Barnes and Harold Rosen.

Britton was committed to establishing national and international frameworks for collaboration and enquiry, and was a central influence in the growth of national and, ultimately, international dialogue. He was amongst the originators of the new National Association for the Teaching of English (NATE), where the style of work through teacher investigations was carried forward, owing much to his influence and commitment. He played a leading role, with colleagues, in the Anglo-American Conference on the Teaching and Learning of English, the Dartmouth Seminar, held in New Hampshire in 1966, and in the first international conference held in York, England in 1971. Following the Dartmouth Seminar, Britton's was a powerful voice in forming the International Federation for the Teaching of English

(IFTE), along with British and American colleagues. Together with his commitment to developing community in English teaching, Britton was immensely skilled in moving enterprises forward.

Reflecting on his time in English teaching and on his own work, in an article originally written in the seventies, Britton points to a new emphasis in education emerging in post-war years. He refers to this as a 'movement' he has shared in:

> a movement towards a conception of *learning* that gives a quite different meaning to *teaching* – reduces it in fact to an ancillary of learning.
> (Britton, 1982a, p. 172)

Simple as the formulation is, it lies at the heart of the contribution that Britton made, a transition to a new understanding of the priority of learning in thinking about work in classrooms. We turn now to a brief introduction to some of the ideas informing this perspective.

An operational view of language

Much in Britton's work draws on his conception of the nature of human living in the world and the role of symbolic representation. This general, philosophical level of his thinking is the starting point for his approach, with its sense of the human construing of experience, the building up of a picture of the world – in favourite words of his, accumulating a retrospect which enables a prospect. This approach offers us a vision of children and young people as already active thinkers and users of language. It thus becomes imperative for educators to take account of, and work with, this agency. A commitment is required to forms of education that are properly responsive to learners as active participants in their own learning, not mere recipients or consumers.

Language is not the only means available for construing and representing experience, but it is key in the development of concepts and thinking. Britton focuses on the inward, organising, structuring face of language. For the external, communicative face depends, in turn, on the tools provided by language to organise and structure meaning.

The shaping power of words is central to how young people acquire language. In the marvellous second chapter of *Language and learning*, Britton draws on his studies of his daughters to make connections with contemporary investigations of language acquisition and with developmental studies of thought and language. His commentary makes available a reading of the work of Luria and Vygotsky, well before these thinkers were taken up within the educational and psychological mainstream.

Britton develops the point that the key to understanding how children acquire language, and how they come to use it, lies in the relation between thought and language. Young children are identifying meanings in the words that they acquire. Every new word learned is also an act of mind. So, meanings evolve for young children, over time, as their concepts form. Britton introduces here the notion of a word as a filing-pin for experience. It is a notion he will refer to again in the often-cited passage in the Bullock Report where he makes the argument for learning as the necessary precondition for instruction.

Following Vygotsky, Britton notes how skills in using language are acquired first in children's social speech and then how a further use of language emerges. The running commentary appears, alongside social speech, as children come to use language to guide their activity. In time, the structure of the commentary gradually abbreviates. External utterance passes inward. The analysis shows how resources first developed in social speech are internalised, as inner speech and as verbal thought.

Through all this, play, fantasy, make-believe and feeling accompany cognition. From his studies of his daughters, and later of his granddaughters, Britton shows how strong is the part of emotional development in releasing the powers of language. Vygotsky's point that in play the child stands a head taller is borne out in the vivid account of Britton's granddaughter playing shops in *Literature in its place* (Britton, 1993, and see 1.3 below), or in his daughter's play with her farm (Britton, 1970, and see 1.1 below).

To summarise, Britton's framework of ideas begins with the notion of symbolic representation, supported by the insights drawn from language and learning, which show how children take over and make use of the resources of language as they learn about the world.

The priorities for the classroom follow from this:

- an operational view of language – language used for real purposes, reflecting young people's intentions and experience;
- complete acceptance of the pupils' language, for the words that children possess from their everyday living are part of who they are;
- talk as central – in acquiring the resources of language and for internalising ideas, including awareness of the part played by listening in spoken language;
- the supportive role of adult listening in developing young people's linguistic resources;

- the principle that written language, both reading and writing, should be developed alongside children's spoken language, with the new resources brought by literacy related to resources acquired through talk.

These are not just simple, child-centred slogans. They derive their value from the thinking that lies behind them – and they have influenced generations of educators. At the same time, we must acknowledge that they represent a very different set of priorities and a very different approach to teaching and learning from the approaches that have become common across much of the anglophone world in recent decades. Britton's ideas represent a challenge to the assumption that teaching involves a simple process of transmission of knowledge, or that the role of the school is to compensate for the linguistic deficits of its students, or even that talk is a distraction from the serious business of learning.

The concept of 'participant' and 'spectator' roles

We come now to the distinction Britton makes between participant and spectator roles, and to the research on the development of writing abilities.

'Once we suppose,' Britton writes in an article outlining categories of writing functions, 'that man operates in the actual world by means of his representation of it, we can see for him an alternative mode of behaviour: he may operate *upon the representation itself* without seeking any effect in the actual world' (Britton, 1971, p. 208).

These two kinds of behaviour – acting on the world by means of the representation and acting on the representation itself – he distinguishes as 'being in the role of participant' and 'being in the role of spectator'.

A favourite example of Britton's is discussion after a party where the talk may shift from a participant search to discover 'who it could have been who left a ring on the wash basin' to spectator-role reflection on the different guests. As he puts it, 'you find yourselves discussing the behaviour of your guests in order to *enjoy* their behaviour in a way you couldn't when they were still behaving. And that's pure spectator role' (Britton, 1982b, p. 104, and see 3.1 below).

The distinction provides the starting point for Britton's discussion of the teaching of literature. It also underpins the taxonomy of functions he went on to develop in his work on writing. More broadly, he saw work in the spectator role as of fundamental concern for English teaching.

To start with literature, Britton knew of course the claims made for the study of literature, based in the promotion of critical reading and the development of judgement. His thinking about literature, though, began in a different place. He wanted to relate the impulses towards storytelling and reflection on experience, found in everyday life and in the lives of children, to the fully developed work of poets and other writers. In the notion of the spectator role, he found a way to carry forward this intention.

In part, the concept helps to mark off literary art from exchange of information or the interchange of knowledge. The creativity of the storyteller or the poet is work on the world picture, elaborating or reconsidering experience, not seeking impact in the world's affairs. But as importantly, the notion of spectator role allowed for connections between everyday storytelling and more developed literary art. Through it, Britton reclaimed the notion of gossip as the informal end of a spectrum of activities – and he was interested, from the first, in children's narratives, in their poetry writing and in their make-believe.

The taxonomy of written language

The thinking about participant and spectator roles is also carried forward in Britton's taxonomy of written language, developed in the course of research into the development of writing abilities. Britton saw the two roles as marking the end points of a continuum determining different kinds of writing. Writing in a participant role is writing to inform or to explain or to persuade, writing carrying forward action in the world. Writing in a spectator role includes the forms of literary art, of poetry and narrative, as well as more informal working on the world picture.

In working out this approach, Britton and his colleagues went on to develop two taxonomies: one, of function – broadly the purpose of the writing, what the writing is for – and, the other, who the writing is for, the audience. In composing, writers make choices within a particular language function and at the same time write for a particular audience. These, in combination, modify the linguistic choices that they make.

The research identified expressive language as a function, at the centre of the continuum, connecting both ends of the model. This was language close to the writer's thinking and to everyday speech: a personal letter, for example. Writing of this kind could be seen as the matrix of other functions, as a starting point, from which it was possible to move in either a participant or a spectator direction. Importantly for teaching and learning, expressive writing was close to the writer's thinking, and, like expressive talk, could serve as a vehicle for the first draft of ideas.

Classifying young people's writing according to these two taxonomies of function and audience provided insight into their development as writers, but the taxonomies also helped to reveal the choices on offer in the school curriculum at that time. The distributions of function and audience showed that options narrowed in the secondary school. A relatively open pattern in the early years was overtaken by a closed one: the dominant model of writing in the secondary school was low-level factual report and the generalised re-presentation of previously given information for a teacher as examining audience. This reflected, of course, curriculum and assessment pressures. It demonstrated the need for changes in pedagogy if the priorities identified by the research were to be taken forward.

In summary, Britton claimed that the writing and thinking processes illuminated through the notion of spectator role are of particular concern for English teachers. Literary study was not abandoned or marginalised; it was re-allocated in the connections made with informal gossip, storytelling, reflection on experience and children's own talking and writing. Through the concept of the spectator role, Britton put literature into touch with processes in the everyday lives of children.

Britton's work on writing is presented in greater detail in this book in 1.2 and in Section 3.

Throughout his career, Britton was guided by a sense that the sharing of experience was central to the wellbeing of young people as they meet the challenges of growing up, a vital emphasis in an educational provision seriously intended to meet the needs of all. There is a philosophical level in this, too: a sense of this activity as intrinsic to human living and a recognition of its human value.

Closing thoughts

A striking feature of the time in which Britton began his work is the joint exploration of new practices and ideas. Within English teaching, there was a sense of an endeavour shared by teachers, by teacher trainers, and also by government inspectors. The goal of secondary education for all called out new energies and new commitments. There is much that we can learn today from this spirit of shared enterprise: it represents an approach to the development of practice markedly different from the experience of teachers today, who are expected merely to implement policies that are devised at a great remove from the classroom, to adhere to notions of 'best practice' handed down from on high, and to meet performance targets that reduce the complexity of their work to a set of pre-specified outcomes.

Britton contributed greatly to the spirit of shared enterprise. The focus of his work gave intellectual leadership to developments in English teaching based on language's role in learning – and he helped to build a set of understandings that was widely shared. He opened up the study of language in classrooms, and at the same time provided a perspective that illuminated these enquiries.

Britton saw the educational questions confronting teachers not as rooted in any one discipline but located at their intersection. His writing therefore draws on several disciplines – philosophy, psychology, linguistics as well as literary study. This is not the usual way in universities, where scholars tend to sit, as he puts it, in 'the dens of their disciplines'. He raided scholarship for teachers and for children in a synthesis drawn from many sources. The breadth of his enquiry is an important aspect of his legacy, together with the quality of his reading of others' work. In the synthesis he offered, he drew attention to and made available a wide range of other perspectives and related thinking, coordinated by his own perceptive commentary. His work raises the discussion of practice to a different level.

His picture of young people, active in using language, working on experience, sorting out the world, changes everything. It throws the focus onto process. It insists on our attending to what is happening in and for the child. It re-allocates the balance between learning and instruction. Quotations from children were never just illustrations in Britton's writing. They are part of the thinking. And it is in this, above all else, that Britton's work offers an approach and a set of resources that might enable us to rethink current priorities and practices: to become properly attentive to what is going on in classrooms and in other more informal sites of learning; to appreciate the agency of children and young people, and to involve them as full participants in their own learning and development; and to question the reduction of school to mere exam factories.

In a collection published for Britton's 80th birthday, friends and colleagues were asked for personal impressions. The Labour politician, Merlyn Rees, recalling Britton as a teacher at Harrow Weald, catches at a memory that, as writers, we also share:

> Increasingly as pupils . . . we knew also that Jimmy treated us differently from others. As adults? Perhaps. As equals? Yes, in a certain sense. The phrase eludes me, but it is something to do with lack of condescension. There was no sloppy friendliness, and in retrospect there never could have been from him, for he is nothing if not sharp in his approach to people and to things.
>
> (Rees, 1988, p. 255)

Rees goes on to emphasise Britton's 'spirit of service' and his commitment to the building of 'community'.

> It mattered to Jimmy Britton as, from his family background, he brought and transmogrified a spirit of service to a fledgling community. It was not a matter of imposing a tradition from older generations of schools; it was creation of a tradition for a new type of school, for different sorts of people, living in a different environment.
>
> (Rees, 1988, p. 256)

Commitments of this sort – to community, to a new vision for new times, and to taking forward a shared enterprise – catch something fundamental about the values that Britton brought to English teaching across the years. It is a commitment that we seek to illustrate in what follows.

Note on gendered language

As a man of his time, it did not occur to Britton, until later in his life, that the use of gendered language in his writings, such as 'man' to mean 'person', 'he' to mean 'he, she or they', 'him' to mean 'her, him or them', was problematic. After some discussion, the editors have decided to leave Britton's usage as it stands; it seemed wrong to force one of the conventions more recently preferred into his work. Readers will notice, however, that in the last of Britton's writings collected here (1993), the man of his time was aware that times were changing, and glad of it.

References

Britton, J. (1934). *English on the anvil: A language and composition course for secondary schools.* London: Foyles Educational.

Britton, J. (1952). 'An enquiry into changes of opinion, on the part of adult readers, with regard to certain poems, and the reasons underlying these changes.' MA in Education, University of London.

Britton, J. (1970). *Language and learning.* Harmondsworth: Penguin Books.

Britton, J. (1971). 'What's the use?'. *Educational review*, 23 (3), pp. 205–219.

Britton, J. (1982a). 'How we got here' [1973], in Pradl, G. (ed.), *Prospect and retrospect: Selected essays of James Britton.* London and Monclair, NJ: Heinemann Educational and Boynton/Cook, pp. 169–184.

Britton, J. (1982b). 'Writing to learn and learning to write' [1972], in Pradl, G. (ed.), *Prospect and retrospect: Selected essays of James Britton.* London and Monclair, NJ: Heinemann Educational and Boynton/Cook, pp. 94–111.

Britton, J. (1988). *Record and recall: A Cretan memoir.* London: Lightfoot Publishing.

Britton, J. (1993). *Literature in its place.* London and Portsmouth, NH: Boynton/Cook Heinemann.

Britton. J. (1994). *The flight-path of my words. Poems 1940–1992.* Bristol: Loxwood Stoneleigh.

Britton, J., Burgess, T., Martin, N., McLeod, A. and Rosen, H. (1975). *The development of writing abilities (11–18).* London and Basingstoke: Macmillan.

Department of Education and Science (1975). *A language for life* (the Bullock Report). London: Her Majesty's Stationery Office.

Gibbons, S. (2014). *The London Association for the Teaching of English 1947–67: A history.* London: UCL Institute of Education Press.

London Association for the Teaching of English (1947). *London Association for the Teaching of English Constitution.* London: LATE Archive, UCL Institute of Education Library.

London Association for the Teaching of English (1950). *The meaning and marking of imaginative composition.* London: LATE Archive, UCL Institute of Education Library.

Martin, N. (1976). *Writing across the curriculum, 11–16.* London: Ward Lock Educational.

Rees, M. (1988). 'Starting a school: Learning with Jimmy Britton', in Lightfoot, M. and Martin, N. (eds), *The word for teaching is learning: Essays for James Britton*. London: Heinemann Educational Books and Portsmouth, NH: Boynton/Cook, pp. 255–256.

The Schools Council (1966). *Multiple marking of English compositions. An account of an experiment conducted by J.N. Britton, N.C. Martin, H. Rosen. Examinations Bulletin No. 12.* London: Her Majesty's Stationery Office.

SECTION

The language of young children

James Britton began his career as a teacher of English in secondary schools. Throughout the 1950s and 1960s, the period which saw the founding of the London Association for the Teaching of English and the publication of some of its earliest studies, the emphasis of his work was on secondary English teaching.

But Britton had a parallel interest in the language development of very young children. He devoted over half of his best-known book, *Language and learning* (1970), to discussing young children's language development at home and at school. Like several other researchers into children's language development in the 1960s and 1970s, many of his observations were based on his own children, whose talk he recorded from their earliest years. Britton's focus, though, was broader than that of most developmental linguists; he was interested not only in the shifting form of children's utterances, or how children acquired speech through interaction, but also in the insights that speech provided into children's pictures of the world and their developing thinking.

In *Language and learning* he also discussed the development of language beyond the early years, and showed how later forms of language, spoken and written, developed from young children's early speech. He described the continuity between young children's pretend play and their later dramatic improvisations, and between their early monologues and their later extended writing. This lucid and coherent view of children's language growth gives teachers at any stage of schooling a longitudinal view of the children they teach, and of the contexts and activities that favour their development.

Britton had read some of the works of Lev Vygotsky – what was then available – and of Vygotsky's colleague Alexander Luria. He was completely convinced by Vygotsky's argument that when children's language, especially in their solo running commentaries, seems to 'die out', it is actually becoming inner speech, and ultimately 'thought itself'. How language changes as it goes through these transformations, what is the nature of 'thought itself', and how dense clots of pure meaning can subsequently be drawn on and drawn out into verbal thought, translated first into inner speech, then expressed in oral language, talk or sometimes indeed as writing (the most elaborated form of language) – this whole process was of the deepest interest to Britton.

1.1 The development of language
'Learning to speak'[1]

In the first passage in this section, from *Language and learning*, we begin with the domestic. These are relaxed scenes in the Britton family home, but not quiet ones. Britton (1970) remarks that in homes 'the talking mainly consists . . . of highly active, sociable and inquisitive exchanges with parents and other members of the household' (p. 51). But when adults are not present, or are otherwise engaged, the children volubly pursue their own concerns, with an adult as a sometimes absent-minded listener. In these examples Britton is present, recording what is going on, and probably keeping his own notes to supplement the tape recording. He recorded his two daughters, Clare and Alison, for several years and, some 30 years later, he also recorded his two granddaughters. His archive contains a considerable number of cassette tapes, all dated, from both these periods. The recordings were not done on particular or special occasions: they were a routine way of capturing the normal, the everyday, the easy and sometimes slightly chaotic life of a household with young children.

Here Britton eavesdrops on the girls' world-making play, which is often accompanied by what he calls 'a highly characteristic and important kind of talk, the running commentary' (Britton, 1970, p. 54). He is fascinated by children's power to initiate, to generate new expressions, and to be creative users of language from very early on.

Vygotsky's theory of the development of thought is Britton's constant point of reference, and these domestic recordings serve as a concretisation and an amplification of Vygotsky's more abstract theorising.

Exploration of the here and now begins from birth, becomes a more evident activity once a baby can crawl, continues on a new level when names give an additional dimension to objects, and goes on to make full use of talk as a further instrument of inquiry and a means of facilitating activities. From about two years of age most children are prolific talkers. (Valentine [1942] notes that a transcript of one day's talk by a two-and-a-half-year-old occupied 27 pages of a learned journal.) At this early stage, the talking mainly consists, where this is possible, of highly active, sociable and inquisitive exchanges with parents and other members of the household. It is from listening to conversation that children gain experience of language before they can talk, and conversation provides the framework for their first efforts in speech.

The verbal exchanges will normally accompany, or rather form a part of, a continuous chain of activity. A transcript of such talk is meaningless unless we are given some idea of what is going on. The two-and-a-half-year-old (Alison) in the following record has her four-and-a-half-year-old sister (Clare) and her father to talk to (though her father is rather occupied with what he is doing):

ALISON: Mummy give me some milk! I'm a baby. Hna-hna! Hna-hna! I'm a baby – listen to this baby! Hna-hna! Hna-hna!
CLARE: What's she say? 'Hna-hna: hna-hna'?
ALISON: . . . have my Teddy and tucker.
CLARE: Get on, get on! (*addressed to a stool with a belt around it for stirrups*).
ALISON: What are you going to do?
CLARE: Get on this. Dad, don't think these stirrups are very good 'cos your knees stick up over the horse's back. Dad. Just can't get my knees down. (*She starts to sing, gets off the stool and says to Alison who is by now playing with the doll's house:*) Now get on my back. And I'll take you round and round.
ALISON: I want to sweep. Now all going to have a lovely sweep. Sweep the kitchen.
CLARE: That's not the kitchen. That's the bedroom. And that's the bathroom. (*Silence.*) I'll ask that ole Mum if dinner's ready. (*She goes out.*)
ALISON: I tripped with my shoe lace. . . . Open door! Open door! Want to go shopping. (*At the door.*) Want to go shopping this way Dad! Open door! (*He does so. Alison goes out, comes back with a large shopping basket filled with odds and ends. Clare is with her.*)
CLARE (*sings*):

> I danced over water I skipped over sea
> All the birds in the air couldn't catch me

The development of language

> I skipped as slow as I could over water
> I danced as slow as I could over sea
> All the silly birds in the air couldn't catch me.

ALISON: I've gone shopping. Could you have any spouts today?
CLARE: What?
ALISON: Could you have any spouts today?
CLARE: Spouts? You mean sprouts.
ALISON: No, spouts.
CLARE: Of teapots and things?
ALISON: Yes.
CLARE: Well, did you know that I have?
ALISON: No.
CLARE: Well I have.
ALISON: Where?
CLARE: In the kitchen.
ALISON: Dad, will you open the door – I want to find the teapots.
CLARE: No, spouts. Teapots and spouts's the same thing.
ALISON: Open the door, Daddy! (*But she is persuaded to stay.*) I'm just going shopping for a minute. I'm going to get Henry. (*Henry, a stuffed toy dog, is on the table.*)
CLARE: Well get him.
ALISON: Can't . . . heavy. You . . . (*Clare takes her basket for her.*)
CLARE: Surely you can!
ALISON: Can't.
ALISON: Put one foot on one, and one on . . . and get him. Only put one foot on.
ALISON: Can't.
CLARE: Well have your heavy things, then, and I'll get it. (*Does so.*) Didn't try hard enough, did you? If you want to fall down just put *both* feet on the doll's house. . . . Don't suppose you want to.
ALISON: I'm going to school. Going to leave my things. You have him. (*Gives Teddy to Father.*) You have him. (*Gives Henry to Clare.*) Good-bye.
CLARE: Good-bye.
ALISON: See you soon.
CLARE: See you soon.
ALISON: Good-bye. Just going to school. Good-bye.

The two-and-a-half-year-old uses talk to initiate activity, to carry the action in the make-believe scenes, to comment upon what she is doing, and to get cooperation from other people. Her talk at this stage with an adult tended to be rather more inquisitive, and rather less 'active' than is found here.

There is at first not a great deal of difference between talk of the kind we have looked at and the talking aloud that accompanies solitary activity. In the following example, Clare at 20 months is sitting on the floor surrounded with things and talking to herself. While her language is quite obviously less advanced than Alison's at two and a half ('Buy shoes', 'Going shopping' as compared with Alison's 'I want to sweep', 'Want to go shopping' and 'I've gone shopping'), it shows a similarly close relationship between what is happening and what is said, and it is spoken in a similar conversational tone.

> Oh, nice comfy comfy girl. Nice comfy comfy girl.
> Put shoes on. Show Mummy.
> (*Her mother puts her head in the door for a moment and withdraws again.*)
> Mummy come back. (*Not as a request but a flat statement.*)
> Cee's bricks. Ballee. (*She gets it.*)
> In there. And Cee's nappy. (*Putting things in a shopping basket.*)
> Shoes. Shoes shoes. Shoes shoes.
> Look Teddy. See-saw Margery Daw,
> Johnny ave a noo mas-sur. (*Sing-song, rocking to and fro.*)
> (*Puts shoe on her hand.*) Glove.
> Buy shoes. Buy shoes for Cee. Going shopping. Nice.
> Take-a your basket. Going shopping.

I quote this for its interest as a forerunner. Such fragmentary talk accompanying fragmentary activity leads to a highly characteristic and important kind of talk, the running commentary. This is a monologue that many children use frequently to accompany the sort of sustained activity they are capable of at three or four years old.

This is Fiona, aged four years and one month, drawing a picture. She spoke in rather soft tones except where she addressed a remark to her granny, and here she spoke in clear conversational tones. (The remarks of this kind are printed in italics.)[2]

> *I'm going to draw a picture now.*
> Big park and another bit of it coming below. Two bits of it. Colour it in and make it all into one park. Draw St James's Park.
> *Look! Now I'm going to draw a person walking around.*

A little round head. A little eye and another little eye. A little nose. A little mouth. And how big the body is and there's the feet. Hands. *I'm drawing a little girl in the park.*
That's a little girl walking round.
What nice coloured clothes she's got on. What lovely coloured clothes. Clothes. Coloured clothes . . . (*she whispers to herself*).

Clare at four years seven months is playing with a set of model farm animals and farm buildings. Again, the remarks made to her mother (italicised) were spoken in quite different tones from the rest of the talk:

Mummy look, the horses and cows in the same field – they're changing their field.
'N the farmer went and took his own cow and brought it in. Then the land-girl took her big horse back in and got Buttercup calf and brought it back and stayed and looked after it. 'N the chook-lady took its own mum and brought it beside. Then she went back and got the other calf and. – This one hadn't any. – She went back. – She went and took a horse into that field.
And then Mummy they all, all of them took the cowshed in the other field.
Last – when they could get. – Then sheep came through into the cows' field, and another one followed her. And she went and took the biggest horse carefully through the gate and put it down. And then the farmer came along and opened the gate and took the bull through. They couldn't let him stay there very long without a cage. And then they did it all up into one whole side 'cos the next thing they were going to – going to put the cowshed in so all the people, the land-girl and everything – the farmer – all the people went – all round the cowshed – the milk-lady and chook-lady and the bull-man, the milk-man and the land-girl. They all went at the front – then he went there and he went there. – Nobody holded the side they didn't need anybody. Then all of them lifted up and put it in the other field. Oh dear, some of the horses needed coming back so she went and took a donkey back. The land-girl and the milk-girl came in. – And one field was only for cows not for any other except cows. – One thing the cowshed – quite a lot were in the shed – two calves could go in one place in it. They put the bull in one corner – put his pen there – the bull in the pen. The cows and the milk – she went and – the milk – those people – and the land-girl stayed close beside her foal in an empty corner where there was quite enough room for her. And the sheep – they went in the horse field.

The pigsty was put in. . . . (*The game goes on many minutes more, but there are no more comments.*)

So many features of the original speech are of course missing from the written version that it is perhaps difficult to draw satisfactory conclusions. I hope it may be clear nevertheless that in both extracts the differences between the remarks addressed to somebody and the running commentary did not lie only in the tone of voice used. At several points in the commentary there are gaps: sometimes what is unspoken can be supplied but even when it cannot there is no breakdown in the stream of speech. ('Last – when they could get. – Then sheep came through . . .'; 'The cows and the milk – she went and – the milk – those people . . .') It seems likely that satisfactory moving of the pieces was enough, left no sense of incompletion arising from the utterance. That is to say, joint action-and-speech remains continuous though the utterance is broken. The conversationally directed remarks, on the other hand, are pretty firm statements complete in themselves; usually they are statements of intention or recapitulations of the situation.

Both extracts illustrate the fact that the commentary has a tendency to 'go underground'. In particular, the second one suggests that with the end of a problem in sight the support of the commentary was no longer felt necessary, and the activity was satisfactorily concluded in silence.

This introduces an important new hypothesis: that the verbalising does in fact provide support for the activity. Clare has her toy farm laid out in front of her – fields with fences and gates and full of people, animals, sheds; and she sets herself the problem of organising by, so to speak, 'realistic' methods a general exchange of positions. There are 'rules' obviously arising from previous play – whose job it is to look after what, which cow the calf belongs to, and so on. As she makes her successive moves, new aspects of the problem and further possible moves reveal themselves; and – to come to the point – I think we can perceive her verbalising these as they arise. Thus, 'She went back' seems to be amended, as the idea strikes her, to, 'She went and *took a horse*'; when the farmer arrives with the bull it becomes apparent to her, we presume, that being a dangerous animal he can't be left unpenned and untended; again, she seems to work, in speech, towards the problem of disposing the people who are to lift the cowshed – the first move by which they are all at the front has to be amended to put the two men at points elsewhere, and the problem of the un-manned side is then solved, aloud, by dismissing it: 'Nobody holded the side they didn't need anybody'. Finally, it is clearly indicated that when all that is successfully managed a new problem arises: 'Oh dear . . .'.

The running commentary is in fact a characteristic form of what Vygotsky called 'speech for oneself'. The child, he suggests, learns to speak in the to-and-fro of talk with those about him, that is to say in speech that has the form of *social speech*. But once he has learned to speak, he uses speech to serve his own development – or, roughly speaking, as an aid to his own exploratory activities. What Fiona was doing when she drew St James's Park and what Clare was doing in manipulating her models were, in this general sense, 'exploratory activities'. Such activity is not of course restricted to solitary occupations and running commentary: it was actively present in the social exchanges between Clare and Alison quoted above, and it characterises talk with an adult. The point to be made is that when activity *is* solitary, the child at this stage may still need to use talk in support of his activity, whether or not anyone is listening. The speech is both *to* himself, in the sense that it seeks no response from a listener, and *for* himself in that it helps him do whatever it is he is doing.

Obviously, a child does not give up social forms of speech when he begins to use 'speech for himself'. The two forms are at first undifferentiated, being early social speech in substance, put to two uses. But as the two uses become established, modification of the form takes two directions: social speech becomes better communication, while speech for oneself becomes *less* communicative, more individualised, better able to serve the particular purposes and interests of a particular child. Thus, the early monologue at 20 months [quoted above] is a form of speech that differs in some respects from the remarks addressed by Fiona and Clare to their listeners, and in other respects from the language of their running commentaries.

It has been shown, on the basis of a number of observations, that the running commentary grows in prominence in the speech of most children from the age of about three, is at a peak at four and five (incorporating some changes in its character which we shall describe shortly) and declines until at seven it is a comparatively rare occurrence. Alternative explanations have been given to account for its decline. Piaget believed that it disappeared as a child's speech became more effective *as communication*. He described monologue, including the running commentary, as 'egocentric speech' and in doing so made an important point which we must consider before going any further.

We have indicated that a child's first speaking takes the form of a conversational exchange; we could have added that a young child is a poor conversationalist. He speaks from his own point of view and is incapable of taking up any other. Effective communication, on the other hand, demands that a speaker take into account the viewpoint – and the knowledge and experience and interests – of his listener. It is common enough to find mothers and fathers acting as interpreters to other people of what their small child is trying to say. From intimate knowledge of the child and all his circumstances (including of course his speech habits), they are able to understand his speech in spite of the egocentric viewpoint he expresses.

> Children [says Piaget] are perpetually surrounded by adults who not only know much more than they do, but who also do everything in their power to understand them, who even anticipate their thoughts and their desires. Children, therefore . . . are perpetually under the impression that people can read their thoughts, and in extreme cases, can steal their thoughts away.

When they talk to other children, therefore, they usually fail to understand each other for the very reason that 'they think that they do understand each other' (Piaget, 1959, p. 101).

Perhaps the best illustration of a child's egocentrism of viewpoint is that given by Piaget when he says, 'a boy of six to seven years old is ready to declare that he had a brother but that that brother has himself no brother'. It is a matter of being unable to step outside himself in order to see the world from another person's point of view; thus it is equally a sign of egocentrism that a young child will often omit himself altogether when he tries to count how many people there are in the room (Piaget, 1959, p. 275). This limitation of viewpoint will affect in some degree everything a child says: it is Piaget's point that attempts to converse run counter to this egocentrism, whereas the running commentary and other forms of monologue run with it. (He divides early speech into two categories: *egocentric speech* – the monologue; and *socialised speech* which includes questions and answers, requests, and information that has undergone some kind of adaptation to take into account the demands of a listener.) Piaget regards the gradual disappearance of the running commentary as a natural consequence of a child's improved ability to internalise his listener, to escape from the limitations of his own viewpoint: egocentric speech is, according to Piaget, gradually replaced by a more mature form, socialised speech.

It was Vygotsky who, in commenting upon Piaget's ideas, pointed out that a child's first speech derives from conversations he has listened to and takes the form of social interchange as we have seen; and that only later does the speech thus acquired come to be used in monologue. He stressed the function of monologue, that of assisting activity, organising a child's experience.

This function, exhibited for all to hear in the running commentary, was one which Vygotsky felt continued to be necessary; and if the need continued it seemed unlikely that the speech process would merely wither away. Vygotsky did not therefore speak in terms of 'egocentric speech' developing into 'socialised speech', but of 'social speech' developing in two distinct directions under the influence of two distinct uses. In continuing to serve the purposes of social exchange it becomes, as we have already seen, more *communicative*, better able to take account of a listener's point of view, and increasing in range and complexity. As *speech for oneself*, or egocentric speech, it becomes individuated and abbreviated: individuated in order to suit, as we have seen, an individual child's own interests and purposes; abbreviated in the sense that parts of the utterance would be left unspoken – since the child is talking to himself he needs to verbalise only the changing elements in his theme and not those that stay constant. (For example, in Fiona's commentary: '*[Now I'm drawing]* a little round head. *[Now I'm drawing]* a little eye and another little eye. *[Now I'm drawing]* a little nose . . .') Thus social speech and speech for oneself in this respect develop in opposite directions: a listener's needs are more and more taken into account in social speech and less and less considered in speech for oneself – appropriately enough since in this case a listener is, so to speak, 'vestigial'.

The drift of all this towards Vygotsky's final explanation will be clear enough. He believed that the monologue did not fall out of use or wither away, but became internalised, became what he called 'inner speech'. As such it continued its function of supporting a child's activities, but in accordance with the simple logic that if we talk to ourselves and not to a listener we do not need to talk aloud. Vygotsky saw the increasing individuation as indicating both the adaptation of speech to the purpose of serving individual needs and by the same token as a reason for its becoming silent: its vocalisation became 'unnecessary and meaningless and, because of its growing structural peculiarities, also impossible' (Vygotsky, 1962, p. 135). It is conceivable that some of the incomplete utterances in Clare's monologue are half spoken because they are too difficult to find words for. She seems, for example, to be concerned with some sort of calculation as to whether there will be room for all the animals when she says, 'And one field was only for cows not for any other except cows. – One thing the cowshed – quite a lot were in the shed – two calves could go in one place in it.'

There will presumably be times when the commentary raises problems which cannot be solved either with or without the help of speech; and other times when the commentary is used to raise a problem and a strategy is worked out for its solution with the help of egocentric speech at a level more advanced than that at which it can be uttered (in accordance with Vygotsky's thesis). Which of the two situations is represented in this example cannot be inferred from the record.

Here, at all events, is Vygotsky's explanation in his own words:

> To explain this [i.e. the decrease in egocentric speech] let us start from an undeniable, experimentally established fact. The structural and functional qualities of egocentric speech become more marked as the child develops. At three, the difference between egocentric and social speech equals zero; at seven, we have speech that in structure and function is totally unlike social speech. A differentiation of the two speech functions has taken place. This is a fact – and facts are notoriously hard to refute.
>
> Once we accept this, everything else falls into place. If the developing structural and functional peculiarities of egocentric speech progressively isolate it from external speech, then its vocal aspect must fade away; and this is exactly what happens between three and seven years. . . . To interpret the sinking coefficient of egocentric speech as a sign that this kind of speech is dying out is like saying that the child stops counting when he ceases to use his fingers and starts adding in his head. In reality, behind the symptoms of dissolution lies a progressive development, the birth of a new speech form.
>
> (Vygotsky, 1962, pp. 134–135)

The new speech form is 'inner speech', the child's 'new faculty to "think words" instead of pronouncing them'.

The respect, therefore, in which the speech of the 20-month-old child talking to herself differs from the monologues of the four-year-olds . . . is in the degree to which the utterance represents the total verbal activity. Both kinds of utterance are fragmentary, but in different ways.

1.2 Early literacy
'Young fluent writers'[3]

For the second passage in this section, we turn to an account of the development of writing. Britton draws again on Vygotsky's thought, referring throughout to Vygotsky's seminal text, 'Prehistory of the development of written language' (1978, 1997).[4]

Britton quotes Vygotsky's central argument, that writing is not, and cannot be taught as, 'a motor skill', but must instead be viewed as 'a particular system of symbols and signs whose mastery heralds a critical turning point in the entire cultural development of the child'. Britton is in complete agreement with Vygotsky in seeing the beginning of writing in other symbolic activities, such as make-believe play and drawing.

The central case study of Clare supports Vygotsky's argument by providing brief but vivid glimpses of a young child's gradual growth in confidence and control of the possibilities of writing, especially story-writing. The prehistory of Clare's writing lies in her playful and inventive oral language, her extended make-believe story-making play, her drawings with their accompanying commentary, her experiments in making little books with scribbled lines standing for 'grownup's kind of writing', and her attention to the detail of writing (plastic letters, alphabet books). Britton, in charting these different moments in her development, is underlining Vygotsky's focus on 'the effect of *intention* on a child's performance'. Britton sees Clare's intentions as arising primarily from her interest in the story-making possibilities of writing.

There follows a brief review, like a speeded-up film, of Clare's writing development from age 6 through to age 14, with snapshots of her writing at several ages. For all its brevity, this is a revealing longitudinal study of the genres and influences that shape Clare's progress, from Beatrix Potter-like animal stories to pony stories to romantic fiction. Britton's commentary keeps both

DOI: 10.4324/9781003532873-4

Clare's reading and her writing in play, seeing them (as Vygotsky does) as two aspects of one process.

I have known a number of children who by the age of 5 or 6 had taught themselves to write. In each case it was stories that they wrote, and usually the stories were made up into little books, with pictures as well as writing. I take it as some evidence of the extraordinary ability human beings have of succeeding in doing what they want to do. One of these young children, under the age of 4, began by producing a little book with 'pretend writing' in it — and surely, just as we pretend to *be* someone we want to be, so we pretend to *do* something we want to do. Some 20 months later the scribbled lines had given place to a decipherable story. Evidence of this kind is too often ignored, and it takes a Vygotsky, speaking across the decades since his death, to observe that the attempt to teach writing as a motor skill is mistaken (Vygotsky, 1978, p. 117); that psychology has conceived of it as a motor skill and 'paid remarkably little attention to the question of written language as such, that is, a particular system of symbols and signs whose mastery heralds a critical turning-point in the entire cultural development of the child' (p. 106). It was his view that make-believe play, drawing and writing should be seen as 'different moments in an essentially unified process of development of written language' (p. 116). And this he contrasted with what he found in schools: 'Instead of being founded on the needs of children as they naturally develop and on their own activity, writing is given to them from without, from the teacher's hands' (p. 105).

I suggest that the 4-year-old I have referred to made what Vygotsky (p. 115) calls 'a basic discovery — namely that one can draw not only things but also speech'. Since pictorial representation is first-order symbolism and writing is second-order symbolism (designating words that are in turn signs for things and relationships), Vygotsky saw this discovery as a key point in the development of writing in a child, yet he recognised there was little understanding of how the shift takes place, since the necessary research had not been done.

Outline for a case study

My records on the development of Clare, the 4-year-old whose pretend writing I have referred to, may illustrate some of the points Vygotsky has made in his account of 'the developmental history of written language'.

(1) Her conversational speech was quite well developed by the time she was 2 years old. Much of her talk was playful (seeing me at the washbasin, *What have*

*you got **off**, Daddy?* – at 2:3 [2 years 3 months]) and she used made-up forms freely (*I'm spoonfuling it in, I'm see-if-ing it will go through, smuttered in your eyes* – for uncombed hair – all at 2:7). Her curiosity about language was in evidence early (*When it's one girl you say 'girl' and when it's two three four girls you say 'girl **s**'. Why when it's two three four childs you say 'child **ren**'?* – at 2:10; *'Fairy girl with curly hair,' that makes a rhyme, doesn't it?* – at 2:11; on hearing something described as 'delicious', *Is delicious nicer than lovely?* – at 3:1).

(2) Extended make-believe play, involving her toy animals in family roles, was established by the time she was 3. Storytelling developed from it, the animals becoming the audience. The toy animals (she was given dolls from time to time but they were never adopted into the family) seem to have sustained a key role. They were the dramatis personae of her make-believe play, the subject of the stories she told, of her drawings, and later of the stories she wrote. Vygotsky's point that in make-believe play the plaything is free to take on a meaning that does not rely on perceptual resemblance is amusingly illustrated by the fact that when Clare enacted a queen's wedding, the least suitable of the animals – a scraggy, loose-knit dog – was chosen for the role of queen!

(3) Her earliest recognisable drawings came just before she was 2, and though they are clearly attempts at human figures, the talk that always accompanied the drawing was often in anthropomorphic terms (the mummy bird, the daddy bird). A picture drawn in coloured chalks at 3:5 shows a large figure of a girl on the left-hand side and a house on the right. Her commentary as she drew explained: *The girl is carrying a yellow handbag and she has a brown furry dog on a lead. Her feet are walking along. . . . I have put a car outside the house. I am putting blue sky, now I am putting in the sunshine.* (Here the diagonal blue strokes that had indicated the sky were interspersed with yellow ones.) *She's got a tricycle with blue wheels and a chain. Mrs Jones across the road has yellow and brown on her windows. I shall put yellow and red on mine.*

It is an important part of Vygotsky's thesis that a young child's drawing is 'graphic speech', dependent on verbal speech: the child draws, that is to say, from the memory of what he knows rather than from what he presently observes; and that what he knows has been processed in speech and is further processed in the speech that accompanies the drawing. The space in Clare's picture is well filled, but not in terms of topographical representation: the girl and the house are upright; the car is drawn vertically standing on its head; the dog vertically sitting on its tail; and the tricycle has its frame, wheels and chain spread out, looking more like an assembly kit.

(4) What circumstances could be supposed to facilitate the process that Vygotsky calls the move from drawing objects to drawing speech? Imitating the general pattern of writing behaviour, Clare at the age of 3:6 produced parallel horizontal lines

of cursive scribble, saying that she was *doing grownup's kind of writing*. At 3:11 she produced the little storybook I have described with similar lines of scribble but interspersed with words she could actually write ('mummy', 'and', 'the') and with a drawing on the cover. The stories she wrote from 5:6 onward were in cursive script with headings in capitals. She was by this time reading a good deal, mainly the little animal stories by Beatrix Potter and Alison Uttley.

Turning from the general pattern to the detail, Clare at the age of 3 played very often with a set of inch-high letters made of plastic in various colours. Among more random, playful uses, she learned to make her name in these letters and she was interested in what each letter was called. (One effect of this play was evident: when first she attempted to write words, an 'E' for example was an 'E' for her whether it faced right or left or up or down.) One of her activities represented a link between letter recognition and writing behaviour in general: at 3:5, in imitation of picture alphabets she knew, she was drawing a series of objects and writing the initial letter of each beside the drawing. Most of them she knew, but she came to one she did not: 'rhubarb'. When I told her, she said, *R – that's easy – just a girl's head and two up-and-downs!*

(5) The final stage in Vygotsky's 'developmental history' is that by which the written language ceases to be second-order symbolism, mediated by speech, and becomes first-order symbolism. I can offer no evidence of this from the records of Clare, and indeed I seriously doubt whether that transition is ever entirely appropriate to the written language we have been concerned with, that of stories.

(6) I think the most important conclusion to be drawn from the case of Clare and other children who have taught themselves to write by writing stories is a point that is central to Vygotsky's argument, that of the effect of *intention* on a child's performance. It would appear that the spoken language effectively meets young children's needs in general, and we must surmise that it is only as they come to value the written language as a vehicle for stories that they are likely to form an intention to write. Much of Clare's behaviour indicated that she had done so. Slobin and Welsh (1973) have effectively demonstrated that mastery of the spoken language cannot be adequately assessed without taking account of 'the intention to say so-and-so' – a lesson that as teachers or researchers we have been slow to learn.

Writing and reading

Clare continued to read and write stories for many years. Animal fantasies predominated until the age of 7, pony stories and adventure stories (often featuring an animal) followed until, from the ages of 12 to 14, she gave herself up almost entirely to reading women's magazine stories and writing herself at great length in that vein. Here, to represent successive stages, are some opening lines:

At 6: I am a little Teddy Bear. I've got a pony called Snow and I live in a little house with a thatched roof.

At 8½: Mrs Hedgehog had just had three babies. Two of them were like ordinary hedgehog babies, covered with soft prickles. But the third had none.

It was a dead calm as the Sand Martin and crew glided out of the small harbour at Plymouth. Phillip and Jean were the eldest. They were twins of fourteen.

At 11: Fiona Mackenzie lay in bed in her small attic bedroom. She turned sleepily over, but the morning sun streaming in at her small window dazzled her, and she turned back. (A story about horses in the Highlands.)

At 12: Derek looked into her face, and his green eyes burning fiercely with the white hot light of intense love gazed into the liquid of her melting, dark brown ones.

At 14: The dance was in full swing, and Giselle was the acknowledged belle of it. More radiant, more sparkling than ever before, she floated blissfully in the arms of James Wainforth.

Her comments on her reading and writing were sometimes illuminating. At 3:8 she described the Cinderella story as *A bit sad book about two ugly sisters and a girl they were ugly to.* At 8:7 she was asked what sort of things she liked reading. *Well,* she said, *there's* Treasure Island *– that's a bloody one for when I'm feeling boyish. And* Little Men, *that's a sort of halfway one.* 'And don't you ever feel girlish?' she was asked. *Yes. When I'm tired and then I read* The Smallest Dormouse. At 10:2 she wrote a story about children finding a treasure: *It's like Enid Blyton's story mostly,* she said, *except longer words.* A few months later she was struggling to get through Mrs Craik's *John Halifax, Gentleman,* but gave up with the comment, *It's a bit Lorna Dooneish, a lot of cissy boys in it. It's so sort of genteel – I can't stand it!*

Spectator role and the beginnings of writing

In the light of current school practices, it is as important as ever today to stress Vygotsky's view that learning to read and learning to write must be seen as inseparable aspects of one process, that of mastering written language. We have come to recognise the way this process is grounded in speech but have not yet acknowledged the essential contribution of other forms of symbolic behaviour: gesture, make-believe play, pictorial representation. In my account of Clare's development, I have added one other activity, that of manipulative play with the substance of written language. Bruner (1975) has pointed out that such play contributes to learning because it is a 'meta-process', one that focuses on the nature itself of the activity. (Children learn to walk for the purpose of getting where they want to be; *play* with walking – early forms of dancing – involves a concern with the nature of the walking process, an exploration of its manifold possibilities.)

It remains for me to point out that make-believe play (embracing the social environment children construct with their playthings), storytelling, listening to stories, pictorial representation and the talk that complements it, story reading and story writing: these are all activities in the role of spectator. As I have suggested, I believe it is this characteristic that develops a need for the written language in young children and the intention to master it. In such activities children are sorting themselves out, progressively distinguishing what is from what seems, strengthening their hold on reality by a consideration of alternatives. Clare, for example, at the age of 8:6, writes what at first sight appears to be a variant of the kind of animal fable she was familiar with from earlier reading of Beatrix Potter:

Hedgehog

Mrs Hedgehog had just had three babies. Two of them were like ordinary hedgehog babies, covered with soft prickles.

But the third had none. He was like a hedgehog in any other way. He ate like a hedgehog and he lived like a hedgehog and he rolled up in a ball like a hedgehog, and he went to sleep in the winter like a hedgehog. But he had no prickles like a hedgehog.

When he was a year old a fairy came to him, and said, 'Go to China and get three hairs from the Emperor Ching Chang's seventh guinea-pig. Throw the hairs in the fire, and then put it out with six bucketfuls of water. Put some of the ash on your head, and leave it for the night. In the morning you will be covered with prickles.' Then she faded away.

[The story tells how he carried out these instructions, and concludes:]

He went to sleep beside the stream. In the morning he woke up feeling rather strange. He looked at his back. It was covered in prickles. He spent four days in China, then he went home in the boat. His family were very surprised to see him! . . .

It has often been pointed out that in one sense a tiny infant is lord of his universe, and that growing from infancy into childhood involves discovering one's own unimportance. But the world created in the stories children write is a world they control and this may be a source of deep satisfaction. As one of the children recorded by Donald Graves remarked, she liked writing stories because 'you are the mother of the story'.

Whether to read or to write, a story makes fewer demands than a piece of transactional writing since one essential element of the latter process is missing in the former. The reader of an informative or persuasive piece must construct himself the writer's meaning and inwardly debate it (an essential part of the piecemeal contextualisation process); the reader of a story accepts, so to speak, an invitation to enter a world and see what happens to him there. The writer of a transactional piece must attempt to anticipate and make provision for the reader's inner debate; the writer of a story constructs a situation to his own satisfaction, though thereafter he may be willing, even eager, to share it . . .

What the young writer needs to know

My argument has been that Vygotsky's account offers an explanation of the phenomenon I have noted: that of Clare and the other children who mastered written language by producing storybooks at an early age. Let me now go on to ask, 'What does a writer acquiring mastery in this way need to know?'

First and foremost, he must know from experience the *satisfaction* that can come from a story – perhaps first a story told to him, but then certainly a story read to him. Sartre (1967, p. 31) has commented on the difference. Accustomed to having his mother tell him stories, he describes his experience when first she reads to him:

> The tale itself was in its Sunday best: the woodcutter, the woodcutter's wife and their daughter, the fairy, all those little people, our fellow-creatures, had acquired majesty; their rags were magnificently described, words left their mark on objects, transforming actions into rituals and events into ceremonies.

Then the writer must know something of the structure of a story, a learning process that Applebee (1978) has very helpfully described in developmental terms for stories told by children between the ages of 2 and 5 (but with implications for later stages). He sees two principles at work: one of *centring*, a concern for the unity of a story, and one of *chaining*, a concern for sequence; and in terms of these two principles he outlines a series of plot structures that parallel the stages of concept development described by Vygotsky (1962). It should be noted, at the same time, that recall of events in narrative form is something that all children achieve a year or more before they are ready to tackle the written language.

Some forms of story writing will only be possible if the writer is familiar with the conventional associations that govern our expectations in listening to stories – the role expected of a wolf, a lion, a fox, a witch, a prince, and so on (Applebee, 1978). Such built-in associations are, of course, a resource that a young writer may in his own stories exploit, improvise on, invert, or ignore.

Knowledge of the linguistic conventions of stories – the *Once upon a time* and *happily ever after* conventions – are often familiar to children before they can read or write, as are more general features of the language of written stories. (I saw a story dictated by a 3-year-old which contained the sentence, *The king went sadly home for he had nowhere else to go* – a use of *for* which is certainly not a spoken form.)

But production of these and all other written forms relies, of course, on a knowledge of the written code itself, the formation of letters, words, sentences. How this is picked up from alphabet books and cornflake packets, picture books, TV advertisements and street signs remains something of a mystery, though two governing conditions seem likely: a context of manipulative play and picture-making, and the association of this learning with the purpose of producing written stories. I am sure we underestimate the extent of such learning when a powerful interest is in focus. In my recent experience of reading stories to a 3-year-old, I have been amazed at her ability to fill the words into gaps I leave when the story I am reading is one she cannot have heard very often. Michael Polanyi's (1958) account of the relation of subsidiary to focal awareness certainly helps us to see this learning process as feasible.

Finally, the writer must know from experience the *sound* of a written text read aloud. How else can he come to hear an inner voice dictating to him the story he wants to produce? An apprenticeship of listening to others will enable him later to be aware of the rhythms of the written language in the course of his own silent reading.

A final speculation

I believe the successful writer learns all these things implicitly; that is to say, in Polanyi's terms, by maintaining a focal awareness of the desired performance that acts as a determining tendency guiding and controlling his subsidiary awareness of the means he employs. I believe, further, that any attempt to introduce explicit learning would be likely to hinder rather than help at this early stage. When we are dealing with poetic writing, there is much that could not in any case be made explicit: we simply do not know by what organising principles experience is projected into a work of art.

It is this problem that Susanne Langer has been investigating over many years. Her distinction between discursive and presentational symbolism – between a message encoded in a symbol system and a message embodied in a single unique complex symbol; her recognition of the key role of the arts as offering an ordering of experience alternative to the cognitive, logical ordering achieved by discursive symbolism – these are foundation stones in our theory of language functions.

From her exploration of the laws governing a work of art she makes one very interesting suggestion: that in all works of art there is a building-up and resolution of tensions, and that the intricate pattern of these movements, this rhythm, somehow reflects the 'shape of every living act' (Langer, 1967).

To speculate on her speculations: we give and find shape in the very act of perception, we give and find further shape as we talk, write or otherwise represent our experiences. I say 'give and find' because clearly there is order and pattern in the natural world irrespective of our perceiving and representing. At the biological level man shares that order, but at the level of behaviour he appears to lose it: the pattern of his actions is more random than that of the instinctual behaviour of animals. In learning to control his environment he has gained a freedom of choice in action that he may use constructively and harmoniously or to produce disharmony, shapelessness, chaos. When, however, he shapes his experience into a verbal object, an art form, in order to communicate it and to realise it more fully himself, he is seeking to recapture a natural order that his daily actions have forfeited. Understanding so little of the complexities of these processes, we can do no more than entertain that idea as a fascinating speculation.

1.3 Meaning-making, interaction and play

'The anatomy of human experience – the role of inner speech'[5]

Drama and play have a key place in Britton's late book, *Literature in its place* (1993). The final passage in this section is from that book's first chapter, on cooperative make-believe play. With its enigmatic title, the book is a celebration of the imagination:

> At the earliest stage, children must rehearse in active play the scene that strikes their fancy; if they do not enact – rehearse perhaps – a make-believe performance, there is no imagined construction. But at a later stage, make-believe play that is rehearsed in the mind, make-believe without action, becomes possible – and the power of the imagination is born.
> (Britton, 1993, p. 85)

For Britton, the place of literature was at the centre of children's development, and he saw imagination as the driving power behind much of children's writing and reading and their work in what he calls the 'verbal arts'. *Literature in its place* was a testimony to his vision of the importance of young children's language play for all their later creative learning and thinking.

Imaginative play and drama constitute a space where children are free to go beyond their everyday speech and become, as Vygotsky (1978) said, 'a head taller' than themselves. Britton's theoretical models of language don't often refer specifically to drama, but it is plain that he saw drama, make-believe and imagination as fundamental to the development of language and learning. (As we noted in the Introduction to this book, he organised regular 'Friday afternoons' for the students at the London Institute of Education, when the normal timetable was suspended in favour of poetry, drama and other arts activities.)

The passage which follows includes three interactions between Britton and his granddaughter Laurie: one in which she is asking him for information in a realistic setting, and two where she engages with him in imaginative play, first as a customer in her cake shop, and then as a baby being put to bed.

Waking in the morning, throwing back the bedclothes, already assailed by an unfocused sense of the day's responsibilities; parting the curtains and looking up at the sky – to approve or disapprove. Emerging into the silent house, moving in a way that will preserve its silence as a kind of freedom, yet at the same time submitting to the routine activities that respond to the needs and expectations of others – the acts of an automaton fulfilling inbuilt neuromuscular instructions. But look far enough into the past and it will be clear that the patterns were probably first recognised in other people and imitated – clumsily perhaps, playfully perhaps, certainly with deliberation. Experience grows for me as I take over these discovered behaviours, adapted to my biological self and the social environment in which I operate.

'Recognising', 'discovering', 'observing' – these indicate too passive a process for what appears in fact to take place. If we begin at the earliest stages of infancy, the active world starts to impinge on the infant as a kind of invitation to miming. Routines or formats of interactive behaviour which are instituted by an adult (most often the mother), by becoming recognisable – that is to say 'familiar' – emerge as distinct from the meaningless flux of other, unfamiliar events. They are likely to be accompanied by talk on the mother's part – talk that puts into words the activities she initiates, but at the same time embeds them in a more general, if fragmentary, representation of the life of the family. While the infant at this stage can respond only to the emotional intonations of the talk and not to its encoded meanings, it will not be long before such talk begins to fulfil the crucial role of providing her/him with the key to linguistic meaning. What had become meaningful from enacted routines may then be matched with what is communicated by the mother's verbal behaviour; and we must assume that it is that matching process that leads to a gradual mastery of the spoken language. Thereafter, talk becomes a principal means of interacting with other people, and it is this continued interaction that constitutes the recognition/production of meaningful behaviour.

So the interacting, responding, observing provide the indispensable key to the origins of those patterns of behaviour and then to their subsequent modification on my part as they constitute my accumulating experience. And on this aforementioned morning, glancing at the weather, contemplating the day's activities, interacting with members of the household, making some demands and responding to the demands of others, it is still the alert and sensitive interacting that holds the key. Should that become something I am no longer capable of, I might as well go back to bed and stay there!

If I were to complete a detailed account of the morning's activities – describing the food and the utensils, the drink and the layout of the table – I should be likely to create an increasing certainty that my home belonged to a particular geographical and social area. There might, of course, be anomalies – reflections of activities observed and imitated during periods of my life when I lived in other surroundings, foreign countries, perhaps, or came under alien influences. Patterns of behaviour will distinguish not only my individual self but also my family, and beyond that my social groups – local, regional, national.

A closer look at adult/child interaction will make quite clear how important is the role played by exchange of talk. Here is a brief interaction between Laurie, my grandchild, at three years eight months, and myself. She is paying a visit to our home and we are in the garden, talking about a thrushes' nest, now empty.

Laurie: Where's the birds' nest?
Me: It's still there, darling, but . . . they're not . . .
L: Are the birds coming?
M: No, they're not coming, darling, because . . .
L: Why?
M: Because they've left the nest.
L: When will they be little babies?
M: They were little babies – they're not now – they're big birds now.
L: When were they little babies?
M: Oh, about six months ago.
L: 's a long while ago.
M: Yes.
L: And I was BIG!
M: Were you?
L: Yes – big.
M: How big were you?
L: Not like Mummy and Daddy.
M: Mm?
L: Not like Mummy and Daddy . . . (*a distraction*) Fluff!
M: That's fluff from the tree – that's seeds that fall down from that tree. Do you see where it's coming down? . . . Do you see that coming down? That's where all that comes from.
L: How are they coming down here?
M: Well . . . that's . . . see, lots of it – some more there – everywhere there's fluff – come down from that tree – that's called a . . . an aspen.

Meaning-making, interaction and play

L:	Why is no more birds going in there – in the nest?
M:	Eh, I don't know, love – I think – they've gone somewhere else, perhaps.
L:	Why are they leaving all the nest there?
M:	Well, p'raps they'll come back to it next year when the birds have another family – p'raps they'll come back.
L:	Why?
M:	Well, they built it there, didn't they?

(*Other members of the family arrive on the scene and the conversation is over.*)

It will certainly not be true of all children everywhere, but with a great many of the children I have known, or learned of from records, by far the greater number of exploratory, interactive meaning-making occasions have been in the context of make-believe rather than in daily real-life activities. In cooperative make-believe the child is likely to be the one who calls up the scene and directs the action; and in doing so, Vygotsky (1978, p. 96) points out, 'the child learns to act in a cognitive, rather than an externally visual, realm, by relying on internal tendencies and motives and not on incentives supplied by external things.' In this way the number and variety of activated concerns is vastly increased, but – even more significant – these concerns are inherently representative of the child's state of experience. There is no shortage of recordings to illustrate this aspect of interaction: here Laurie and I take part in a game of shops earlier on the same day as the garden encounter recorded above. In one form or another, playing shops had become a favourite make-believe scenario with the three-and-a-half-year-old:

(*A shop space is marked out by a tea-trolley [a pretend cooking stove] and a gate-legged coffee table.*)

Laurie:	Switch. I turn 'em all on – they're cooking – switch. What cake do you like?
Me:	Have you got chocolate cake? I like chocolate cake.
L:	Yes . . . Why does this fall over? It's . . . Why does this tip over – this one doesn't tip over – it's got wheels! Why? (*The coffee table versus the tea-trolley*) Look there. Are you coming? There! I turn the cakes off: they're READY!
M:	Oh, good – are they cooked?
L:	I'm going to pass these – I'm walking did you see – Come here! Come in my shop and I'll give you one. What kind?
M:	I'd like chocolate cake please.
L:	O.K. How much money?
M:	Two shillings – twenty pence – twenty pence.
L:	Here 'tis then.

M:	Do I give it to you, then? O.K. There's twenty pence for the cake . . . What's that cake?
L:	A shallow cake?
M:	Yes.
L:	A brown one or a yellow one or a pink one.
M:	Chocolate – a brown one. Do you say these are shallow cakes – do you call them? What are these then?
L:	Those are chocolate cakes with banana.
M:	Oh, that sounds lovely. How much are they?
L:	Fifty pence.
M:	How much?
L:	These will be . . .
M:	Fifteen pence?
L:	Thank you.
M:	Thank you . . . Lovely. What kind of cakes are those?
L:	China cakes.
M:	Chung cakes. . .? What's the word?
L:	Chi-i-i-ina cakes.
M:	China cakes – oh – I'll have one of those.
L:	[*abashed*] Well – there are only these many. *Please can you go to another shop?*
M:	Oh – yeah – O.K. O.K.
L:	Ask Alison for one.
M:	Bye-bye, thank you.
L:	Bye!

Spoken dialogue is at this stage the principal means by which a child's linguistic resources are recruited and experiences internalised. Some children will, as early as this, attempt spoken monologue, but when they do their utterances are likely to be of the somewhat dream-like, loose, illogical kind that I have called *spiels* (Britton, 1970, p. 83) – word-spinning performances, jigsaw collections of remembered phrases – offered as entertainment to admiring listeners, not as conversation. Utterances as celebration would designate some of these performances, as for example the following, spoken in a sing-song voice by my daughter Clare at three years zero months:

> Angels at head, fairies at foot
> The stars are shining with golden light
> Hit on the ball with golden light

Loo-ing, loo-ing. Darling child
The children in bed
  it's the big one that's saying it, you see –
Lighting up the candles so early
Holy night – silent night.

I should add that the sources of the language of most *spiels* would be more diverse and less easily recognised than those of this example.

Genuine monologic speech is another matter – and a later development, though, as might be expected, the transition may not be at all clearly marked. That is to say, expressive, performance-directed speech may play some part in utterances that would otherwise be recognised as communicative monologue carrying cognitive messages.

The transition from dialogic to monologic speech in young children has been helpfully described by Luria. He traced the development of a child's problem-solving speech from its beginnings as expanded – fully verbalised – vocal speech through speech for oneself, where it becomes abbreviated in the process of being internalised – becoming, that is to say, inner speech.

> Only when external speech has become abbreviated and converted into inner speech does it become possible to carry out the opposite process, i.e. the expansion of this inner speech into an external, connected text with its characteristic semantic coherence. . . . We would argue that once a child has mastered these operational components of expanded speech, he/she goes through an equally complex path to develop real speech activity. This activity is guided by a motive, is subject to a specific goal, and constitutes a constantly regulated, closed semantic system.
>
> (Luria, 1981, p. 158)

These are developments that Luria would have expected to occur as a child approaches school age and the earliest monologues, he suggested, are likely to take a narrative form.

An early example of what I take to be essentially monologic speech is provided by Laurie at four years one month, in a make-believe situation in which she is the mother and I play the part of her small child. The situation she implies is fictional (she has in reality only one younger sister), although it clearly represents some aspects of her own real experience. The tape-recording shows hesitations that suggest she is improvising as she speaks – that is to say, in Luria's terms, that her utterance is an expanded version of her inner speech. I think it is a fair description to call the piece as a whole *enacted* (rather than related) *narrative*. Finally, if we accept Vygotsky's view (1978, p. 102) that in make-believe play a young child is able to act some months – or even years – ahead of his/her chronological age, it may well be that true monologue is likely, in the case of many children, to make its earliest appearance in make-believe play.

Laurie: Now it's time for little darlings to go to sleep.
Me: Yes.
L: You've got to go to sleep now. Your blanket – pillow. Lie down! Now you're going to have a little – if you don't want to go to sleep – you *must* go to sleep, 'cos – or you will be afraid of night, 'cos the *owls* come at night. . . . Yes, they go to-whoo! They don't frighten *you* – they don't eat you, only rats or mice – that's good, isn't it?
M: Yes.
L: Now I've got to sort your cover, 'cos you messed it up last night, didn't you?
M: Yes, I wriggled about so much, didn't I?
L: Yes, 'cos you're afraid of the *owl*, aren't you?
M: Yes.
L: Tonight I have to sleep in my own room which is downstairs and Dad sleeps downstairs too and you only sleep *up*stairs. And the baby *sleeps* (*pause*) downstairs too and the big girls – and your two sisters sleep down too and you only sleep up, don't you? So you have to be very quiet. If you hear – if you – um – hear a *monster*, I'll come running up. I hope – if you dream about one, just cry and come down and say 'Oo-oo, Mummy, I had a bad dream.' Yes. Now you're going to go to sleep, aren't you? Close your eyes!

It seems to me that the play of imagination illustrated in transcripts of this kind provides a key to the continuing role of creative language in human existence – whether manifested in the verbal arts or in the probing curiosity that empowers scientific inquiry. Vygotsky has spelled out his account of the transition from make-believe behaviour to the birth of the imagination:

> Imagination is a new psychological process for the child; it is not present in the consciousness of the very young child, is totally absent in animals, and represents a specifically human form of conscious activity. Like all functions of consciousness, it originally arises from action. The old adage that child's

play is imagination in action must be reversed: we can say that imagination in adolescents and school children is play without action.

(Vygotsky, 1978, p. 93)

It will raise no eyebrows to acknowledge here the existence of a close developmental link between make-believe play in infancy and the practice of the arts at all stages from kindergarten to the grave. The link has been widely and variously formulated. In *Play, dreams and imitation in childhood*, for example, Piaget (1951, p. 155) characterises make-believe as *symbolic assimilation* and concludes that it is 'reintegrated in thought in the form of creative imagination' or 'spontaneous constructive activity'. Freud (see Vygotsky, 1971, p. 73) claims that 'the poet does the same things as the child at play: he creates a world, which he takes very seriously, with a lot of enthusiasm and animation, and at the same time very sharply sets it apart from reality.' Vygotsky goes on to state his own view that art functions for the child in ways that differ from its role for an adult, and he explains this by referring to the work of Chukovsky (1963) on the young child's use of nursery rhymes: the way their topsy-turvy nonsense appeals to a child at a time when he is consolidating his mastery of the actual. 'By dragging a child into a topsy-turvy world,' Vygotsky (1971, p. 258) writes, 'we help his intellect work, because the child becomes interested in creating such a topsy-turvy world for himself in order to become more effectively the master of the laws governing the real world.' If rhymes and stories – seen as works of literature – have this effect, they will clearly be serving a purpose that diminishes as the child grows older: as what T.S. Eliot – in his poem 'Animula' – called 'the imperatives of is and seems' grow less insistent. Vygotsky goes on to suggest that while adults have no such predominance of 'seems' over 'is' to contend with, there is also for them in art something of the same dualism – that art serves to present modified, even somewhat distorted, views of reality, and thus has the effect of strengthening in the viewer his/her grasp of the nature of reality, while at the same time, let me add, exploring the structures of what it might become. In short, art by this view is 'a method for building life'.

It is an interesting feature of Vygotsky's book that while it bears the title *The psychology of art*, its subject matter – its exemplification throughout – is, in one form or another, literature, the verbal arts.

It is my purpose in the rest of this chapter to ask how central a function in human development is the use of language in creative, constructive modes – how important to us, in other words, are social products of a literary nature, and what do we achieve by experimenting in the production of such works? In pursuing this inquiry, there are two ideas put forward by early Soviet students of language – contemporaries and probably professional associates of Vygotsky – that we need to consider at this stage:

1. The notion that meaning is, in the first instance, interpersonal, constantly created, adapted, modified in the course of person-to-person verbal exchange. (The same idea has been elegantly put by Georges Gusdorf, the French philosopher [1965, p. 48]):

> In essence, language is not of one but of many; it is between. It expresses the relational being of man. . . . The self does not by itself alone have to carve out for itself an access to being – because the self exists only in reciprocity with the other. An isolated self can truly be said to be only an abstraction.

2. The idea that human experience in its organised and recoverable form is a network of verbal meanings. Volosinov spells out this view in the course of answering the question: 'How, in fact, is another's speech received?'

> Everything vital to the evaluative reception of another's utterance, everything of ideological value, is expressed in the material of inner speech. After all, it is not a mute, wordless creature that receives such an utterance, but a human being full of inner words. All his experiences . . . exist encoded in his inner speech, and only to that extent do they come into contact with speech received from outside. Word comes into contact with word.
>
> (Volosinov, 1973, p. 118)

However, it does seem to me that the encoding process is a selective one, and that the selection will entail an element of individual responsibility. What I encode will reflect to some degree on the biological, psychological, and social aspects of my life, and what is encoded will shrink or expand or suffer other transformation in the light of my changing conception of the world I inhabit. Verbal interaction will be the means by which what I encode will be shaped and stored, and my choice will come to influence what counts as experience in the social group to which I belong.

Volosinov introduces this notion of individual initiative early in the first chapter of his book *Marxism and the philosophy of language*:

Although the reality of a word, as is true of any sign, resides between individuals, a word, at the same time, is produced by the individual organism's own means without recourse to any equipment or any other kind of extracorporeal material. This has determined the role of word as the *semiotic material of inner life – of consciousness* (inner speech).

(Volosinov, 1973, p. 14)

Finally, Volosinov tackles what he regards as 'one of the most important problems in the science of meanings, the problem of the *interrelationship between meaning and evaluation*'. He stresses that the overriding purpose in speaking is an evaluative purpose: 'All referential contents produced in living speech are said or written with a specific evaluative accent. There is no such thing as word without evaluative accent' (Volosinov, 1973, p. 103).

Having embarked on an attempt to specify the purposes of literature, I must now go on to raise a question that Volosinov does not at this point consider: what are the consequences of an evaluative utterance upon the choice of subsequent action on the part of the speaker? If for example an experimental inquiry fails to yield any evidence upon the hypothesis that underlay it, what effect might that be expected to have on the inquirer? Will he/she merely reframe the hypothesis in alternative terms and try again? Or might the failure matter so much that life no longer seems worth living? (And of course there have been cases of such disillusionment.) I believe we would have to conclude that what is evaluated in any, broadly speaking, scientific activity is likely to be within limits prescribed by professional practice and epistemological levels, or the current state of knowledge in a field.

Consider in contrast the evaluative scope of such a document as the suicide note discovered and reported by Aldous Huxley in *Texts and pretexts* (1932, p. 139): 'No wish to die. One of the best sports, the boys will tell you. This b, at Palmers Green has sneaked my wife, one of the best in the world; my wife, the first love in the world.' Not that I wish to call that heartfelt cry *literature*, but I would claim that it represents a type of discourse that is in every way responsive to human evaluative needs – and a type of discourse that is capable of the highly sophisticated and influential expression we cannot fail to recognise as literature.

Such discourse, across such a range, must be seen to occupy a key place in the functions of language, and to be of vital importance not simply to addicts, scholars, writers, and critics, but to every man, woman and child alive in a literate society.

Notes

1. The source of this text is Britton (1970), pp. 50–61.
2. 'With acknowledgement to Mrs E.W. Moore, formerly of the University of London Institute of Education, for permission to use this extract.' Britton's note.
3. The source of this text is Britton (1982), pp. 58–66.
4. The version of 'The prehistory of the development of written language' from which Britton quotes is the partial text included in Vygotsky (1978).
5. The source of this text is Britton (1993), pp. 1–10.

References

Applebee, A. (1978). *The child's concept of story*. Chicago: University of Chicago Press.
Britton, J. (1970). *Language and learning*. Harmondsworth: Penguin Books.
Britton, J. (1982). 'Young fluent writers', part of 'Spectator role and the beginnings of writing', in Pradl, G. (ed.), *Prospect and retrospect: Selected essays of James Britton*. London and Monclair, NJ: Heinemann Educational and Boynton/Cook, pp. 58–66.
Britton, J. (1993). *Literature in its place*. London and Portsmouth, NH: Boynton/Cook.
Bruner, J. (1975). 'The ontogenesis of speech acts'. *Journal of Child Language*, 2, pp. 1–19.
Chukovsky, K. (1963). *From two to five* [1933]. Trans. M. Morton. Berkeley, CA: University of California Press.
Gusdorf, G. (1965). *Speaking*. Trans. P. Brockelman. Evanston, IL: Northwestern University Press.
Huxley, A. (1932). *Texts and pretexts*. London: Chatto and Windus.
Langer, S. (1967). *Mind: An essay on human feeling*. Baltimore, MD: Johns Hopkins Press.
Luria, A. (1981). *Language and cognition*. New York: Wiley.
Piaget, J. (1951). *Play, dreams and imitation in childhood*. Trans. C. Gattegno and F. Hodgson. London: Heinemann.
Piaget, J. (1959). *Language and thought of the child*. Trans. M. Gabain. London: Routledge and Kegan Paul.
Polanyi, M. (1958). *Personal knowledge*. London: Routledge and Kegan Paul.
Sartre, J-P. (1967). *Words*. Trans. A. White. Harmondsworth: Penguin Books.
Slobin, D. and Welsh, C. (1973). 'Elicited imitation as a research tool in developmental linguistics', in Ferguson, C. and Slobin, D. (eds), *Studies of child language development*. New York, NY: Holt, Rinehart and Winston.
Valentine, C. (1942). *The psychology of early childhood: A study of mental development in the first years of life*. London: Methuen.
Volosinov, V. (1973). *Marxism and the philosophy of language* [1929]. Trans. L. Matejka and I. Titunik. Cambridge, MA and London: Harvard University Press.

Vygotsky, L. (1962). *Thought and language* [1934]. Trans. E. Haufmann and G. Vakar. Cambridge, MA: MIT Press.

Vygotsky, L. (1971). *The psychology of art* [1925]. Cambridge, MA: MIT Press.

Vygotsky, L. (1978). 'The prehistory of written language' [1931], in Cole, M., John-Steiner, V., Scribner, S. and Souberman, E. (eds), *Mind in society*. Cambridge, MA: Harvard University Press, pp. 105–120.

Vygotsky, L. (1997). 'Prehistory of the development of written language' [1931], in Rieber, R.W. (ed.), *The collected works of L.S. Vygotsky. Volume 4, The history of the development of higher mental functions*. New York: Plenum Press, pp. 131–148.

SECTION 2

Language and learning at school

The pieces in this section are of interest not only for their insight into some of Britton's key ideas concerning language in school, but also for the different contexts in which these ideas are worked out and presented. Britton's thinking in these pieces is informed by the set of understandings about language in the early years already illustrated in Section 1. He is concerned not only with language but with language's role in young people's development and with the way they come to master its resources. He now draws on these understandings to set out an approach to language in the classroom that is 'operational' in emphasis, directed toward active use: a fundamental and recurring insistence.

Britton's *Language and learning* (1970) provides the fullest explanation of his thinking. In the chapter from the book which forms the opening extract of this section, he draws on the perception of language's role in learning to argue the case for the importance of classroom talk. In a lengthy consideration of home language, he stresses that schools must accept and build on children's home experience and on the language that young people bring to school. He focuses on the value of talking in school and on the cultivation of cooperative talk in learning.

Subsequent pieces in this section pursue in different ways this central emphasis. They include the argument presented in Chapter 4 of the Bullock Report (Department of Education and Science, 1975), and 'Language in the British primary school' (Britton, 1982a), a lecture originally given in 1979 to a conference of primary teachers, in part reflecting on the take-up of the report. The final piece is taken from a talk prepared for a pioneering conference of the London Association for the Teaching of English (LATE) on language across the curriculum, and originally published in 1969 with talks by Douglas Barnes and Harold Rosen in *Language, the learner and the school*. (We have used here the third edition of the book: Barnes, Britton and Torbe, 1986.)

We offer fuller descriptions of the different contexts for these pieces in what follows. Before these separate introductions, we need to highlight one further important preliminary, and to say a little more about the political and social context that Britton is meeting in his later writing. The political dimension of Britton's understandings, not always foregrounded but always subtly present, underpins the stress on language and learning in this section. The climate of educational discussion had become increasingly shaped by criticisms of so-called progressive teaching in the primary and comprehensive schools. To make the argument for an operational approach to language and for a practice based in developmental understandings had become increasingly important in support of public education and the work of teachers.

In the form that Britton was encountering them, the criticisms contained a not unfamiliar mix of genuine, though often uninformed, concern, prejudice, and underlying political motivation. The political edge to the discussion was given fresh momentum by reactions to the Plowden Report (Central Advisory Committee for Education [England], 1967) and by resistance to the boost for comprehensive schools proposed by Anthony Crosland, Secretary of State for Education 1965–1967, in Circular 10/65. A central influence in promoting and building up a range of critical voices were the Black Papers, a series of documents published between 1969 and 1977 by the journal *Critical Quarterly*.

Guided by the accounts that featured in these papers, a picture of schooling emerged in which teachers had abandoned the transmission of knowledge and the maintenance of standards as prime purposes of education. The status given to spoken language was undermining the priority for literacy. The teaching of grammar had been neglected, and as a result the training afforded to young minds and the grasp of grammar perceived as essential to learning to write. Young people were being denied the aid of phonics in the teaching of reading. The canon of the English literature had been abandoned in exchange for demotic, 'socially relevant' texts.

Such criticisms were not new minted. They can be sourced in pre-war forms as well as in those that Britton was encountering. They have equivalents today. Cumulatively, their impact was decisive in promoting a climate of concern for public education. The picture presented of what was happening in schools, however disproportionate, was something to which the government needed to respond in the mid-1970s, and indeed this was the outcome.

An immediate response was a speech by James Callaghan, the Labour Prime Minister, given in Ruskin College, Oxford in October 1976, which is widely regarded as having begun 'The Great Debate' about the nature and purpose of public education. In due course, Black Paper criticisms and Callaghan's response played a part in the climate leading to the stronger intervention of government through the National Curriculum and the coming of Ofsted during the 1992–1997 Conservative government. Their influence can be heard in the critical tone in which these interventions have successively been conducted.

We must end the historical story at this point, for present purposes. There have of course been other influences on public policy and the teaching of English since that time, notably the programmes and educational strategies of the Blair years, and the reforms instituted by Michael Gove as Secretary of State for Education in the Conservative/Liberal Democrat government of 2010–2015. How Britton might have responded to these more recent developments, had he lived to see them, is not difficult to imagine.

In his own time, as an educator, Britton responded to the issues that were emerging in the seventies and eighties, and the chapter from the Bullock Report included here is of particular interest for indicating how he took up in his own way the criticisms directed toward teachers and their work. Set alongside the other extracts included in this section, Britton's positioning of central understandings about language as well as his robust defence of teachers' insights and experience have continuing relevance. As he comments, movingly, at the close of 'Language in the British primary school':

> the 'enlightened' view of teaching and learning we profess is not an outmoded bandwagon, representative (as I have heard it said) of 'the dependent sixties'. It is, in fact, not a bandwagon at all, nor a pendulum swing. It is a steady, slow growing movement that has roots in philosophy back to Dewey and beyond; and is deep-rooted in the intuitions of the most successful teachers over a much longer period than that.
>
> (Britton, 1982a, p. 199)

2.1 The value of talk
'Now that you go to school'[1]

Here, Britton follows young children as they begin schooling. The school experiences he describes, including the emphasis on doing rather than sitting at desks, may not be quite those of today. In some respects they may be found to be in advance of what happens in the early grades of 21st-century schools. In this chapter from his major work, Language and learning (1970), he is building on the insights established in previous chapters.

Key insights in his earlier discussion were that talk is a major instrument of learning in infancy and that the infant *learns by talking* and that she *learns to talk by talking*. The thinking behind these insights, illustrated in Section 1, had drawn on consideration of his daughters' talk, together with Britton's reading of Luria and Vygotsky. From these developmental insights Britton draws out two key implications for schooling: first, that the processes of school learning must merge into the processes of learning that begin at birth and are lifelong; and second, that what children use language for in school must be 'operations' and not 'dummy runs'. He adds, as elaboration:

> They must continue to use it to make sense of the world: they must *practise* language in the sense in which a doctor 'practises' medicine and a lawyer 'practises' law, and *not* in the sense in which a juggler 'practises' a new trick before he performs it.
>
> (Britton, 1970, p. 130)

Britton regards it as essential, then, that schools accept and build on children's home experience and home language. Differences in speech should be accepted. Awareness of other forms of speech from one's own can be encouraged through drama, and through growing experience of written language, but early forms of language are tied to our primary experiences, acquiring vitality from these connections. He quotes a brilliant passage about home dialect from the Italian writer Luigi Meneghello to underline how this earliest language is stored 'deep down in the mind', forming a bedrock to all subsequent experiences.

Britton focuses on the value of talking in school and of the cultivation of cooperative talk in learning. The rich quotations that he offers from Connie Rosen's classroom illustrate the way in which talk becomes the basis for children's thinking; the expressive talk that comes from shared experiences in a busy and interesting classroom leads to comments, criticisms, questions and reflections. Britton sees a classroom which is alive with this kind of talk as a 'web of human relations' through which a community is constructed.

The idea that learning is something you do sitting in a seat is a highly sophisticated notion and, to a young child, a very peculiar one. It symbolises, probably more sharply than anything else, the long-standing traditional distinction between school learning and the kind of learning we all undertake from time to time at home, in the street, in strange cities, in the countryside – and many other places. Yes, we may also visit a library and learn a good deal without stirring from the seat, but to do so betokens a high level of verbal sophistication on our part.

It is to our national credit, then, that only in very rare instances do children in our infant schools spend the day sitting at desks. Rather, they are here, there and everywhere, up and about; going off to ask somebody something or tell him something else; going off to see for themselves; standing at a bench or a table, moving round to get a better grip or take a longer look; working or playing in different parts of the room or the building in accordance with what is to be found to do there. And the area given over to these operations, indoors and out, tends to grow greater and more diversified as the advantages of such active learning become clear to the people who control the design of schools.

The point itself is far from trivial, but it is here to introduce an even more important general principle: that in school we cannot afford to ignore all that has gone on before. So often in the past we have tried to make a fresh start, at the risk of cutting off the roots which alone can sustain the growth we look for. It is not only that the classroom must more and more merge into the world outside it, but that the processes of school learning must merge into the processes of learning that begin at birth and are lifelong. We can no longer regard school learning as simply an interim phase, a period of instruction and apprenticeship that marks the change from immaturity to maturity, from play in the nursery to work in the world.

School learning must both build upon the learning of infancy and foster something that will continue and evolve throughout adult life.

We have seen that talk is a major instrument of learning in infancy: that the infant *learns by talking* and that he *learns to talk by talking*. In trying to explain why it is that normal children succeed in this astonishing task of learning to talk, we suggested [earlier in the book] it was because the two tasks – learning in the most general sense, that is, making sense of the world, and learning to talk – are so closely enmeshed. When we arrive at the school stage we must add writing and reading to talking, but the stress upon the operational value of language use remains the same, and teachers should rely on a similar motive – on the dividends that language learning pays.

Putting this at its simplest, what children use language for in school must be 'operations' and not 'dummy runs'. They must continue to use it to make sense of the world: they must *practise* language in the sense in which a doctor 'practises' medicine and a lawyer 'practises' law, and *not* in the sense in which a juggler 'practises' a new trick before he performs it. This way of working does not make difficult things easy: what it does is make them worth the struggle. It is, of course, subject to a good deal of criticism: it has been called 'language learning by osmosis', or 'learning by soaking' and the like. Teachers need to defend themselves against such criticism in two ways: in theory, by insisting that learning is an evolutionary process in which the fullest possible development at any stage is the best preparation for ensuing stages; and in practice (or 'more commodiously') by ensuring as far as they can that the operations undertaken by their pupils offer genuine challenge, and result in the extension and deepening of their experience. And where classes of young children are so organised that 'there are forty feeding as one' (as Wordsworth said of cattle), this is all but an impossibility.

The talk that goes along with the activities I referred to earlier is essential to the learning, and it is a direct continuation of the small child's talk in his family. In due course, moreover, writing will grow from that talk: by 'grow' I do not mean to suggest that it comes without effort on the part of the child and of the teacher, but that their efforts are directed towards that growth from those roots. Yet no longer ago than 1925 teachers were exhorted by their advisers in one instance to 'make a fresh start' when the time came to teach their children to write. A Board of Education publication entitled *General report on the teaching of English in London elementary schools, 1925*, drawn up by His Majesty's Inspectors, has this to say:

> As long as children are expected to write for the most part upon subjects which afford them no opportunity for imitation of what has been well

done in speech by their teacher, or in writing by the authors they are studying, they are not likely to express themselves well. And when the subjects are such as deliberately throw them into the atmosphere of their out-of-school life, it is almost certain that they will express themselves in the language of the home and the street, which, teachers constantly assure us, is ever in conflict with the language the school is trying to secure. And this language cannot be corrected by talking about it; a more correct language must be built up by the imitation of better models of speech and writing.

If this view is accepted, it is important that in the earlier stages the child's exercises in writing English should be based upon what he reads and hears in school, and not until he has acquired some familiarity with the language, which the school is trying to build up, should he be asked to express himself upon other topics.

(Board of Education, 1929, p. 19)

The writers of this report, in spite of the wise things they say in other sections, could not have held an 'operational' view of speech: not appreciating its essential role in bringing a child from helplessness at birth to a five-year-old's grip on his world, they are prepared to discount it as 'incorrect', antagonistic to a teacher's purposes. An inevitable consequence of this would be to discredit a child's speech in his own eyes, at least in so far as his school career was concerned. (It is perhaps worth noting that the inspectors were not so sure of their position as they make themselves out to be: why otherwise do they hedge over that last half-sentence? To state their case logically, it should have read: 'and not until he has acquired some familiarity with the language which the school is trying to build up should he be asked to express himself upon other topics'. That would have been to distinguish 'the language which the school is trying to build up' quite clearly from the language the children possess; by enclosing the words 'which the school is trying to build up' in commas, they make it a non-defining clause – an explanatory addition – so implying that what they referred to is 'the language' – the English language. This constitutes a quite unsupported claim that what the teachers teach is 'the language' whereas what the children use is *not*!)

We cannot afford to be in doubts over this matter: what the children speak is an operationally effective form of the English language. We may not like their speech, but if this is the case we should at least be clear on the grounds of our objection. Effective communication is a social good: for that reason it is desirable that the forms of our speech should be appropriate to the occasion and intelligible and acceptable to our listeners. But such a statement goes no way towards justifying the absolute judgements of right and wrong we have so often applied: it calls instead for judgements that are *relative* to particular circumstances. Speech cannot be effective if it is unintelligible: but the chatter of two West Indian children over a game of five stones is none the worse for being unintelligible to me as I walk by. Oaths and blasphemies that offend one regional group or one generation are often acceptable currency in another. And grammar – that King Charles's head of any talk about talk – must be seen for what it is, a system of relationships that makes language possible: something therefore that is to be found in any and every dialect or variant of any language. As Henry Sweet put it in 1891, 'Whatever is in general use in a language is for that very reason grammatically correct' (Sweet, 1891, p. 5). Thus the grammatical features that we may find unacceptable in a child's speech are not examples of 'bad grammar': they are the grammatical features of *a language we find unacceptable*. I need not labour the point that it is no solution in such a case to attempt to 'teach grammar'. The forms of speech we find acceptable will be adopted by children only as they gain experience of them by listening and only as they are disposed (for one reason or another) and encouraged (by one means or another) to imitate what they have heard. And in this respect a grammatical feature ('them strawberry ones') is in no sense different from a vocabulary item (say a four-letter word), a mode of address, a pronunciation, or any other speech form.

When we speak of acceptable forms we probably have in the backs of our minds the variety of English that has been labelled 'Standard English'. It has been defined as 'that type of English used by educated people when carrying on their affairs publicly, in writing and in speech' (Cassidy, 1966). What is important is to recognise that the term indicates in fact not one but many varieties of English. The Standard English used in Glasgow differs from that used in Edinburgh, that of Boston differs from that of San Francisco – and so on for Melbourne, London, Toronto and the rest. Over and above differences in vocabulary and – less prominently – in syntax, Standard English is spoken in a great variety of regional accents. Nevertheless, all these differences are of far less importance than the common intelligibility and the common functions of Standard English – and this of course is seen at its greatest in the written forms.

Standard English will be the mother tongue of some of the pupils in our schools; others will have acquired it, in addition to the language of their homes, by the time they leave school. On the other hand, in some situations the question of whether or not they should acquire it simply will not arise: other matters will be of obviously greater importance.

All living languages are subject to change and Standard English is no exception. Though we change our speech habits in the course of a lifetime, nevertheless there is likely to be a greater difference between speakers of an earlier and a later generation at any one time than there will be between, for example, my speech at the one age and my speech at the other. Educators have often ignored this difference between the generations and wasted a good deal of energy over battles they were destined to lose: battles to preserve – so it seemed to them – decent standards of speech; battles that were in reality attacks on quite trivial changes from the forms of their own speech (for example, 'different to' where they said 'different from', 'due to' where they said 'owing to', or 'disinterested' where they said 'uninterested'). 'Change and decay in all around I see' is what the hymn says; the real pedant sees change in everything that leads to the language as he learnt it, but regards all subsequent changes as decay.

Let me suggest one way of approaching the problems of this confusing situation. In ordinarily favourable circumstances no one has a greater influence than the teacher in determining what speech is acceptable in his classroom: the language of that group in that situation will evolve in the light of the standards of acceptability set by the teacher. Clearly a great deal depends therefore upon his own speech, to which the children listen: again, even from this limited point of view of acceptable forms, it is important that no child in the class should be a non-talker, for the listening and the producing need to interact. Given such a situation, the first thing I would say is that we must begin from where the children are: in other words there can be no alternative in the initial stages to total acceptance of the language the children bring with them. We cannot afford to 'make a fresh start'. From there I would go on to develop an awareness of difference among forms of speech: at a fairly explicit level this might lead to the recognition of interesting differences in the way different people speak and the way they speak for different purposes. Much less explicitly, it will enter into dramatic improvisation – the need for a king to talk like a king and his wise men, perhaps, to talk like a book. An acceptance of differences seems to me more important throughout the whole junior school age-range than any sense that approval narrows down upon one form, the socially acceptable. And from awareness of differences can grow, without anything of the sort necessarily being formulated, the habit of adapting speech to suit different purposes and occasions.

However, a teacher must in the end face for himself the complexities of our present social situation and make his own decision with regard to the children he is responsible for. We have moved quite rapidly in recent years away from the public dominance of the 'BBC voice'; we can all point to individuals whose lack of acceptable speech does not appear to have held them back. Yet the ordinary child who grows up to apply for one of a range of jobs may well need to call upon his listening experience of Standard English – as things are today. Perhaps it is patience that a teacher needs most: opportunities for his own speech to influence that of the children arise mainly in areas where new experiences demand new language, and in particular where problems are discussed in a way that is more *general* and more *abstract* than talk in many homes is likely to be. Again, as children grapple with the written language, first by listening to stories read to them, and later in their own writing and reading, they move more directly into the sphere of influence of Standard English. Above all, patience is required in the form of trusting to the total process of schooling – despite its evident failures. If in the early stages we can increase the range of a child's choice, encourage acceptance of difference and adaptability to changing situations, and at the same time leave him in unimpaired command of the speech of his home, then I believe we shall have produced the best possible foundation for all his later uses of language, including that of taking over – if and when he feels the need for it – some spoken form of Standard English.

★ ★ ★

Language, as we have seen, is one way of representing or symbolising our experience of the world. . . . As adults, we rely upon language as a means of making other people's experiences our own – and, through our reading, a vast field of secondary experience lies open to us by this means. The quality of the experience we gain must rely upon the effectiveness of the instrument we use, that is to say upon the vitality of the connexions between our language and our primary experiences, our encounters with reality via the senses, emotions, intuitions. And this vitality probably derives above all from early experiences of words with things.

Luigi Meneghello, an Italian writer and scholar, has this to say about words learnt in childhood, words in the home dialect as distinct from those acquired later:

> There are two layers in the personality of a man; the top ones are like superficial wounds – the Italian, French and Latin words: underneath are the ancient wounds which on being healed have formed scars – words in dialect. On being touched the scars set off a perceptible chain reaction, difficult to explain to those who have no dialect. There is an indestructible kernel of *apprehended* matter, attached to the tendrils of the senses; the dialect word is *always* pegged to reality, because they are one and the same thing, perceived before we learnt to reason, and never to disappear even when we have been taught reason in another language. This holds good, above all, with names of objects.

> But the kernel of primitive matter (whether in connexion with names or any other word) contains uncontrollable forces because it exists in a pre-logical sphere where the associations are free and fundamentally unstable. Dialect therefore is in certain respects reality and in others instability.
>
> I feel an almost physical pain in the nerves, deep down inside me, which produce words like *basavéjo* (sting of a bee) and *barbastrijo* (bat), *anda* (snake) and *ava* (bee), even *rùa* (wheel) and *pùa* (doll). It comes shooting up through me like a *lamposgiantizo* (flash of lightning), I feel conscious of that ultimate fusion of what we call life, that indestructible core, the very bedrock.
>
> (Meneghello, 1967, pp. 90–91)

'Instability' is at first sight difficult to reconcile with 'the very bedrock'; I think it is a *rational* instability that is intended, indicating the absence of a systematic or logical framework, and 'the very bedrock' suggests the kind of conviction that multiple associations forged in successive first-hand experiences might convey.

Be that as it may, I would put forward the notion that much of the later detail of a person's world representation, filled in by relating idea to idea, or one verbally communicated experience to another, may retain its intimacy with actuality, its fidelity to things as they are, by virtue of the fact that elements in his individual language have remained from childhood 'always pegged to reality' – and enough of them to act as focal reference points for the structure as a whole.

All this goes to support the claim that talking-and-doing must be given major stress throughout the primary school. Language must continue to grow roots in first-hand experience. The headmaster I heard of recently who said uneasily as he began to show his American visitor round the school, 'I don't know what's the matter – it isn't usually as quiet as this', was splendidly unaware that his comment might sound odd! Most of our primary-school buildings were not planned for the kind of work that goes on there today, so if the tide of busy and talkative children washes right up to the door of the headmaster's room, that may be taken as a good sign. For the smaller the working groups – down to a pair – the greater the total of relevant talk that can go on at any one time. And the more experienced the class in this way of working, the greater the amount of useful consultation between groups, and with the teacher. What in a traditional curriculum would have been history or science or geography or number-work or painting or English – all this may go on without distinction and all equally capable of contributing to the forging of links between language and first-hand experience.

Talk in a participant role provides also the most efficient schooling in *listening*. Young children, in their egocentrism, have to learn to cooperate and they have to learn the language of cooperation: if talking is to assist cooperative doing, it must move out of egocentrism towards reciprocity, and success in a joint undertaking is a built-in incentive. It has too often been assumed in the past that young children without any such schooling were capable of listening to the sustained monologue of a teacher. A London junior schoolgirl knew better when she commented recently upon a visitor in some such words as, 'Yes, I liked some of what she said – but she talked so much that there wasn't any time to learn.'

Much that is shared between children in this cooperative talk, however, will not be practical but expressive. (Sapir [1961, p. 10] referred to the 'colour' as well as the 'requirements of actual contexts'.) Such talk will express in fact 'the way I feel about things' as well as communicate 'the way things are'. And if we are to pick up the implications of Meneghello's statement, the expressions of feeling may well be of particular importance, contributing strongly to the 'ultimate fusion of what we call life'.

But talk is quicksilver. It is all very well to record that a joint activity may generate both practical and expressive talk, each with its own importance. The truth is that almost any sort of talk, given favourable circumstances, may break out at any time. The children in the following example were gathered round the teacher's desk, with the bits and pieces they had been working on, ostensibly to consult her:

B.C.   I could buy a whole sack of potatoes with the money I've got at home. (*Referring to a bill he was working out.*) This isn't really a shopping list it's more a grocer's list. It's two sacks of potatoes. I'll need a five pound note.

P.S.   In the olden days they didn't spell penny with a 'p' but with a 'd', didn't they?

G.H.   You know carrots, those brown things on the top. Well my friend told me how to do it. You cut it off and wet the cotton wool and put it on and all the flowers grow out. You're the best lady I met in my life.

F.S.   I wonder why rhinos are so fat yet they can run sixty miles an hour?

B.C.   I'm going to live in a castle in the south of France in the summer. It was before gunpowder was invented and it's liveable, but it's got dungeons and arrow slits and gallows.

P.S.   I can run sixty miles an hour in these shoes.

G.H.   You know Little John in Robin Hood, well I thought he was little but he's about ten feet tall.

(Rosen, 1966, p. 3)

The teacher receives what each has to say and needs, on this occasion, to say nothing in return.

A great deal of the most useful talk arises in connexion with events and activities that *have* taken place, inside or outside the school. Much of this will be in the participant role – talking to piece together the history of an old building or the accurate record of a pond-hunt, to make sense of facts and figures about the weather, or arrive at a solution to some such problem as 'How did they get the chains across the gorge to build the suspension bridge?'. And much of it will be in the spectator role – individuals recreating in story the events of the day, or celebrating some precious moment of it – some notable find, or triumph, or disaster or even – occasionally – grief. Such talk merges, in the spectator role, with all the talk that arises from poems and stories, read or heard, told or written.

Two final points remain to be made in brief. It can hardly be doubted that the talk of young children is the direct precursor of their later thinking. Much of our thinking as adults seems to us to bear the guise of an inner debate: the 'voice of reason', the 'voice of conscience', the 'voice of ambition' – these dramatis personae have often enough been named, figuratively of course, but the figure seems right. In an earlier chapter [of *Language and learning*] we have considered Vygotsky's suggestion that speech for oneself becomes internalised as 'inner speech' and then, by a further metamorphosis, becomes verbal thinking. James Moffett, of the Harvard School of Education, elaborates on this point with some conviction:

> In order to generate some kinds of thoughts, a student must have *previously* internalised some discursive operations . . . Elicitation [e.g. 'asking stimulating questions'] has a place certainly at some stage of instruction, but more basic is to create the kinds of social discourse that when internalised become the kinds of cognitive instruments called for by later tasks.
>
> (Moffett, 1968, p. 70)

Connie Rosen, from whose article I quoted the example of talk with a teacher given above, introduces my second brief point with these comments on the talk in her own class of nine-year-olds:

> . . . I'm not the type to say to them, 'Look here, I'm terribly sympathetic and understanding and you can tell me anything you like, my dears. Was that your mummy in that nice car? What a pretty dress you have on!' I know

some people can and produce some kind of nice, warm conversation with young children, but I can't.

I can only aim at making a triangle of myself, the children and the activities outside both of us, but in which we are both involved for different reasons. We must make and do things, paint and stick and cut, go for walks, collect things, feel things and discuss them together. In some ways there is too much talk that needs pruning and trimming, and too little of the purposeful reasoning talk. The talk I am aiming for is the talk that arises from shared experiences, experiences enjoyable and interesting to all of us, organised and yet allowing the children freedom to express themselves. Talk that will encourage comment and criticism and lead them to think about what is happening to them. In the course of such activities I would hope to build a relationship where they could feel safe to talk about anything that concerned them, and then because they had learnt to talk in class in a particular way, we might produce the kind of remarks and questions and individual approach that Stephen can make.

(Rosen, 1967, pp. 27–8)

It had been Stephen who, on the first day of the new term in a new school, had created the right orientation for the whole class by asking the question that lay buried in everybody's minds: 'When are you going to tell us the names of the teachers?'

Yes, the talk that constitutes learning of so many varieties is at one and the same time the means by which we must spin in the classroom the web of human relations.

2.2 'Language and learning'[2]

The second text in this section is key amongst Britton's work for its political intervention and for its promotion of understandings about language and learning in wider public discussion. *A language for life* (Department of Education and Science, 1975) is the report of a committee of enquiry chaired by Alan Bullock, appointed in 1972 by Margaret Thatcher, then Secretary of State for Education in Prime Minister Edward Heath's administration (1970–74). The background to this enquiry included a report by the National Foundation for Educational Research (NFER), entitled *The trend of reading standards* (Start and Wells, 1972), which had registered strong reservations about the information that was available through current tests. Critiques of the teaching of reading and writing and the perception of a decline in educational standards initiated by the writers of the Black Papers had given the issue of reading standards a political significance in educational discussion.

The chapter included here was intended as a theoretical basis for the coverage of different aspects of language and literacy which followed. The chapter draws extensively on Britton's ideas and introduces key themes in his thinking. It highlights the role that language plays in interpreting and reinterpreting the world, and the individual's active participation in that process through talk and writing as much as through listening and reading. Britton challenges 'the simplistic notion that "being told" is the polar opposite of "finding out for oneself"', maintaining, rather, that an understanding of the heuristic function of language informs the teacher's task and that children learn language most powerfully through their use of it.

It is a masterly statement of Britton's thought, and masterly, it must be added, in relation to the politics developing in relation to comprehensive schools, public education and the teaching of literacy – never addressing this directly but faultless in its positioning of understandings.

> *Man interposes a network of words between the world and himself, and thereby becomes the master of the world.*
>
> Georges Gusdorf [1965]

It is perfectly obvious that asking and telling play a persistent role in the day-to-day behaviour of human beings, and that without the exchange of information in words we should not be able to achieve a fraction of our customary activities. Add to this that we write and read letters, listen to radio and television, read newspapers and look things up in books, and it will be evident that verbalised information plays a crucial role in our affairs. This, however, if current theories are to be believed, is no more than the tip of the iceberg. It is the role that language plays in *generating* knowledge and *producing new forms* of behaviour that typifies human existence and distinguishes it from that of all other creatures.

These current theories stem from a powerful movement of ideas developed over the past fifty years, according to which man's individual, social and cultural achievements can be rightly understood only if we take into account the fact that he is essentially a *symbol-using animal*. By this account what makes us typically human is the fact that we symbolise, or represent to ourselves, the objects, people and events that make up our environment, and do so cumulatively, thus creating an inner representation of the world as we have encountered it. The accumulated representation is on the one hand a storehouse of past experience and on the other a body of expectations regarding what may yet happen to us. In this way we construct for ourselves a past and a future, a retrospect and a prospect; all our significant actions are performed within this extended field or framework, and no conscious act, however trivial, is uninfluenced by it. We interpret what we perceive at any given moment by relating it to our body of past experiences, and respond to it in the light of that interpretation. No doubt the processes of representation and storing are selective. Some things we are unable to interpret and their meaning is lost to us; some we may interpret but fail to store, and much that has been stored is certainly beyond the reach of deliberate recall. (Experiment has shown, however, that this does not necessarily mean we cannot be influenced by such things in interpreting fresh experiences: see, for example, Luria and Vinogradova [1958].)

Language is one of a number of ways in which we represent the world to ourselves, and if its workings are to be seen in perspective it is necessary first to look briefly at one of the other ways. The most obvious example of an 'inner representation' is probably the visual memory we carry away of some object we have looked at and can no longer see. It is this memory which enables us, in confronting a new scene on a later occasion, to recognise an acquaintance among a crowd of strangers. We could hardly expect, however, that the person recognised will look *exactly* as he did on that first occasion. It must be that our memory enables us to generalise beyond the situations on which it is based, or we should fail to recognise an old friend wearing a new expression. By generalising from our visual memories, in fact, we may make a good deal of sense of something we have never set eyes upon before. Thus, from much looking at many faces we come to recognise that a stranger is middle-aged rather than young, male rather than female, European rather than Oriental – not to mention the prior recognition that it is a human face that confronts us and not the face of a cat or an ape.

One of the keys to an understanding of language lies in realising that it is the prime means by which we construct *generalised* representations. At its simplest level of operation, a word that names an object is for a young child a filing-pin upon which he stores successive experiences of the objects themselves. As his experience grows, he uses the word to refer to an increasing range of objects, and applies it more and more consistently in the ways the adults do about him. He becomes increasingly aware of the characteristics of the category of objects named by the word. Thus he is employing language to assist him in generalising from visual (and indeed all other) modes of representing his experience. He does not, of course, do this without assistance. He may invent some words and apply them to categories of his own creation, but the vast majority of the words he uses will be taken over from the speech of the adults around him; and the objects these words refer to will be principally those to which the adults refer in using them. To sum up, then, we have to generalise from particular representations of past experiences in order to apply them to new ones, and language helps us to do this by providing a ready means of classifying these experiences. The important thing to remember is that as long as every event is experienced as unique and different from all other events, we cannot set up expectations regarding the future. It is by recognising recurrences that we learn from our experience.

This brief account began at the simplest level of operation of language, with what a *word* can do. But of course, language is more than a mere inventory of words; it also includes highly complex rules for combining words into continuous speech or writing. An obvious example of such rules is the relation of the subject of a sentence to the predicate or the relation of a verb to its object. In addition to a vast array of grammatical rules, there are also lexical and semantic relationships built into language. The term 'flower', for example, is part of a hierarchy of terms: it subsumes the categories named by 'buttercup' and 'daisy' and is itself subsumed under other categories such as 'plant'. A speaker profits from the constraints upon his language behaviour, because they are the rules of the 'language game' that make communication possible. Having taken a word into his speech vocabulary, a child learns by degrees to use it for more purposes, for more complex purposes, and for purposes approximating more and more to adult uses. A similar process operates with respect to the rules governing language. For example, a child will first use the words 'buttercup', 'daisy', 'flower' and 'plant' without regard for their values in this hierarchy; later, however, when he is able to use the hierarchical distinctions, he will have acquired a very useful strategy of thinking, as any player of the 'Twenty Questions' game will recognise. Some psychologists go so far as to claim that the language rules gradually 'internalised' in this way 'become the basic structures of thinking'; indeed, that 'a child's intellectual growth is contingent on his mastering the social means of thought, that is, language' (Vygotsky, 1962). For other psychologists, this would be too close an identification of thought with language. However, there is no need to enter this controversy, since it is enough to state what would be generally agreed: (a) that higher processes of thinking are normally achieved by the interaction of a child's language behaviour with his other mental and perceptual powers; and (b) that language behaviour represents the aspect of his thought processes most accessible to outside influences, including that of the teacher.

The plausibility of this claim has been greatly strengthened in recent years by the work of Chomsky and his associates in attempting to discover structural features to be found in all languages. If all languages embody some rules in common and those common rules are seen to be closely related to universal modes of human reasoning, then clearly the link between language and thinking is one that must be acknowledged. The simple fact would appear to be that people of all races have developed languages as their means of organising their experience of the world; and in doing so they have acquired, in common, characteristics specific to the human race. As a child gains mastery of his particular mother tongue he learns by degrees to apply its organising power to his own experience, and as a result his mental processes take on new forms. So complete is the transformation that it is impossible for us to reverse the process and conceive of our situation in the way we saw it as inarticulate infants.

The familiar facts with which each of us goes armed to meet new experiences are in origin statements about the world, and we require language to make those statements. However, it would be perfectly possible to state here that the page the reader has before him is green in colour, and that is patently *not* a fact. Language used in that way is the language of hypothesis, the formulation of possibilities. It is crucial in the sense that *what is* can be said to exist in its own right, open to contemplation, whereas *what might be* takes a form in which it may be contemplated only when it is in some way represented or symbolised. It may be said that all behaviour is experimental: that, for example, as we walk from one part of a building to another, we test out the hypothesis that an aperture is indeed open and not protected by a plate-glass door. And there may be occasions when the hypothesis is abruptly disproved. It would be very rash, however, to claim that in such a situation language had any direct role to play. It is when our behaviour moves into more problematic situations that the need arises for a hypothesis to be elaborated, to take on the form of a statement of the possibilities, and here we must use language. The effort to formulate a hypothesis, to put into words some possibility we have envisaged, results in a 'spelling out' to which we may then return, in the light of further experience and in search of further possibilities. By a kind of spiral, the formulation itself becomes a source from which we draw further questions, fresh hypotheses. The statement we have made becomes an object of our own contemplation and a spur to further thinking. It is probably true to say that the higher thought processes become possible to the child or adolescent who in this way learns to turn his linguistic activities back upon his own formulations.

If such claims are to seem feasible, two things must be remembered. One is that language provides us with a generalised representation of experience, and generalising has the effect of reducing the multiplicity of experience to a more manageable form. The other is that the complex rules governing the combination of elements when we speak or write impose order upon the experiences we succeed in putting into words. There are implications here for two familiar enough forms of classroom activity. In group discussion the spoken contribution of each member may be worked upon by speaker and listeners alike, and in the immediacy of face-to-face speech they make corporate enquiry a powerful mode of learning. Secondly, in the practice of writing, the child left alone with his evolving utterance is engaged in generating knowledge for himself, particularly when the writing is frequent, brief and strenuous rather than occasional and at length. At the same time he is developing mental operations which will afterwards be of service to him in writing, speaking, reading, listening or thinking.

It is a confusion of everyday thought that we tend to regard 'knowledge' as something that exists independently of someone who knows. 'What is known' must in fact be brought to life afresh within every 'knower' by his own efforts. To bring knowledge into being is a formulating process, and language is its ordinary means, whether in speaking or writing or the inner monologue of thought. Once it is understood that talking and writing are means to learning, those more obvious truths that we learn also from other people by listening and reading will take on a fuller meaning and fall into a proper perspective. Nothing has done more to confuse current educational debate than the simplistic notion that 'being told' is the polar opposite of 'finding out for oneself'. In order to accept what is offered when we are told something, we have to have somewhere to put it; and having somewhere to put it means that the framework of past knowledge and experience into which it must fit is adequate as a means of interpreting and apprehending it. Something approximating to 'finding out for ourselves' needs therefore to take place if we are to be successfully told. The development of this individual context for a new piece of information, the forging of the links that give it meaning, is a task that we customarily tackle by talking to other people.

In the Committee's view there are certain important inferences to be drawn from a study of the relationship between language and learning:

(i) all genuine learning involves discovery, and it is as ridiculous to suppose that teaching begins and ends with 'instruction' as it is to suppose that 'learning by discovery' means leaving children to their own resources;
(ii) language has a heuristic function; that is to say a child can learn by talking and writing as certainly as he can by listening and reading;
(iii) to exploit the process of discovery through language in all its uses is the surest means of enabling a child to master his mother tongue.

The ideas briefly set out in this chapter are intended, therefore, to provide a theoretical foundation for the chapters that follow.

2.3 In defence of 'progressive' practice

'Language in the British primary school'[3]

> *'Language in the British primary school'* confronts the public/political issues arising from the implementation of the kind of language and learning policy that Britton and his colleagues have been advocating for so many years.
>
> Gordon Pradl, from his introduction to
> *Prospect and retrospect* (Britton, 1982b, pp. 5–6)

This paper is the published version of an address to a conference on primary education held in 1979. In its conclusion, Britton looks back movingly at the tradition in which he is writing, not as 'a bandwagon . . . nor a pendulum swing. It is a steady, slow growing movement that has roots in philosophy back to Dewey and beyond; and is deep-rooted in the intuitions of the most successful teachers over a much longer period than that.' Now more than ever, he reflects, it seems to him important that 'the ideals that created the image of the British primary school, and the practices that supported it, should be kept alive'. The paper is a powerful defence of those practices and of the tradition that they represent. It speaks to us now precisely because the threats to that tradition which Britton identified have become, in the intervening years, ever-present, dominant features of the terrain of schooling.

Although Britton felt that the Bullock Report was less radical than the Plowden Report, in particular having too little to say to teachers in our inner-city schools, he confesses that by 1979 it was beginning to feel like 'a beacon that shone ever more brightly as the skies around it darkened'. He addresses the dangers and shortcomings of the polarised arguments that were coming to surround the notion of 'literacy': how it is learned and should be taught. He also confronts the emphasis on 'evaluation' – assessment – that was already increasingly prevalent in public discussion. Britton notes that 'the focus of the reactionary attack is now on the primary school', seen as the locus of progressive practice, or 'child-centred' education. Behind such attacks lie the influential lines of criticism of the Black Papers, which Britton is able, here, to address directly.

Britton reminds the reader of the distinctive ideas embodied in the Bullock Report, which recognise the unique role of language as an organiser of knowledge and the crucial part that talk plays in that process. He recalls the counter offered to the simplistic view that 'being told' is the polar opposite of 'finding out for oneself', once again showing how peer talk and teacher talk, reading and writing interweave as young people move towards mastery. Developing these remarks, he confronts the 'Note of Dissent' voiced by a member of the Bullock Committee, who had questioned in particular 'the notion postulated in Chapter 4 that a child can learn by talking and writing as certainly as he can by listening and reading'. Britton defends the notions of expressive language – expressive talk and writing – as lying at the centre of the teacher/learner relationship.

Building on this re-articulation of the positions taken in the Bullock Report, Britton continues by extending his account of the part played by expressive language as the starting point for children's engagement with curriculum learning.

> I believe a concern for the mastery of theoretical concepts begins with a respect for the common-sense concepts from which they must grow: that the mastery itself is a process of modifying common-sense concepts, and that mature thinking involves moving *back and forth* along a continuum from theoretical to common sense, from abstract to concrete, from the fruits of analysis to the data of experience.

It is an important statement of position based on illustrations drawn from the writing of young people and explored more fully in accounts of findings in Britton's research on writing.

Turning to his second line of warning about directions in contemporary discussions, Britton considers the nature and role of evaluation, or assessment, in teaching, and also of teaching and the work of teachers, and warns against evaluation's misuse as an instrument of enforcement upon teachers and a distortion of what it means to teach. He emphasises the role of the teacher as trusted listener and observer whose aim is to discover, however tentatively, the intentions of the learner (to read or write something) and to find ways of responding to those that encourage growth. In recognising the subtle and particular nature of the teaching/learning relationship, he shows how a teacher's self-evaluation and reflection is integral to that process. The centre of gravity is with noticing and responding. A preoccupation with 'marking' either the teacher or the child can distort how we teach and how we learn and, ultimately, narrow the education we offer in schools. Britton's warning of the dangers 'when trust gives way to surveillance' was prescient, indeed.

Every thoughtful primary-school teacher would agree, I believe, that it is a very difficult matter to assess the quality of learning that is going on in any classroom. But if it is difficult for the teacher, who is *there*, what of the parents and the public, who are not? No wonder they are so easily misled by the dogmatic pronouncements of the Black Paper campaigners. This may be one of the main reasons why popular opinion tends to fall in behind such views. Clearly, five minutes in a formal teaching situation is enough to demonstrate that useful information is being retailed; but to judge the quality of *learning* on this basis is like estimating the state of nurture of a nation by considering the size of its butter mountain or its reserves of dried milk. As every teacher knows, when you tell thirty children something, only some of them will have been told.

The 'British primary school' has not lacked for enthusiastic supporters in many parts of the world. Long before the Plowden Report (Central Advisory Council for Education [England], 1967) came out this was true, but the 'image' and the report have certainly sustained each other, and have made, I believe, an effective contribution to the work of innovators in other systems. Of course, when overseas visitors spend time themselves in our schools they often report that the 'image' and the reality fall far apart. It must be recalled that the survey of teaching procedures carried out for the Bullock Committee gave pretty convincing evidence that informal or 'progressive' methods had barely a foothold in our primary schools so far as language work was concerned. Yet the detractors continue to ignore this evidence. A recent edition of *The Times* (13 September 1978) reports publication of a document prepared by the Monday Club which reiterates the familiar charge: 'Literacy and numeracy standards among 10-year-olds were a national disgrace,' the paper says. It attributes the alleged decline in standards to too much 'progressive' teaching, and it calls for 'national standards to be set in both literacy and numeracy'. The focus of the reactionary attack is now on the primary school because the one view it shares with its protagonists is a belief that the most promising solution of our undoubted secondary-school problem would be to get things right in the preceding stages.

The Bullock Report (Department of Education and Science, 1975) has also been influential in other English-speaking countries, but it is, I believe, a less radical document than Plowden. The Bullock Committee was set up to represent all factions, yet both Mrs Thatcher and the Chairman she appointed were eager to secure a unanimous report, presumably on the grounds that the issues that really matter lie at a more fundamental level than those that divide us. I don't think a reading of the report bears out that view; what comes over, I believe, is a somewhat watered-down form of a 'progressive' view, with some important anomalies and ambiguities. In particular, I think it offers cold comfort to radical innovators who, in their classrooms, are beginning to devise solutions to the most difficult of the inner-city secondary-school problems.

The year the report came out was the year of my retirement, and I spent most of the next two years teaching in Canada and Australia. I returned to what seemed, from the point of view of educational climate, a very different England. The 'Great Debate' was in full swing, launched by a speech from the Prime Minister which had a good deal to say about literacy but made no reference to the Bullock Committee's views on that topic. 'Literacy' in fact was one of the words on everybody's lips, and 'evaluation' was the other. I soon began to feel that the Bullock Report was a beacon that shone ever more brightly as the skies around it darkened. Not that 'literacy' and 'evaluation' as concerns are in themselves agents of darkness, but they require wise handling and are all too easily mishandled for ulterior purposes. A narrow focus on literacy may result in the rejection of the spoken uses of language from which literacy must grow; notions of evaluation become threatening when they see it, not as a way of generating information useful to the system, but as a means of enforcement, whether upon teachers or upon pupils. On both literacy and evaluation, the hidden protagonists are two sharply divided views of teaching and learning.

The Plowden Report was clear about the importance of talk as a means of learning. It placed a high value on 'the direct impact of environment on the child and the child's individual response to it' (para. 544), recognised the unique role of language as an organiser of experience, and so found that there was 'every justification for the conversation which is a characteristic feature of the contemporary primary school' (para. 535). The Bullock Report in its earlier chapters is equally forthright and pursues the ideas a little further:

> (i) all genuine learning involves discovery, and it is as ridiculous to suppose that teaching begins and ends with 'instruction' as it is to suppose that 'learning by discovery' means leaving children to their own resources; (ii) language has a heuristic function; that is to say a child can learn by talking and writing as certainly as he can by listening and reading; (para. 4.10)

To a teacher in the old tradition, as to the public, it is common knowledge that a child learns by listening to the teacher and reading the textbook, and there is no need to look any further. But this view is based on a misunderstanding of the processes involved:

> Once it is understood that talking and writing are means to learning, those more obvious truths that we learn also from other people by listening and reading will take on a fuller meaning and fall into a proper perspective. Nothing has done more to confuse current educational debate than the simplistic notion that 'being told' is the polar opposite of 'finding out for oneself'. In order to accept what is offered when we are told something, we have to have somewhere to put it; and having somewhere to put it means that the framework of past knowledge and experience into which it must fit is adequate as a means of interpreting and apprehending it. Something approximating to 'finding out for ourselves' needs therefore to take place if we are to be successfully told. The development of this individual context for a new piece of information, the forging of the links that give it meaning, is a task that we customarily tackle by talking to other people.
>
> (para. 4.9)

[These two quotations, of course, are taken from Britton's own Chapter 4 of the Bullock Report – see 2.2 above.]

Teaching by seminar, a strategy based on this principle of learning by talking, is sometimes ridiculed by its opponents as a 'pooling of ignorances'. But there is one sort of gain to be had from discussing a topic with those who share our ignorance, and our struggle to understand, and another complementary gain from discussing it with an expert, the teacher. Good teaching consists in relating these two processes in a productive manner. But this account of language in learning is incomplete until we have admitted also learning by reading, learning by listening to the teacher's monologue. Rightly phased, these can be crucial highlights; but that phasing implies that the reading and listening should be spaced out with intervals for the students' own talk, sometimes with the expert, sometimes with each other. Finally, learning by writing is most typically the 'harvesting' stage, when what has been talked about and thought about is worked on, solitarily, from the standpoint of the writer's own synthesis. A little hard evidence on the learning value of writing was shown in a report of an experiment by Howe (1975): half the students attending a lecture undertook to make notes, the other half not to; after a brief revision session, some little while later, at which the note-takers had their own notes and the others had the lecturer's notes, a series of recall tests demonstrated the superior recall of those who had undertaken the writing, that is, the note-taking.

The Black Paper retort to the paragraph I have quoted from the Bullock Report did not have to await the publication of the report; it was voiced by a committee member in his 'Note of Dissent':

> It is doubtful if children's talk in school does much to improve their knowledge, for free discussion as a learning process is notoriously unproductive. As for children learning by writing, this seems a very doubtful proposition. The writer can only write from his present knowledge and experience and in the case of children these are very limited.
> (Department of Education and Science, 1975, p. 558)

A similar view is put forward by Williams (in the juggernaut she calls 'a critique' of our writing research) [see 3.1 and 3.2 below], when she complains that encouraging a child to use expressive talk and writing is 'in a sense imprisoning the child in a web of common-sense concepts' (Williams, 1977, p. 47). We must infer that behind the two opposing views of the nature of teaching and learning lie very different conceptions as to the nature of our knowledge of the world.

George Kelly began one of his psychological papers: 'This paper, throughout, deals with half-truths only. Nothing that it contains is, or is intended to be, wholly true. The theoretical statements propounded are no more than partially accurate constructions of events which, in turn, are no more than partially perceived' (1969, p. 66). And he goes on to explain:

> When a scientist propounds a theory he has two choices: he can claim that what he says has been dictated to him by the real nature of things, or he can take sole responsibility for what he says and claim only that he has offered one man's hopeful construction of the realities of nature.

This agrees in substance with things said by Karl Popper, a philosopher whose conclusions in other respects have been very different from Kelly's. Popper showed that scientific hypotheses cannot be established as true: they can be proved false, but unless and until that happens they 'forever remain hypotheses or conjectures'. For his part, he draws no hard and fast line between our common-sense and our theoretical or scientific concepts:

In defence of 'progressive' practice

I tried to show that our knowledge grows through trial and error-elimination, and that the main difference between its prescientific and its scientific growth is that on the scientific level we consciously search for errors: the conscious adoption of the critical method becomes the main instrument of growth.

(Popper, 1976, p. 115)

Such methods, he claims, are widely applicable beyond the bounds of science.

I believe a concern for the mastery of theoretical concepts begins with a respect for the common-sense concepts from which they must grow: that the mastery itself is a process of modifying common-sense concepts, and that mature thinking involves moving back and forth along a continuum from theoretical to common sense, from abstract to concrete, from the fruits of analysis to the data of experience.

Here is a nine-year-old writing about his first 'scientific experiment' in school:

1. The *paper* crinkled up and then went smaller and black. It was very brittle and thin at the end. It turned to ashes so if we breathed on it hard it flew all over the place . . .
2. The *cotton cloth* burned and fringed at the same time. But the amazing thing was that the threads separated or in other words parted so that you could see through them like from the inside you can see through net curtains . . .
5. The *cotton yarn* at first looked like little worms crawling about and then the flame covered and smoothed it like a sheet covering your face.[4]

Learning to observe and record is an essential part of the learning process in science. It involves sorting the objective from the subjective aspects of the experience recorded and the rejection of the latter for the purpose of mustering and organising the former. But our everyday speech and expressive uses of writing demand no such separation: what happened and how what happened affected us, our feelings about the events, are intertwined in our experience and we normally expect our listeners or readers to be interested in both aspects. Expressive speech and writing naturally carries both: the very words that denote the events are likely also to carry something of our feelings about them (as when we say, 'I hear Arsenal made mincemeat of Chelsea' rather than the announcer's 'Arsenal 4, Chelsea nil'). Thus scientific recording requires the use of informative writing, not expressive; but the move from one to the other on a child's part involves the difficult piece of learning I have been describing, and that must be given time. To allow expressive writing (like that of the nine-year-old above) in the early stages enables the teacher to monitor that learning in progress, and plots for the student its gradual achievement. It seems to me that attempts to hasten the process threaten to divorce the scientific facts to be handled from the experiences that give rise to them. It is all too likely then that rote learning from the textbook will replace the development of a true scientific understanding. What is true for science is true also for all environmental and historical studies. The philosopher Ernst Cassirer (1944, p. 187) once said of learning in history: 'If I put out the light of my own personal experience I cannot see and I cannot judge of the experience of others.'

Expressive speech and writing are forms of discourse which come naturally to us in situations of mutual trust, and as such they embody the teaching/learning relationship we try to establish with every child. Further, because there is trust there is also a willingness to take risks, and the exploration of new experiences, the acceptance of new information, the move to a new viewpoint, demand that a learner should take risks (Britton et al., 1975). A campaign for literacy can all too easily be used as a weapon in the hands of those who oppose these educational processes because they do not understand them.

Among the things currently being said about evaluation is the statement that evaluation is an inseparable part of teaching. I want to claim that while evaluation is part of a teacher's responsibility it should be kept as distinct from teaching as possible, and we should know when we are doing the one and when we are doing the other. Clearly, we can take the argument no further until we have broken down the term 'evaluation' and seen the different things that it might refer to.

Since education is a public expense, I believe it has to be accountable to the public, and that there must therefore be some form of national 'monitoring' to provide a comprehensible glimpse, as it were, of what goes on in schools. The Bullock Report goes into some detail as to how this might be done without interfering with the processes it [the monitoring] sets out to evaluate. The essential features are that it should assess what teachers in fact try to teach (wherever this can be done), that there should be no single test or 'instrument' which might have the effect of distorting or restricting what they teach, and that no attempt should be made to measure the whole performance (in a given subject) of a particular pupil or a particular school. This form of national assessment is thus kept clear of other forms of evaluation and their purposes. From the evidence of the document 'Language performance' (Assessment of Performance Unit, 1978), I am very happy with the plans devised by the unit for carrying out this national evaluation of work in language.

Consider next the evaluation procedures required for the management of local resources: psychological services, additional teaching strength, specialist teachers, supplementary budgets and so on. I think we need to keep a careful watch at this level: do the testing procedures yield information which will be used to benefit children? – both because it is the right information and because resources exist to respond to it. Evaluation of innovative programmes – which might be within a school or an education authority or more widely – is yet another distinct purpose and one that need not concern us here. Very little such work is done because very little is known about how to do it. That brings us to the heart of the problem for my purposes here – evaluation by the teacher.

Before tackling it, however, I want to suggest that in all these other forms of evaluation there is a danger that the procedures will be misused as instruments of enforcement upon teachers. This was notably the case with the behavioural objectives movement in North America. For many administrators the enforcement aspect was overt and systematic: teachers were to formulate their objectives in accordance with approved policies *in order to be held to them*. Similarly in the United Kingdom, Rhodes Boyson has expressed the view that Her Majesty's Inspectors ought to return to their one-time role, and go round classrooms checking that the teaching of the 3Rs is satisfactory – as a direct counter-measure, I assume, to the spread of 'progressive' teaching methods. Claims of this sort at this time could, I believe, be multiplied. I think they are ill-based because enforcement by this means does not achieve what it sets out to do and because in the long run it lowers the quality of teaching. It is ineffective in the general sense that what happens in any classroom is the result of interacting teacher and pupil behaviours: the gap between any regulation, guideline or other sort of 'recipe' and the actual behaviour of the teacher is one that only the teacher can fill. At his most effective he fills that gap from *conviction* – indeed, so many second-by-second decisions contribute to it that anything more remote than inner conviction has little chance of being consistently applied. I would use this argument equally to oppose the notion of 'teacher-proof' project kits and enforcement by evaluative procedures. The long-term adverse effects are best described as the substitution of a 'regime of surveillance' for a 'regime of trust'. The productive value of a regime of trust between teacher and pupil can be matched by that expected from a relationship of trust between teachers and the public and the intermediary agents, parents, principals and administration. Admittedly, it can be shown that not all teachers are trustworthy: but the loss we sustain when, in a more open regime, they are able to 'get away with things' is nothing, in my view, compared with the effects of loss of morale on the part of the average teacher and, more particularly, on the part of the best teachers in the system, when trust gives way to surveillance.

To deal briefly with evaluation in school, I think, as teachers, we have to accept responsibility for generating information about pupil performance which will be useful to parents, succeeding teachers, placement agencies, and, at a later stage, employers and admission agencies. If for the moment we can restrict the term evaluation (in school) to that process, I would stress that this evaluative function should be kept distinct from our teaching function. 'Teacher didn't want to *read* my story, she only wanted to *mark* it!' was the comment of a six-year-old in an infant school, and it is the distinction he recognised that concerns me here. We are more than ever supported today in a belief that children demonstrate a mastery in achieving their own intentions that they do not show in working to somebody else's purposes. Linguists have discovered that a young child's mastery of syntactic structure cannot be truly assessed from their responses to presented test questions, but only by observing their spontaneous utterances (Slobin and Welsh, 1971). With this support, primarily from cognitive psychologists, we have grown more expert in our attempts to tap children's own intentions in school, and at arousing new intentions in directions in which we foresee their developing needs and powers. Yet it is my contention that the 'evaluative frame of mind' that we have allowed to become a part of the teacher's stance – the readiness to 'mark' rather than 'read' – prevents us from reaping the full benefit of these attempts. Courtney Cazden comments on one aspect of this evaluative habit of mind:

> But teachers, over the decades if not over the centuries, have somehow gotten into the habit of hearing with different ears once they go through the classroom doors. Language forms assume an opaque quality. We cannot hear through them; we hear only the errors to be corrected. One value of knowledge about language is not to make the language of our children more salient to our attention. Quite the opposite. That knowledge reassures, and it lets language forms recede into the transparency they deserve, enabling us to talk and listen in the classroom as outside, focussing full attention on the children's thoughts and feelings that those forms express.
>
> (Cazden, 1976, p. 80)

If we succeed in harnessing or arousing a child's intention to write something, perhaps, or to read something, we shall release in him tacit powers favourable to his success, and it is in that process of satisfying his own intention that he will learn most effectively. But if we then 'evaluate' his performance – in my present sense of the word, that of giving a mark or grade or comment which will indicate a 'verdict' upon his performance – then we are in effect providing an alternative objective to his own satisfaction. In fact the evaluation becomes the real objective, his satisfaction no more than an ostensible one. The evaluating procedure, in fact, *drives a wedge between a child's intention and its satisfaction.* A typical intention for a piece of expressive writing on the part of a ten-year-old, for example, might be his wish to establish and maintain a relationship with the teacher who reads it: he will know whether his writing has succeeded by the way he feels about the growing relationship. The teacher's response will aim at maximising this aspect of the exchange as the best way of ensuring its learning value. In reading and responding appropriately he will have fulfilled his teaching function: for his evaluating function, he will, at the end of the term or the year, help the child select some of his writings (perhaps including this particular piece), and this work will be multiply marked (by the teacher and a colleague) to arrive at the informative evaluation of the child's progress which will go to parents, other teachers and so on. 'Responding appropriately' may, of course, include very helpful detailed 'feedback' – the comments of someone better able than the child to overcome the difficulties we meet in trying to say what we mean: but this, in my terms, is not 'evaluation' but 'guidance' – the heart of teaching.

That leaves one gap to be filled: since a teacher's intention is to teach, he must continually monitor his efforts in terms of the learning that goes on in those he teaches. This is indeed inseparable from teaching, but the information generated is for the teacher's guidance, is constantly sought, interpreted and applied, and may have no relevance to the child, his parents or any other agency.

I want in conclusion to remind readers that the 'enlightened' view of teaching and learning we profess is not an outmoded bandwagon, representative (as I have heard it said) of 'the dependent sixties'. It is, in fact, not a bandwagon at all, nor a pendulum swing. It is a steady, slow-growing movement that has roots in philosophy back to Dewey and beyond; and is deep-rooted in the intuitions of the most successful teachers over a much longer period than that. It is under attack in many countries today as an effect, I believe, of the worldwide inflationary recession. I am not thinking primarily of budgets, a setback we can survive; I think the psychological effects of the recession are much more intractable. Psychologists have often enough pointed out that one of the first effects of anxiety in a person is a reduction in the number of factors he is prepared to take into account in arriving at a decision; and I believe the same can be seen at the level of whole societies. People today are asking difficult questions in all directions, but the educational system is particularly vulnerable. Typically of the USA, the question there has taken the form of 'How much for the dollar?'; but the formulation fits well enough what is going on elsewhere in the world. The narrowing of educational perspectives is variously reflected here in the views of the public, of parents, in the Black Papers, in the administration at all levels, and in the views of many teachers themselves. However, I think we can already see signs of the worst being over: as recession itself recedes I believe perspectives will widen again. But meanwhile, in the difficult five years, say, that lie ahead, it seems to me more than ever important that the ideals that created the image of 'the British primary school', and the practices that supported it, should be kept alive.

2.4 The disorderliness of learning
From 'Talking to learn'[5]

Language, the learner and the school, by Douglas Barnes, James Britton and Harold Rosen, was first published in 1969. Its origins lay in the work of the London Association for the Teaching of English (LATE), under whose aegis practising teachers had been investigating the importance of language in learning. Britton's contribution to the book is a chapter, 'Talking to Learn', which focuses on the learners and on what can be accomplished in and through talk. The chapter appears here, somewhat abbreviated, in the form which it took in the book's third edition (Barnes, Britton and Torbe, 1986).

The preface to the third edition contains a trenchant statement about the relationship between research and teaching:

> Teaching will not be enhanced by handing over to teachers a 'knowledge' developed elsewhere. It is they themselves who have the capacity to sharpen their judgements: other people – in person or in books – can only point a direction, offer a framework, or give encouragement or support.
>
> (Barnes, Britton and Torbe, 1986, p. 8)

Britton's quite remarkable contribution might be construed as an enactment of these principles. Immediately striking is the length of the transcripts included in it: what we are presented with are not mere highlights, snippets of classroom interaction that might exemplify a point, but rather the ebb and flow of dialogue among students. This requires us to respond differently as readers: to pay careful attention to what is being said, to tune in to the conversations and to begin to make sense of them for ourselves. We are thus learning how to 'sharpen our judgements' as we travel with Britton through the chapter.

Recognising from the outset that the relationship between what is taught and what is learnt is complex and unpredictable, Britton announces that the focus here is on learning, which will sometimes, he suggests, 'take place in a very disorderly fashion'. This point is illustrated by the contrast between the first two transcripts. The first involves five 16-year-old girls talking about their homes; the second has three 14-year-old girls working together to translate some English sentences into Latin. This second instance might be taken to exemplify all that is most obviously productive about the use of collaborative talk in classrooms. A student who might struggle if confronted with the task working alone is supported by her peers, while the one who is most competent (and/or confident) benefits from having to explain to her peers the reasons for the choices she makes. And what is abundantly clear is that the talk among the students is 'on task': it is all directed towards the goal of accomplishing the translation, and that objective is, to a very large extent, achieved through the discussion that takes places among them.

But talk in the first transcript does not appear to operate in this way. There is no obvious goal, no objective to be met, nor even, on the face of it, a problem to be solved. The relation of the subject matter – the students' homes and families – to any form of curricularised knowledge is a distant or tangential one. This conversation requires more time to develop – and a different form of attentiveness from us if we are to begin to grasp what might be achieved through it. From it, Britton develops a vitally important argument about the affective and social dimensions of learning: 'Our knowledge of the world,' he suggests, 'is inextricably bound up with the way we feel about the world, about people and things and events and ourselves.' And he makes the bold proposal that much might be gained through 'teachers' attempts to make in-school learning more like out-of-school'.

Drawing on Vygotsky and Polanyi, Britton fleshes out a model of learning as 'a process in which meaning is negotiated by constructing a version of the unfamiliar from the raw material of the familiar'. In this process, the everyday knowledge that learners bring with them to the classroom has to be the starting point for any engagement with the curriculum: with the organised, 'scientific' concepts that schooling has to offer. In this negotiation of meaning, Britton assigns a central role to expressive language, spoken and written: such language, close to the language of everyday speech, is the means whereby learning is accomplished, in the exploratory, dialogic interactions of the classroom. It follows, therefore, that this is the language to which teachers need to pay attention, rather than seeking to suppress it in favour of more public, formal or 'academic' registers.

In the final section of the chapter, Britton reflects on what had been learnt since the book's first publication 17 years previously. First, there are the implications for pedagogy. It wasn't enough for teachers merely to indicate a tolerance of different linguistic forms and resources: 'We learned from experience that expressive talk has to be earned rather than simply allowed in.' What need to be established first, as a precondition of productive, collaborative talk, are relationships of mutual trust. This also involves, Britton indicates, a shift in teachers' view of their own knowledge and expertise: as vital as any sort of disciplinary knowledge is the capacity to develop relationships with the learners: 'The listening is . . . crucial: with all the pressures of class teaching it has to be fought for strenuously.'

There are also implications for how English is conceptualised as a subject. Here, as elsewhere in Britton, the two main strands, the rendering in language of personal experience and the experience of literature, are brought into close alignment. In both strands, what is salient in the learning process is 'the generation and refinement of our value systems' – how we feel about the world, rather than merely what we know about it. It is a process that is sustained by learning with and from each other.

We teach and teach and they learn and learn: if they didn't, we wouldn't. But of course the relation between their learning and our teaching isn't by any means a constant one. From any given bit of teaching some learn more than others: we teach some lessons when everybody seems to learn something, and other lessons when nobody seems to learn anything – at all events, not anything of what we are 'teaching'. As the syllabus grows longer we teach more – but do they learn more? And if we get three lessons a week when we ought to have five, presumably we teach more to the minute than we would otherwise: but again, do they learn any quicker? How *do* we judge how much is being learnt, in any case?

It's easy enough to test simple rote learning of course (from nonsense syllables through Kim's Game to the Thirty-Nine Articles), but this goes no way towards satisfying our idea of what learning and teaching *are*. We want children, as a result of our teaching, to *understand*; to be wise as well as well-informed, able to solve fresh problems rather than have learnt the answers to old ones; indeed, not only able to answer questions but also able to ask them. Information as to how well they're getting on in this kind of learning – even if we could spend half our time devising and setting and marking tests – would be terribly hard to come by.

With considerations of this sort in mind, it seems useful to take time off to think about learning, look for examples of it in progress, forgetting teaching altogether for the moment. If the teacher could be more certain what learning looked like, in some at least of its many guises, he might find it easier to 'monitor' his own teaching.

Since learning doesn't take place to numbers, however, and will probably sometimes take place in a very disorderly fashion, it is impossible to set it out, marshalled and docketed like the exhibits in a museum. Glimpses of it are to be found, first, in what people say to each other.

The first example presents a group of five 16-year-old girls talking about their homes. They come from the leavers' class in a comprehensive school, and the discussion arose as part of work on the BBC Schools Radio programme, 'Speak'. There is no adult present. The starter for the discussion was an extract from a short story, 'Now I lay me', by Ernest Hemingway. The girls followed the suggestion for talk in the teacher's notes on the passage. (Part of their discussion was subsequently used in a BBC radio programme called 'Parents'.)

The transcript cannot show all that was said because every now and then snatches of general — or dual or triple — talk break out, and perhaps only a word or two emerges. But it is as faithful as I can make it. Since such a conversation represents people acting upon each other, I have tried to keep the speakers clear in the record by giving each an identifying letter. Words in brackets are what emerges from general talk or else unidentified interruptions — though as we shall see, the term 'interruption' does not do justice to the supportive tone that most of the interpolations carry. . . .

A	This is always happening in our house. (Really?) My dad brings home things and . . . you know, my mum comes along and she says, 'Right, this is no good, we'll get rid of this, we'll get rid of that, what's this doing here, we don't need this . . . '
B	No, and doesn't ask first . . .
C	Load of old junk . . . throw it out!
A	You can't blame her really . . .
B	Yes, I know, but they have some things that you might think are old junk as well . . . that could be taking up space, you know . . .
A	Like old exercise books . . .
C	Yes, you wouldn't throw *those* away for anything . . .
B	I mean . . . I put certain things down in one place where I know they are and suddenly my mother comes and she says, 'Come on, we haven't got

The disorderliness of learning

	room for that' . . . (Yes, . . . or she says . . .) and I say, 'Well, where *can* I put it?' Or she throws it away and says, 'Oh! did you want it?' [Laughter]
C	Sorry, but it was cluttering up the room . . . you might as well have thrown it away . . . it's no good.
A	It's always causing rows in our family . . . My brother says, 'Where's my cricket set?'
D	I think it happens in any family unit, actually.
B	I think it's just thoughtlessness for the other person . . . they probably think because you're younger, what you do have to put away is not worthwhile but as they're older people . . . you know . . . they . . .
A	Have you ever . . . you know . . . sort of . . . Mum's said to you, like, 'Could you help me clear up?' So you say, 'Yes, OK', and you put your brother's or sister's things away, and then they come up and say, 'Where's so and so?' (Yeah . . . Yes) But then you think to yourself, Well, it's annoying to have . . . to have . . . to leave somebody's coat or something in the middle of the room . . . (Yes . . . Yes, I know . . .) Do you know what I mean?
B	And when they do complain, you feel as if you haven't done your job, but then you say, 'Well, I did pack it away, didn't I?' . . . You know . . . what are they complaining about?
D	It's annoying as well . . .
E	I do the same . . . I mean if I find anything lying around . . . if it's no good I just throw it away . . .
A	It might mean a lot . . .
D	I think in my family . . . I think my mother is the most considerate . . . she'd ask rather than my father . . . my father wouldn't.
A	Well, I'm lucky . . . I've got a room of my own . . . so . . .
D	I'd like a room of my own, but then again, you don't keep everything in your room, do you? My dad or mother goes in there and finds anything that she doesn't think is necessary . . . my mother would ask me first, but my dad . . .
B	Well, frankly, my mother wouldn't touch anything in my room, you know . . . she just doesn't. She feels I've put it there for some purpose . . . but again, if I go into her bedroom . . . (Yeah . . . That annoys me . . .) But say if I have a day off from school . . . or when . . . Or we've got some sort of holiday and I see things around and I say, well, you know, I'll give the place a good old clean, at least it'll help . . . and I put things neatly, it's all tidy . . . I wouldn't throw anything out, because I'm not

	sure whether she wants it or not . . . and then she comes home, and she says, 'Where's this? where's that?' . . . I feel awful . . .
D	And you feel that . . . um . . . she doesn't appreciate . . .
B	. . . appreciate, you know . . . I even the other day moved her bedroom . . . er . . . (Furniture) . . . furniture around.
D	I did that in my house . . .
B	I did . . . I thought it looked awful where it was, you know.
A	But I . . . what annoys me is my room . . . is my room . . . If . . . if it's in a muddle I know where everything is . . . I like my room to be in a mess.
B	But you see, we . . . I keep that as a sort of main bedroom, you know . . . (main room . . .) Yes, sometimes I don't even sleep in my room, it's so cold . . .
C	Ooh, crumbs!
B	How do you feel on this subject, Pamela?
D	[with a great guffaw] Negative!
C	I always know where everything is in my room even if it is untidy, but my mother comes along and I can't find anything anywhere.
A	I like it when you get to that age when your parents seem to realise that you're . . . you're going off on your own . . . (Yes . . . You're growing up . . .) . . . you've got your own life to lead, so you think, Right, we'll leave all her things, she can do what she likes with them. It's her time, she can do what she likes with her time.
B	They start from a certain point, don't they?
E	Well, I don't think they always do that . . . They try to remember that you're growing up and then they forget.
D	Yes . . . they try to protect you . . .
E	They're treating you like children and telling you where to put things . . .
C	. . . going round tidying up after you.
E	You know, I usually arrange my bedroom as I want it and then my mum comes along. Oh, you'll catch a draught there . . . it's no good, you don't want it that way . . . (Yes. Yes.) . . . and they move it around you know.
A	I feel like the bed by the window, but they say no . . . I like to look out you know . . . see what's going on.
B	I like it as well, you know . . . I like the head of my bed to be right by the window, you know, and my mother comes along and she says, 'Where's the North Pole?' you know, Where's north? . . . all this business . . . What's north got to do with it, you know . . . north and south . . . you

The disorderliness of learning

	know, you should have your head facing such-and-such . . . Oo, I think it's just fuss, fuss . . . I don't like it at all.
D	They're trying to do their best to protect us but sometimes they do overdo it.
B	And things like if I don't draw my curtains when I go to bed . . . well, I like to see a half light streaming in, you know.

Already, it seems, the reader will be asking questions. How much of this talk is simply 'for the record' – an effect of the presence of the microphone? Does any individual girl in fact represent ideas that she really subscribes to? Or is each of them merely offering common currency, the small change of talk among their elders? Alternatively, in a different image, are they doing more than taking a nice warm dip together in comfortable beliefs that they all hold, have all talked about often enough before? Is anything happening to anybody in this talk – is anybody changing, or laying herself open to change?

Before pursuing these questions, let us look at a very different example of talk. A class of third-year girls [Year 9] (in their second year of Latin) was set the task of translating English sentences into Latin. They worked in groups of three, and here is a brief record of one trio:

A	[Reading] 'All the pupils are not praised by the teacher.'
B	Where is it? [Laughter]
C	All the pupils are not . . . third . . . (Yes) Are . . .
B	Are not praised . . . ([Several voices] No)
C	Are not being praised . . .
A	Er . . . to praise . . .
C	Um . . . *antur*.
A	So it's . . .
B	Yes, so it's . . . um . . . *laudantur*. [Writing] *Laud-ant-ur*.
A	All right. So we've got that out of the way.
B	We've got to make sure whether it's singular or plural . . .
A	Mm. They are . . .
B	They . . .
A	Yes, so it's right. Um . . . now the subject (Pupils) . . . which is er . . .
B	*Discipulus.*
C	*Discipuli* . . .
B	*Discipuli*, yes, because it's plural.
C	All the . . . all the . . .

B	All the – what's all?
C	Mm . . . don't know, is there a word for it?
A	Yes, *cuncti*.
C	So it'll be *cuncti discipuli*.
B	Or *omnis* . . . which shall we use?
A	*Cuncti*.
C	*Cuncti discipuli*.
B	Mm . . . by the teachers . . .
A	By the teachers . . . so it's ablative . . . So it's . . . Yes, so it's *magis* . . . [Laughter]
C	Um . . . *magi* . . . um . . .
A	You ought to know that.
C	Yes, I know – ablative . . . *Magistra*.
B	I've got . . .
A	Now what does it read?
B	*Cuncti discipuli magistra non laudantur* . . . *laudantur*. [Laughter] Yes – they are!
C	Oh! you've got to have . . . that . . . shouldn't you?
B	Oh . . . um . . . *a magistra*.
A	Why?
C	Yes . . . *a magistra*, I think.
B	*Cuncti discipuli a magistra laudabantur* . . .
A	*Laudantur* . . . [Reading] 'Heavy burdens will not . . . will be carried by the sad slaves.' . . . Heavy.
B	*Gravis*.
C	*Gravis*.
A	*Onerus*.
C	It's a passive verb.
B	I know, but you've got the subject is 'heavy burdens' . . . no, slaves are the subject, so slaves would be . . . er . . . *servi*s Sad . . . *tristis* . . . *tris* . . . *tristes*.
A	*Tristis* . . . *tristes* . . . *tristes* . . .
B	*Servis* . . .
C	Um . . . accusative, isn't it?
A	No, it's ablative. Sad . . . The verb will be 'will be carried'.
C	The subject is . . .
B	*Portatur* . . .
A	*Portabuntur* . . . Will be carried by the sad slaves . . .

B	*A servis . . . servi . . .*
C	No, you should . . . um . . . heavy burdens is the subject, because that's what it's having done to it, you see.
B	I know, but couldn't we . . .
C	Burdens is having the thing done to it.
A	Yes, so you should start with the subject.
C	Which is heavy burdens.
A	*Onerus . . . onera . . . grava . . . gravia.* Um – by the sad slaves, for the last time . . .

The contrast between the two examples is evident enough, but they are not offered in order that one should be accepted and the other rejected. Their differences are of concern, but what is more important is first to consider each as an example of talking to solve problems, talking to learn. The problems facing the third-form girls were highly specific: should it be *laudatur* or *laudantur*, for example. They were able to commit themselves quickly, and their solutions, like the lights in a crossword puzzle, would before very long be proved right or wrong. To reach such solutions, however, they had to operate general principles, a kind of modified code based on the generative laws of the Latin language. Thus behind the problem *of laudantur* lay that of using the passive in Latin.

To a beginner, one might say, the use of the passive in Latin has many pitfalls; and in any situation full of pitfalls, three watchdogs are better than one. To that interpretation of the situation, however, at least three things must be added. First, the girl least adept at manipulating the passive in Latin is likely to learn to do it better by working with those more adept. Secondly, even the girl who is most adept at handling the passive in Latin is likely to improve her understanding of the principles involved under challenge of being asked to *explain* what so far she has accepted as 'obvious' or 'inevitable'. (As teachers we are familiar with that form of the wisdom of babes and sucklings that consists in asking the 'too simple' question.) And thirdly, one can conceive of a situation in which the application of general principles presented a novel difficulty that none of the group could solve at first, but which they *solved jointly* by talking their way through it.

But what is to be said about the first example, the talk about rooms and families by the 16-year-olds? Clearly they commit themselves to nothing that can readily be proved right or wrong. They are not arguing: no one seems particularly concerned to prove anybody else wrong nor is anyone put in the position of having to prove herself right. And as for the speed of the operation, the dominant impression from the extract must be that if anything happens at all it will achieve itself in its own good time. If we ask, 'Are the speakers merely supporting each other in already accepted familiar opinions (whether genuinely held or assumed, and whether prejudices or well-grounded opinions)?', we shall probably find it impossible to arrive at a satisfactory answer for the very reason already given – that the pace is leisurely and we need to see it cover a longer span.

That is therefore what I propose to do. But first something may be said on the basis of the extract already quoted. It seems fair to comment that the speakers do appear to be speaking their own minds: the consensus appears to be a consensus of their own views, not very much affected by the knowledge that adults may later be listening to what they say. There is a mixture here: some of the statements are complaints against their parents, invidious comparisons – things they might voice to their parents in anger, or even in cold blood, but not in the genial cum tolerant cum affectionate cum condescending tones of this talk; others seem to pose an adult view – or perhaps, rather, move towards such a view. Again, there are some observations that are clearly made from their own experience and not that of their parents – as, for example, when the 'good girl', by tidying up for her mother, gets it wrong with her brothers and sisters. In fact, if one were to hazard a formulation of what is beginning to happen in this extract, it might be to say that the group is gently probing to see how far it can go towards reconciling a daughter's viewpoint with that of a parent.

One direct outcome of a few minutes' talk by the third formers was a sentence in Latin: the 16-year-olds have nothing remotely like it, have in fact here no practical outcome directing their efforts. What they achieve in the way of learning – if they achieve anything at all – will have to be measured against some other yardstick. Here then the tape continues – back among the bedrooms:

B	And things like if I don't draw my curtains when I go to bed . . . well, I . . . like to see a half light streaming in you know.
D	The thing is, with my bedroom, I haven't . . . can't have a view really, 'cause it adjoins the bathroom, you see, and . . .
B	Oh, I know.
C	I have to share mine with my sister.
B	You share with your sister?
C	Yeah.
E	I've got my own now but it's rather small. . . .
A	I think it's a shame though . . .
C	A box-room, wasn't it?
E	More or less . . . yes.

The disorderliness of learning

A   I think it's a shame when you live in a flat or a small house and your parents want the best for you and they try to get you a room on your own. My mum often goes round saying, 'Oh, if I had a big house, I'd have a music room and a reading room . . .'

B   Yeah, all different rooms.

A   They really want the best for you, you know . . . you're pleased at that . . . but the trouble is they feel as though they've not done all they could. (Yeah)

B   And you don't want them to feel that way, do you? (No) Because you know, you can only . . .

E   The thing I like, you know, is when you come in in the evenings and there's only one room, one main living-room to go to . . . and you have to get on with everyone, so you talk and say what's happened to you during the day and . . . you know . . . it's good to get on . . . (Yes. Mm)

A   It's also nice to have somewhere to get away from all the time. (Yes . . . Yes, I think so) Because . . . I mean . . . at this stage, parents can be very annoying . . . and ruin you . . . They've got different ideas. I mean . . . you know . . . you might . . . they might say something, you can answer them back . . . and to them, just to answer them is being cheeky or impudent. (Yes) They don't realise you're just . . . because you're talking to them as if they were a friend . . . how I think it should be . . . (Yeah. Yeah) . . . they don't remember that, and they . . . sort of . . . you know . . . sort of think, You're my daughter and so . . . you know . . . (Yeah)

D   . . . especially if I wanted to start a discussion on anything . . . music perhaps . . . my father would say, 'Oh, that . . . symphonies and so forth are rubbish' . . . I mean, go on as if he was telling me off . . . I'm only trying to start a discussion . . . about music, and that . . .

B   Just a general argument. I think the trouble is, they're so used to putting their point and making it. . . . Well, that's that and it's right . . . that when they get somebody that comes along and puts a different point to them . . . makes a different point to the matter . . . it's different . . . they can't understand it, you know.

A   I think that's a good thing . . .

B   And with my mother . . .

E   You do?

A   Yes. To have a row is good . . . it gets it out of your system. (Yes. I think so.)

B   To have a row is good, I think . . . Well, the trouble with me I never stop at one thing . . . I always want to prove I'm right.

E   My parents bring up something else what happened a long time ago. (Yes. . . . Yeah.)

D   My father is always referring back . . . I remember when you were ever so little, you never used to talk to me like that . . . I said, I've grown up.

B   You couldn't, could you? But then again, in this book [the Hemingway story], there's another point, isn't there . . . I think this is the point . . . that the child talks about praying and how many people it prays for . . . and then by the time it's finished, it's daylight you know. And then, near the end, it says, but then again there *are* only two people.

A   Two main people . . .

B   Two main people there, yeah. But then . . . so . . . I think this signifies that whatever might happen between you and your parents, no matter what . . . they are there . . . and it means something, you know, just that they're there, even.

E   There are some people that'll go through things with you that are nice . . . you know . . . to do, but when it comes to you asking someone to do something that's not very nice . . . you know . . . you hate doing . . . (Yeah) . . . they're always there.

B   Your parents, yeah.

E   If you have a row with a friend that you like, you know . . . that you get on well with . . . there aren't many people you can talk about it to, 'cause usually you're in a circle of friends that you all know each other . . . but your parents are always there, you know.

A   It's all right for some people . . . I mean, it's not too bad for me . . . but some people can't talk to their parents . . . and girls can't talk to them. (No) With normal people, you know . . . it's still this, a mother and child.

B   Do you think it's because . . .

A   It's the same as some teachers who still think that . . . you know . . . We're the teachers and we've got to teach you . . . you're just the children . . . You know, they can't talk to each other as if they were sort of . . . on the same level.

D   I don't think there's so much of that in our school though.

B   No there isn't . . . I don't think there is at all . . .

At this point they spend a minute or two talking about school, about the need to learn how to put your own views and the difficulties of doing so. I am reluctant to cut the tape because one of the points I want to illustrate is the slow evolution that is one of the forms learning may take – and the need to give the process time. The

The disorderliness of learning

circularity of much of the discussion will be clear. It moves on, certainly, with little hesitation and very little backtracking: probably the only clear example of backtracking – or a blind alley – in the whole tape is the exchange where a consideration of some relationship between rooms and sleeping – put forward by B – is rejected by D's 'Negative!' But progress is a kind of spiral: thus A drops a hint when she says, 'but the trouble is they feel as though they've not done all they could.' B takes it up and appears to be on the point of offering an explanation, but E interrupts with a point compelling enough to shift the course of the conversation. And the question of guilt – and its infectiousness in the home – does not return for some time.

To return to the tape for another extract or two – for, unfortunately, the record is too long to be given in full: B has firmly steered the talk back from school and related matters to the problems of the family. They talk about having to look after grandparents, with obvious implications about their own parents growing old, and this leads on to a pretty unanimous vote of confidence:

E I think that's part of growing up . . . that . . . um . . . to know what your parents have said to you all along . . . well, it's true (. . . appreciate the fact . . .)

B Well, it's true, I can appreciate them more. To experience it in life and find out that it's true . . . you know . . . 'cause that's the best way . . . when you experience it.

D Yes, it's hard to believe it even though it is your parents telling you.

A You don't seem to believe your parents, do you, until it happens and then you can't believe it . . .

B No . . . until you find out . . . till you find out for yourself.

E I think round about now, you know, you start to realise . . . your parents do know much better than what you do.

B I mean, you might not admit it . . . ten to one you don't! (No) [Laughter]

They go on to elaborate this confidence in their parents' views, mainly in terms of views about boys and dating. Then A breaks into a new vein:

A When we used to live in . . . in Kennington . . . they used to walk . . . we used to walk across the bridge . . . you know, walk round London . . . used to be ever so happy and I can remember my parents walking along hand in hand . . . you know . . . giggling [Laughter] . . . and there's me in between, you know, looking up . . . and laughing our heads off we were . . . and I can remember that clearly as anything. It's one of the first

	things I remembered . . . you know, being very happy, just the three of us. Then the next thing I remember was me having to go away because my brother was born and he had pneumonia . . . and he came along and it was horrible . . . (Yes) [Laughter] . . . It split up the family . . . you know what I mean . . . I was really jealous.
E	You were out of things . . .
A	Yeah, I really got left out . . . and it's been a bit like that ever since. (I think that, like . . . Well, not only that . . .)
B	I think parents begin to get out of touch with each other as husband and wife . . . slightly, I should think . . . I don't know . . . it all depends what the couple's life is like . . . er . . . when they start having children. You see it takes so much of their time . . . and it takes a certain place in their lives.
A	The husband gets left out a lot, doesn't he? (Yeah . . . has a hard . . .) [Laughter] . . . No, you hear such a lot . . . when perhaps . . . when your dad come home in the evening and your mother will say, 'Just a minute I'm getting so and so's tea' . . . Can you wait a bit?' . . . you know, he's probably come home from work . . . (Yeah)
B	Or, I've got my ironing . . . or, I've got to take the children to bed . . . and what not.
A	Yeah, I think that's when they get . . .
D	My dad comes home and sits down and says, 'Will somebody get my slippers?' and nobody moves, you know . . . Everyone's eating their dinner or staring at the television . . . He feels very neglected I think . . .
B	Probably because he feels everything should be done to him, you know. (Yeah)
C	He's the father . . . they should do everything for him . . .
D	Probably been . . .
B	Head of the house . . . as it were.
A	. . . extra special attention . . . which I think is right, you know . . . I hope I remember that when I get married.
D	He's the one that goes out to work . . . earns the money, as he says.
B	But then again, you find some families who . . . don't take this attitude. They feel that . . . both should be the sort of . . . head . . . you know . . . leader.

A's recollection of her infancy encourages other girls to contribute theirs, and they give rise to such matters as parents who like to go out and those who like to stay in, the difficulties mothers have in getting out while the children are small, parents'

The disorderliness of learning

attempts to educate their children, and so on. Then E, who has not yet contributed an early memory (and who has said nothing for a while), launches the group into the topic of our final extract:

E   I think what you mainly remember is when . . . sort of . . . to your knowledge . . . your . . . the first time you see your mother and father having a row . . . Not a fight, but a row. (Yes) You always think . . . you always look at them to be . . . you know . . . you think, That's my mother . . . and father . . . they're always so happy, you know, and I'm happy with them . . . but when you see them angry with each other . . . that just spoils everything. Sort of . . . you can't say, you know . . . then when you get older, you think, what if they got divorced . . . or had to separate . . . (Yes. Oh dear)

D   It's on your memory all the while, isn't it?

E   You think which one would you choose, and you can't . . . well, I can't . . . I couldn't choose between my mother and father.

A   They seem to be one . . . they are one. (Yeah. They are) Parents, you don't think of them as two separate people.

D   You don't split them up into mother and father . . .

A   It's when they have rows that you realise they're two separate people . . . what could go wrong. (Yes)

D   I don't want to take sides . . . I hate taking sides . . . because my mum will explain . . . she gets quite angry and she'll explain to me and tell me what happened . . . and then my dad will explain. But the stories may be different . . . you know, the same sort of thing, but different . . . but I can see one of them isn't quite right and I can't say which one of them it is. (No)

C   Have you ever had them say . . . whichever one it is . . . say you're always on his side? (Yes)

E   I could never take sides, you know . . . if my father is . . . you know . . . shouting at my mother, I'd say, 'Don't shout at my mum like that!' . . . and then my mother will start shouting at my dad and I'd say, 'Don't shout at my dad like that!' . . . You know, I could never choose.

D   I can't.

A   I can remember the first row we ever had. It was . . . I think . . . my brother and I were in the kitchen and my mum and dad were rowing and it was so bad . . . I'd never seen a row like this before, and my mum just started crying her eyes out and my dad felt terribly guilty, he was dead

	silent. Then I started crying, my brother started crying . . . it was hell for about half an hour, you know. We all split up, there was nothing of the family left. And then we all crept back in, giggling and saying, 'Oh, I am sorry, you know'.
D	Yes, that's the best part . . .
B	Well, frankly when my parents . . . when they do have rows, you know, I . . . er . . . always saw both sides, because there was something in each one's explanation that . . . that meant something. (Yes)
D	You know, because each one's explanation was different, wasn't it?
B	Yeah, and there was something right in each one . . . So I just couldn't realise why on earth they did have the row in the first place, because you . . . you both have perfectly good reasons but they just don't fit in.
D	Sometimes they don't realise how upsetting it can be to the child. The child sometimes doesn't want to show they're upset in front of the parents, do they?
B	Yeah.
C	Sometimes it's something silly and the child could see it's silly and wondering why they're rowing over it 'cause they wouldn't think of anyone rowing over it . . . it's just silly.
A	Yes, it's funny isn't it, children don't row so much as adults.
D	Really? [Laughter] My brother and I, we row.
C	My sister and I are terrible . . .
D	I think that happens to all families, doesn't it, when they've got brothers and sisters . . .
E	Yes, but now I think you get most rows because they're *over* you, you know. (Yes . . . Terrible) And you think you're the object of this row . . . and you think, Ooh!
B	You're always getting the blame for everything.
D	. . . and you're not really . . . can't stick up for yourself.
B	This is why sometimes . . . sort of lose contact with each other . . . because you sort of come between them in a way . . . you know.

There it is then: the whole conversation lasted about 30 minutes, and of that I have given you some 17 minutes' worth, extracting first from the beginning and lastly from very near the end.

The language remains 'expressive' throughout, in the sense that it is relaxed, self-presenting, self-revealing, addressed to a few intimate companions; in the sense that it moves easily from general comment to narration of particular experiences and back again; and in the special sense that in making comments the speakers do not aim at accurate, explicit reference (as one might in an argument or in a sociological report) and in relating experiences they do not aim at a polished performance (as a raconteur or a novelist would). I make this sketchy analysis here in the hope of returning to it later.

In their comments and their narration, the speakers offer their own evaluations of the behaviour they talk about: on the whole their individual evaluations agree with each other. Some differences come to light (as when A feels that adults quarrel more than children) and here it may well be that an individual will revise her evaluation – and of course there may be modifications made also to unspoken evaluations. But in general it is a sanctioning process that goes on: each enjoys the valuable social satisfaction of finding her evaluations sanctioned by her fellows.

I would want to call this in itself educative – a kind of learning, though rarely recognised as such. Our knowledge of the world is inextricably bound up with the way we *feel* about the world, about people and things and events and ourselves. Our ways of feeling, taken overall, show a persistent patterning which constitutes our value system. It is our values that make us the sort of people we are, and it is on this basis of shared values that we establish our most intimate network of relationships with other people. To define learning as *coming to know* something about the world that we did not know before, while denying the term to a *change in the way we evaluate* some experience, is to make a false disjunction. We need to recognise, moreover, that the network of people related to us by shared values provides, at every stage of life, the primary context for our learning of both varieties – both coming to know and refining our value systems. The maintenance of the two forms in close association can alone explain how knowledge can be at one and the same time both *personal* and *social*.

We should notice here that for the adolescents who make up the secondary-school population, this network of peers, mutually supportive on the basis of shared values, will be the seed-bed of a 'counter-culture' wherever such comes into being. Dare we hope that the kind of teacher understandings this book has set out to promote might contribute towards harnessing the energy of such a movement for positive ends? Part of the answer will certainly lie in the teachers' attempts to make in-school learning more like out-of-school.

As the talk of these five girls rolls on, we see as it were elements of the family situation laid out for inspection. They are not precise elements like 'subject' and 'passive' and 'third person singular', which when properly inspected and handled may come together as a Latin sentence. But they are there: parents are provided with a history – seen as young couples, with no children, free to go out; and as people with a future, old and needing help from those who now need them; and as separate people with separate likes and dislikes, though they usually feature in our minds as one; and as human beings capable equally of wise control and rows over silly nothings. Laid out also are the bits of the family jigsaw itself: father, the one who goes out to work; mother, the one who tidies – and is perhaps equally 'the leader'; brothers and sisters; grandparents, the not-to-be-neglected. And the various ties that link the pieces in various ways together: love, happiness, protection, anger, guilt.

I am particularly interested in E's last contribution and will try now to explain why. Quarrelling had come into the conversation early on – but then simply as a good way of clearing the air: guilt had been hinted at, as has already been observed. E's behaviour might suggest – though nothing can be said for certain – the gestation of an idea. Silent for some minutes, she then produces, rather belatedly, her contribution to the 'I remember' series: and when it comes it breaks defences that none of the group has yet dared to breach – and goes the whole way. We see her recoiling from the guilt involved in choosing one parent to reject the other, and finally – forcing the conversation back to make her last point – confronting the guilt of being the cause of all the quarrelling. Doubtless she could not say so, yet she seems to know – with us – that, of all the emotions that bind a family together, feeling guilty about each other is the most treacherous. E, if I am right about her, would indicate that there is here more than the laying out of the elements of the problem: something is done with them. There is a spiral movement in all that 'circularity'.

In talk of this kind trivialities may break in at any moment (though it is never easy to be sure what is trivial in somebody else's concern); it does seem, however, that as this conversation moves on it grows in its power to penetrate a topic and resist the trivial distractions. At its most coherent points it takes on the appearance of a *group effort at understanding*, and these coherent passages are more frequent in the later phases than in the earlier. There will be other virtues in argument and the clash of opinions; the mutually supportive roles these speakers play make it possible for them, I believe, to exert a group effort at understanding – enable them, that is, to arrive at conclusions they could not have reached alone and without that support.

If this is learning, it might be argued, then learning must be a very common phenomenon. No one would wish to dispute that: what I would argue is that a mode of learning so frequently practised ought to make more of a contribution to learning in school than, by and large, it is able to do as we organise things at the moment. And if teachers in fact came to the conclusion that it was no concern of the school to foster a better understanding among members of the family, their attention should still be drawn to this talk as exemplifying a means of learning that could be useful in other areas.

The emphasis we have placed, here and elsewhere, on expressive talk and writing has led to a good deal of misunderstanding and misinterpretation. One critic believes that the outcome of such an emphasis will be to 'imprison children in their common-sense concepts' (Williams, 1977, p. 47). But it is our view that the objective or scientific concept can only be arrived at by the modification of existing, common-sense concepts, however naïve these may be.

We believe it is of the very nature of human learning that it proceeds by anticipation. From early infancy we learn to incorporate a sense of the future into our perceptions of the present (Vygotsky, 1978, p. 28). The efficiency of our data-processing, when compared with that of the animals nearest to us in the evolutionary scale, cannot be explained on any other basis than this: we *prepare ourselves* for perceiving, we anticipate in a way that they cannot. And what is true of percepts in the early stages is later true also of concepts: we tackle an intellectual problem fore-armed with alternative possible solutions. In this way human learning represents growth from a centre, a continuing programme. Typically, it is whatever is part familiar and part novel that beckons us on at all stages, from an infant who imitates its mother's gestures, to the scientist whose research investigates the borderline between the known and the discoverable.

Clearly, then, a learner's common-sense concepts cannot be left behind while he or she moves forward to contemplate, *de novo*, the new and unfamiliar – some statement of the scientific concept or evidence as to its nature. Rather, learners must bring with them whatever they already know and believe and attempt to re-interpret that in the light of the evidence offered. Interpreting the new and re-interpreting the familiar are the two faces of one coin. It is the language of their own intimate musings, their inner reflections upon experience, that will serve both to bring their common-sense concepts to the point of engagement with the scientific concept, and to carry out the reconciliatory interpretation.

Expressive talk and writing are means therefore rather than ends. Any expressive formulation of some piece of knowledge about the world is a potentially useful approximation to a more impersonal, objective, 'public' statement. But that is not all we can say: we must then recognise that that impersonal, objective statement will be appropriated and understood only as each individual who meets it is able to translate it into the language of his own reflective processes. Knowledge, in Michael Polanyi's terms, 'is an activity which would be better described as a process of knowing' (Polanyi, 1969, p. 132). 'Engagement', then, is a process of knowing, a process in which meaning is negotiated by constructing a version of the unfamiliar from the raw material of the familiar. In the kind of conversation we have been considering, the talk is itself an enactment of that process of engagement.

I think the reader will agree that those five girls showed considerable skill in the art of expressive speech. If expressive speech is a means of learning, they have at their disposal a pretty effective instrument. But, of course, the skill is something they had to *learn* – a fact that may not readily be recognised since much of that learning may have taken place before they came to school. Families will vary in the degree to which expressive speech is encouraged in the home: anthropological studies in recent years have shown amazing differences in the speech habits fostered and maintained by families in different sub-cultural groups living in neighbouring areas of the same town (Heath, 1983). Moreover, our uses of speech are so intimately dependent upon their context of interpersonal relationships that modes of speech acquired in one social setting (e.g. the family) cannot be relied upon to operate in another – even so open a setting as a self-chosen group of classmates in a school. There can be no doubt, therefore, that the skill shown by these five girls owes a good deal to their experiences in school – that is to say, it is to some degree a reflection of school learning.

★ ★ ★

The last transcript in this section differs from the others in many respects. The occasion is a science lesson with a first-year [Year 7] secondary-school class, and the talk arises out of what the boys are doing and have been doing – heating copper in a flame. Again, though a good deal of talking went on among small groups of boys during the lesson, what is recorded consists in the main of what the teacher says. He talks first to small groups and later to the whole class. The tape comes from a film made by the Nuffield Science Project. (It was not possible to distinguish all the boys who speak, but A, B, C, etc., have been used to differentiate as far as possible the members of the group taking part at any one time.)

Teacher Right, now. What do you think?
A It went . . .
B It's turned silver.
T Turned silver? Are you sure it's silver? Take it up to the front and have a look at it.
A It seems to have gone . . . red.
B . . . green.

The disorderliness of learning

T	Yes, it looks as though it changes colour. What happens if you scrape it? Have a look.
B	It's going . . .
A	It goes pink . . .
T	Do you think that's something that's formed on the outside, or what?
A	. . . think it's . . . er . . . formed . . . er . . .
T	What's happening then?
A	A film's forming . . .
T	A film? You think this is coming out . . . coming from inside the copper, do you?
A	Yes.
B	. . . combined with something in the air . . . to form the film.
T	So you think something in the copper is . . . doing what?
B	Is coming out . . . well, is combining with the air and forms that film.
T	Yes. And what do *you* think?
C	The same.
T	You think the same? Well, *what* do you think – you tell me then . . . since you say you think the same.
C	I think . . . there's something that's . . . er . . . combining with the air . . .
T	Something combining with the air? Do you think you could think up an experiment to see whether the air is important in this?
A	Yes . . . well . . . we could . . .
T	Yes, well you think about it. I'm going to ask you all in a minute when you line up round the bench. All right?
A	Right.
T	OK.
T	Well, what about it then, A . . .?
A	Well, sir, it got . . . with something in the copper.
T	Well where do you think it's coming from, this black powder?
A	From the flame.
T	From the flame? . . . something coming out of the flame? . . . See if you can think up something . . . You think it's coming out of the flame. Do *you* think it's coming out of the flame?
B	I think it's coming out of the copper, sir.
T	You think it's coming out of the copper? Well, B . . . see if you can think of things you could do . . . another experiment which would show which of you's correct. Anyway, think about it and I'm going to have you all up at the bench in a moment.

T	[to the class gathered round the bench] Right, then. We've got three theories as to why the copper turns black when it's heated. We've got A's theory, which has six supporters, saying that it's something coming out of the air. We've got C's theory with four supporters saying that it's something coming out of the flame. We've got F's theory with 18 supporters saying it's something coming out of the copper. Now obviously you can't *all* be right – and you've had some time to think over and work out an experiment to help verify your theory. OK, then, A, what's your experiment?
A	Well . . . suppose that's . . . air, I guess . . . It would be a good idea . . . um . . . to . . . um . . . put . . . a piece of copper foil in a . . . in a . . . in a tube and . . . and put a cork in the end, and then take the air out of it with a vacuum pump. And then heat it. . . . If it turned black again it would prove our idea was wrong, but if . . . if . . . if it doesn't change, our . . . it would be right.
T	Do you agree with that, B?
B	Yes.
T	Good. Now, what do the flame people think? [No answer] What do you think, C?
C	Use another sort of foil and if that turned black then you'd know it was something in the flame. If it didn't, it wouldn't be something in the flame.
T	Yes . . . any idea what particular foil?
C	Lead foil?
T	All right, we might try that. What about D, you got any ideas?
D	No . . . the same one, sir – use aluminium.
T	All right, well we'll try it . . . But can anyone think of a way by which they could heat the copper so that the flame won't actually come in contact with it? What could you do to . . . E, any ideas from this group?
E	Sir, you could . . . er . . . put copper foil in a test-tube over the flame . . . then the flame won't be getting at the copper.
T	Good – that's a good idea, isn't it? If you heat . . . if you heat the copper in something where the flame's not actually touching . . . Now, F, you're the spokesman for the copper school. Now have you got any ideas on this?
F	Well, you . . . you could repeat . . . um . . . A's experiment, and if . . . um . . . if the copper turned black, that would prove us right . . . um . . . but if it turned . . . if it stayed its norm . . . it would prove A's group wrong as well.

It is a brief extract, but even so I believe it will speak for itself to most teachers. 'Alternative possibilities' are very much in the air – indeed certain alternative possibilities are what the lesson is about. And because they are possible ways of explaining something pretty concrete and specific, and because differences in the explanations offered are going to be resolved in the end by further concrete happenings in the laboratory, one may miss the essential importance of the theoretical processes involved.

The first phase – the talk in small groups – is directly concerned with possible explanations. Though the teacher's questions are obviously a great help, he begins on each occasion with a very open question: 'What do you think?' and 'What about it then?' – saving his more directive questions until he finds they are needed. No doubt they will be needed less as time goes on – and more will come from the boys in response to the open question: indeed, in response finally to events themselves, regardless of the teacher. I was struck by his questions to C in the first group: he seems to believe there is some virtue in having C formulate for himself rather than take over B's formulation. I believe also that the movement in words from what might *describe* a particular event to a generalisation that might *explain* that event is a journey that each must be capable of taking for himself – *and that it is by means of taking it in speech that we learn to take it in thought.*

The second phase is the mustering of the alternative explanations and, from there, the devising of means to verify them. The ideal in this – the most difficult part of the task in hand – is that all the possible explanations of a proposed experiment should be taken into account. Are there some that would consider it a waste of time, therefore, that the teacher did not do this part of the job himself? He does in fact lay the burden on the boys' shoulders, and waits patiently while they talk their way through.

They are using in this extract – both teacher and pupils – a spare kind of language very different from that in most of the other examples. The reason for this lies in the nature of the activity of which the language forms a part. At the roots of scientific activity lie empirical operations: what is *done* in the chemical laboratory is of central importance and the language that serves such operations is closely related to processes – a language that may often be barely intelligible to someone who can't see what is being done. And when at the next stage (as in this example) words are used to explain the effects of what has been done or to devise plans for what *shall* be done, the generalisations must maintain firm connections with the concrete data. True enough, wild speculation has its place in scientific activity, but the process of applying it, harnessing it, is one of re-shaping it in appropriately *specific* forms.

The spare look this language has may mislead us into thinking that it can easily be learnt. But the task is not that of learning a language; rather it is that of acquiring, *by the agency of the language*, the ability to perform these mental operations I have been talking about. *A child's language is the means*: in process of meeting new demands – and being helped to meet them – his language takes on new forms that correspond to the new powers as he achieves them. Expressive speech is one of the more accessible forms; the language of scientific hypotheses, spare though it may appear, comes later.

I think at the time of writing this [in the late 1960s] we believed that expressive talk would manifest itself in the classroom if we as teachers merely indicated our willingness to accept it. It seemed to us that the strictures normally set up for classroom discourse prevented its appearance, and once those strictures were removed, expressive talk, so familiar outside the classroom, would prevail also inside it. This certainly proved not to be the case. We learned from experience that expressive talk has to be *earned* rather than simply allowed in. That is to say, mutual trust between teacher and pupil has to be established before expressive talk can flourish, and mutual trust cannot be created in terms of speech behaviour alone. Appropriate speech behaviour on the teacher's part is a necessary but not sufficient condition; rather, teachers must prove to be 'as good as their word'. Martin Buber goes so far as to suggest that this relationship of mutual trust is the key to all that school education can achieve: trust in the teacher breeds trust in the world – trust on the part of the individual child in his own ability to make sense of the world (Buber, 1947, p. 98).

Much that is involved in this notion has yet to be explored: it has powerful implications for our conception of a teacher's authority, for our conception of curriculum, and for our understanding of the purposes of schooling in our society.

Taking a narrow, professional view of ourselves as teachers, we might claim that our authority lies in our expert knowledge of a particular field, our 'subject' on the timetable. In so many words, our successful achievements as a student of that subject conferred on us the right to teach it. Critics have not been slow to point out that this conception of expertise in institutionalised education in a literate society falls a good deal short of the non-institutional, pre-literate view by which the teaching was entrusted to a successful *practitioner*. Our confidence in ourselves as teachers is likely to be more vulnerable when we base our claim on *knowledge about* rather than on *role performance*. More materially, an authority derived from such expertise is effective only in so far as the student covets for himself the knowledge and skill we can teach him. This means that it is destined to meet failures in every classroom, and not least for the reason that the brand of expertise offered appears to the student to have little to do with any social role performance appropriate to his present or predictable life. Thus it is that management techniques, the policeman aspect of a teacher's job, come into play, for to maintain conditions in which learning can take place is an essential part of a teacher's responsibilities in school. It is at this point that we discover that being an authority on Jane Austen does not make us an authority over Tom, Dick or Jane.

In exercising this managerial authority we are the agents (in differing degrees on different occasions) of the corporate group that makes up the class, the social institution that constitutes the school, and the wider community in which the school operates. I have been fascinated by the way new teachers arrive at the discovery that the managerial role is both (a) necessary at times and (b) of no use in the actual process of teaching. Intuitively, they proceed to develop a teaching/learning relationship with each individual pupil, while maintaining a potentially managerial role *vis-à-vis* the group as a whole – exercising it less and less until it becomes no more than a potential role and the teaching/learning relationship has virtually taken over.

It seems to me that intuitive processes of this nature are essential in learning to become a teacher, and continue to be essential to good teaching. Yet so many of our approaches in teacher-education tend to discourage rather than encourage such processes. The conventional concept of 'the student who has earned the right to teach' puts far too much stress on what the teacher knows and directs attention away from what the students know, what they need to know, and the means by which they can be helped to know it. Living with this concept long enough, we as a profession tend to become bad learners, anxious to teach ourselves rather than trust our teachers (Hargreaves 1982, p. 201), and bad listeners. The listening is in my view crucial: with all the pressures of class teaching it has to be fought for strenuously. If it is the students only who have to listen, they are denied a major part of the *action* that makes up *interaction*, and without interaction we regress to a discredited view of learning as a uni-directional process, proceeding from the teacher to the student. The distortions arising from this view lie behind a good deal that Douglas Barnes has criticised in the first section of this book. Take, for example, the way a process of 'guessing what is in teacher's mind' will often substitute for genuine discussion. Yet genuine discussion is *exploratory*, an opening out of possibilities in order to arrive at a configuration, a nexus of some kind; guessing what is in teacher's mind, on the contrary, is a closing-in process, a mental variety of 'hunt the thimble'.

A recognition that talking can be a means of learning; that its effectiveness as such a means relies on a relationship of mutual trust between those taking part in the talk; and that the onus for establishing that relationship in the classroom lies first with the teacher – all this clearly assumes an interactive view of learning; and this in turn has important implications for our view of curriculum.

An 'output' model of curriculum, one which sets out its description in terms of pre-planned outgoing behaviours to be achieved by those taking the course, is clearly consistent with a uni-directional view of teaching/learning: the stress is on what the teacher will do, and this is something he can determine and describe in advance. An interactive view of learning demands something much more flexible. What can be planned in advance is a set of teacher-provided resources which may or may not be called into service. The aim here is to conduct a course that makes sense to a student as he *looks back* over it: a teacher is able, from past experience, to make available resources likely to stimulate learning, even in unforeseen ways; that is to say a degree of planning of the *input* is possible. But the difference is not simply one of the predetermining of either output or input. There is a sharp difference in the amount of pre-planning that is possible, and in the flexible model consistent with an interactive view of learning, a process enters in that has no counterpart in the output model – the process of *negotiation*. Provision is thus made for unforeseen learning to take place, both because of the pre-planned resources, and because input is invited from other sources – from the students themselves and from the shared experiences of all concerned from one day to the next.

We may advocate such a programme in very simple terms – in terms of the advantages of learning with each other and from each other. Yet the processes involved are complex: not only is it true that such a learning programme makes sense to a student as he looks back on it; it is furthermore a *corporate* experience, treading the knife edge between satisfying individual needs and interests and maximising the effect of shared experiences, common interests and social responsibilities.

A good hard look at curriculum by teachers who have learned from experience what student talk can achieve, what interactive learning means, how much students can contribute when curriculum is negotiated, what kinds of cooperative learning flourish as teachers become better listeners – I doubt if there ever was a time when this was more sorely needed than it is today. Where relationships of mutual trust make corporate learning experiences possible, I believe a model is provided and a mode of operating established which could enable school leavers, over a wide range of interests and abilities, to become responsibly independent learners for the rest of their lives; not learners for the sake of learning (or even for the sake of teaching), but learners from experience who plough back into responsible social behaviour the fruits of their individual learning. Such a belief should challenge us as teachers to resist those aspects of the hidden curriculum in our schools that work in a contrary direction, rationing knowledge, reducing perspectives and hostile to change.

There is no doubt that public policies for education are today far less supportive of the ideas we have outlined in this book than they were when it first appeared in 1969. We may, however, find encouragement in the fact that there has been since that time an increasing body of research findings consistent with these ideas and effective in extending our understanding of the mental processes involved. But perhaps we should be encouraged above all by the way sensitive and committed teachers continue, as others have done over the centuries, to find their own way – by honest intuition and a confidence in their own experience – to an interactive view of teaching and learning. I came across this piece of encouragement in my recent reading. Published in 1916, it is a third-person autobiographical account of events that took place in 1895; the writer is Dorothy Richardson – untrained governess turned untrained teacher in a school in Finsbury Park, a north London suburb:

> She had discovered that the best plan was to stand side by side with the children in face of the things they had to learn, treating them as equals and fellow-adventurers, giving explanations when these were necessary, as if they were obvious and might have been discovered by the children themselves, never as if they were possessions of her own, to be imparted, never claiming a knowledge superior to their own. 'The business of the teacher is to make the children independent, to get them to think for themselves and that's much more important than whether they get to know the facts,' she would say irrelevantly to the Pernes [the three sisters who own and run the school] whenever the question of teaching came up. She bitterly resented their vision of children as malleable subordinates. And there were many moments when she seemed to be silently exchanging this determination of hers with her pupils. Good or bad, she knew it was the secret of her influence with them, and so long as she was faithful to it both she and they enjoyed their hours together.
>
> (Richardson, 1979, p. 333)

★ ★ ★

Work in English, as work in any of the arts, has as its principal objective the kind of learning we characterised as concerned with the way we *feel* about the world – that is to say with the generation and refinement of our value systems. I believe learning in all subjects of the curriculum involves both 'coming to know' and the adjustment of *values*; but that in the science-like subjects the former is dominant, whereas in the art-like subjects it is the latter that is dominant.

What is important is that the two modes of learning should complement each other and achieve a kind of balance. . . . Both modes of learning rely upon specific uses of language and . . . the quality of learning in all subjects will improve when we as teachers apply a fuller understanding of the language-using and learning processes.

Acknowledgements

I should like to thank the following for help with transcripts and permission to quote from them; the British Broadcasting Corporation, Margaret Frood, John Kerry, Nancy Martin, Martin Richards, Pat Smyth, Margaret Tucker, Unilever Ltd and the Nuffield Science Teaching Project, and Elizabeth Webster.

Notes

1. The source of this text is Britton (1970), pp. 128–141.
2. The source of this text is Chapter 4 of Department of Education and Science (1975), pp. 47–50.
3. The source of this text is Britton (1982a), pp. 191–200.
4. 'With grateful thanks to Heather Kay for permission to quote this extract.' Britton's note.
5. The source of this text is Barnes, Britton and Torbe (1986), pp. 91–130.

References

Assessment of Performance Unit (1978). *Language performance*. London: Department of Education and Science.

Barnes, D., Britton, J. and Torbe, M. (1986). *Language, the learner and the school* (3rd edition). Harmondsworth: Penguin Books.

Board of Education (1929). *General report on the teaching of English in London elementary schools, 1925*. London: His Majesty's Stationery Office.

Britton, J. (1970). *Language and learning*. Harmondsworth: Penguin Books.

Britton, J. (1982a). 'Language in the British primary school' [1979], in Pradl, G. (ed.), *Prospect and retrospect: selected essays of James Britton*. London and Monclair, NJ: Heinemann Educational and Boynton/Cook, pp. 191–200.

Britton, J. (1982b). *Prospect and retrospect: Selected essays of James Britton*, Pradl, G. (ed.). London and Monclair, NJ: Heinemann Educational and Boynton/Cook.

Britton, J., Burgess, T., Martin, N., McLeod, A. and Rosen, H. (1975). *The development of writing abilities (11–18)*. London and Basingstoke: Macmillan.

Buber, M. (1947). *Between man and man*. London: Routledge and Kegan Paul.

Cassidy, F. (1966). 'Standard English and the schools'. Unpublished seminar paper, Dartmouth Seminar, New Hampshire, USA.

Cassirer, E. (1944). *An essay on man*. New Haven, CT: Yale University Press.

Cazden, C. (1977). 'How does knowledge about language help the classroom teacher – or does it?'. *Urban Review*, 1977, pp. 74–90.

Central Advisory Committee for Education (England) (1967). *Children and their primary schools* (the Plowden Report). London: Her Majesty's Stationery Office.

Department of Education and Science (1975). *A language for life* (the Bullock Report). London: Her Majesty's Stationery Office.

Gusdorf, G. (1965). *Speaking*. Trans. P. Brockelman. Evanston, IL: Northwestern University Press.

Hargreaves, D. (1982). *The challenge for the comprehensive school*. London: Routledge and Kegan Paul.

Heath, S. (1983). *Ways with words*. Cambridge, UK: Cambridge University Press.

Howe, M. (1975). 'Taking notes and human learning'. *Bulletin of the British Psychological Society*, 28.

Kelly, G. (1969). 'Man's construction of his alternatives' [1958], in Maher, B. (ed.), *Clinical psychology and personality*. New York, NY: Wiley and Sons.

Luria, A. and Vinogradova, O. (1959). 'An objective investigation of the dynamics of semantic systems'. *British Journal of Psychology*, 50(2), pp. 89–105.

Meneghello, L. (1967). 'Deliver us from evil', in Trevelyan, R., *Italian writing today*. Harmondsworth: Penguin Books.

Moffett, J. (1968). *Teaching the universe of discourse*. Portsmouth, NH: Boynton/Cook.

Polanyi, M. (1969). *Knowing and being*. London: Routledge and Kegan Paul.

Popper, K. (1976). *Unended quest*. London: Fontana.

Richardson, D. (1979). *Pilgrimage I* [1916]. London: Virago.

Rosen, C. (1966). 'Living language'. *English in Education*, A3(3), September 1966, pp. 2–10.

Rosen, C. (1967). 'All in the day's work', in Britton, J. (ed.), *Talking and writing: A handbook for English teachers*. London: Methuen, pp. 26–34.

Sapir, E. (1961). *Culture, language and personality*. Berkeley and Los Angeles, CA: University of California Press.

Slobin, D. and Welsh, C. (1971). 'Elicited information as a research tool in developmental psycholinguistics', in Lavatelli, C. (ed.), *Language training in early childhood education*. Chicago, IL: University of Illinois Press.

Start, K. and Wells, B. (1972). *The trend of reading standards*. Slough: National Foundation for Educational Research.

Sweet, H. (1891). *A new English grammar, logical and historical*. Oxford: Clarendon Press.

Vygotsky, L. (1962). *Thought and language* [1934]. Trans. E. Haufmann and G. Vakar. Cambridge, MA: MIT Press.

Vygotsky, L. (1978). *Mind in society*. Cole, M., John-Steiner, V., Scribner, S. and Souberman, E. (eds). Cambridge, MA: Harvard University Press.

Williams, J. (1977). *Learning to write, or writing to learn?* Slough: National Foundation for Educational Research.

SECTION 3

Writing

The teaching of writing was among the earliest issues taken up by Britton and by the London Association for the Teaching of English (LATE) in exploring approaches in English teaching. In the context of the times, young people writing imaginatively, and the quality of work they could achieve, still needed to be argued for and demonstrated. The study group that Britton led on 'The meaning and marking of imaginative composition' (London Association for the Teaching of English, 1950) was partly motivated by such considerations, as was the anthology of writing that he and Nancy Martin later edited (London Association for the Teaching of English, 1960).

Questions about marking were of interest for the issues that they raised concerning the status of writing of different kinds, and their educational value. What was the value to the writer of personal writing? How did this compare in value with writing of a more impersonal kind? How was quality assessed? How did writing develop? What was the place in the curriculum of different sorts of writing? What was the place of grammatical accuracy in determining writing's quality? These were questions relevant both to classroom practice and to the examining of writing, for example to the demands of the 'O'-level examination. Research in the 1960s by Britton, Nancy Martin and Harold Rosen, on the *Multiple marking of English compositions* (Schools Council, 1966), partly carried forward such questions.

An immediate stimulus for the work on multiple marking was the coming of the Schools Council in 1964, with its mandate to oversee the introduction of the Certificate of Secondary Education examination (CSE) and to fund educational research. (Before the introduction of CSE, eight out of ten students left secondary school with no paper qualification whatever.) For Britton and his colleagues, a study of multiple marking at 'O'-level provided an opportunity to contribute to the development of assessment practices for the new examination, and also to raise some underlying issues about language variety.

The outcomes of the team's research demonstrated convincingly the superiority at 'O'-level of a system in which the judgements of three markers are pooled, together with a further mark for mechanical accuracy, over the existing arrangement of a single marker guided by examining criteria. As it happened, these implications were not much taken up for the CSE examination, though they have continued to influence discussion of assessment. As important, a further finding was the clear indication of the importance of topic in the 'O'-level examination – and of the choice among kinds of writing that different topics entailed. Quite simply, candidates choosing one topic were likely to be at a disadvantage compared with candidates choosing another. This last consideration was an indication of the very rudimentary understanding of writing development that lay behind the setting of most 'O'-level composition papers, and was key to formulating the subsequent proposal for research into the development of writing abilities, also funded by the Schools Council.

As Britton's thinking had developed, issues about young people's writing had increasingly been set within his wider consideration of language and learning. Drawing on these understandings, in the researches of the sixties and seventies, he was able to place writing within a picture of language generally, relating it to processes of thinking, reading and talk, and offering a rationale for valuing writing of different kinds. The breadth of this perspective underpins his investigation of young people's writing in secondary schools, with its exploration of function and audience, as the extracts which follow will show.

In the first of these, 'Writing to learn and learning to write' [1972] (1982b), Britton offers an extended report of the work on the development of writing abilities then in progress at the University of London Institute of Education. He dwells in turn on the nature of expressive language, the underpinning theory of representation, and the distinction between participant and spectator roles that underlies the account of writing functions. There is no report at this stage of empirical findings. Britton's account is of the thinking in the research, dwelling on the significance of its conceptual framework.

The three passages which form the second extract, taken from the opening chapter of *The development of writing abilities (11–18)* (Britton et al., 1975) are similarly conceptual in focus. Read together, these passages offer an account of the central impetus behind the research, and of key influences underpinning the development of its model. We include some indications of the research's findings in the more detailed introduction to the passages in this extract, but a full account will need to be followed up through further reading.

In the final text in this section, 'Shaping at the point of utterance' [1980] (1982a), Britton considers composing. In a marvellous, speculative piece, moving on from the work on writing abilities, he reviews what can be said about embarking on the process of writing, about a writer's attention to the piece's voice, and to the multiple voices that are dictating meaning. His insistence on composing as an act reliant on the 'untaught lessons' drawn from reading and from spoken language resources complements the earlier extracts in this section, which are concerned with the constituents of development. What is transparent in this account of 'shaping' is the irreducible centrality of writers' attention to meaning, and by implication of young people's investment in what they want their writing to convey. It brings home the necessity often stressed by Britton – always important to recognise – that teachers should first and foremost be real, interested readers of the content of young people's writing. As he has put it in the final paragraph of 'Writing to learn and learning to write' about the teacher as listener:

> And then finally the teacher as listener. We must be careful not to sacrifice to our roles as error spotters and improvers and correctors that of the teacher as listener and reader. I could sum it all up very simply. What is important is that children in school should write about what matters to them to someone who matters to them.
>
> (Britton, 1982b, p. 110)

3.1 Expressive writing
'Writing to learn and learning to write'[1]

The following account (Britton, 1982b) addresses writing as a language process, drawing on the research into the development of writing abilities that Britton and his colleagues were conducting between 1967 and 1975. The text is taken from a lecture to American educators at a conference of the National Council of Teachers of English in 1972. Britton's research was still at a fairly early stage at this point, awaiting analysis of the empirical data; the work was not finally published until 1975 (see 3.2 below). Also, two of the most original concepts of the research, the notions of expressive language and the use, within a typology of language functions, of the distinction between participant and spectator roles – the principal concentrations in Britton's account – would be relatively unfamiliar to his audience at this stage, and possibly controversial.

The interest of the piece that follows is therefore partly in the depth of Britton's presentation, while his ideas are still developing, to a key professional audience of English educators, well informed about English teaching but of a different national tradition and background. Britton provides an extensive account of the expressive function, covering both its role in learning, as a first draft of ideas, and its role as the matrix from which a move into transactional and poetic functions may occur in relation to particular writing projects. He refers to the background of the notion of expressive language in the writings of the American linguist Edward Sapir.

The argument which follows carefully develops the concept of participant and spectator roles in speech and writing. Using a series of simple diagrams and examples, Britton shows how our role as language users changes as we move from participation in an event to reflection upon it. When we are involved in an experience, we respond to it in terms of our existing worldview. It is only when we are able to stand back, to take on the spectator role, that we are able to shape that experience and, possibly, modify our worldview.

Driving Britton's accounts of expressive language and of writing functions in this lecture is his operational view of language and of writing. It is presented towards the close of the lecture in one of his most powerful formulations.

> A child's learning has its own organic structure. Hence, the value of writing in the expressive, which is the language close to and most revealing of that individuality. Hence, also, the importance of individual work and work in small groups, and of the sea of talk on which all our school work should be floated.
>
> Given these conditions I want to suggest that children learn to write above all by writing. This is an operational view of writing in school. The world about the child waits to be written about, so we haven't the need to go hunting around for exercises or dummy runs. We have to set up a working relationship between his language and his experience, and there is plenty there to write about. An operational view implies that we have our priorities. Of course we care about spelling and punctuation, but not more than we care about what the language is doing for the child.

This statement brings together both of Britton's key concentrations in thinking about language in school: concern for continually enhancing our understanding of young people, and regard for their flourishing.

My lecture derives from some work that I've been doing for the past six years as director of the British Schools Council Research Project into the Development of Writing Abilities in Children (ages 11–18). We're still working on the data of that, so I shan't be referring to it very much more. But we began by collecting writings in all subjects from children 11 to 18 from about 65 schools. We had about 2000 children in all and we drew a sample of 500 children's work in English and other subjects. And what I want to discuss is the thinking that has arisen in connection with sorting and interpreting those papers. I shall be quoting one or two of them to you.

The first of these was written by an eleven-year-old called Jacqueline, for her science teacher. She writes on how to make oxygen and this is what Jacqueline says:

> It is quite easy to make oxygen if you have the right equipment necessary. You will need probably a test tube (a large one), a stand with some acid in

it. You will also need a Bunston burner, of course you must not forget a (glass) tank too. A thin test tube should fix neatly in its place. When you have done that, fill the glass tank and put the curved end upwards. Put the (glass) tank on the table and fill with water. Very soon you will find that you have made oxygen and glad of it.

It's the 'glad of it' that interests us here. I wonder where that came from. On the whole she is trying to tell you what she did, so if you are really keen to make oxygen, well, you know how she went about it and you can go about it. That is what she is trying to do, but that bit at the end seems to come from somewhere else, doesn't it? I can just imagine her mum saying, 'Yes, I dropped in and had a chat and a cup of tea, and glad of it.' It comes straight out of speech. It is a sort of spoken fragment. I wonder what her science teacher thought of it. Do you think *he* would think he was glad of it, or that this was something she might well have left unsaid? I think from what I know of the situation that he was glad to know that Jacqueline was glad she'd made oxygen and wasn't simply going through the hoops for him. On the other hand, while I would welcome that expressive feature, that feature taken from speech, in that writing at that stage, I hope you would agree with me that in the long run, ultimately, if she's out to inform us and wants us to have the information necessary for making oxygen, that at least is inappropriate – is not required.

What about this? This is another piece from the research by a 15-year-old boy from a school just off the Old Kent Road, which is a dockland area of London.

School, ugh. Dad is up having a wash, Mum has gone to work, sister has got up, and me, I don't get up till I'm told to. If I had my way, I wouldn't get up. Still I get up, have a wash and go to school. On the way you see some funny people about these days. Take that old man who lives round the corner. He says that he cannot go out to get his pension [that's the old age pension, and he has to go to the labour office to get it] but when someone gets it for him, he is round the pub like a shot. Crafty old man. At any rate, to get back to walking to school. School, what a terrible word, whoever invented it should have been shot. I know parents say schooldays are the best days of your life but that was in those days. School was good because you started work when you were twelve so school was good. For the time you were there.

Obviously a good deal of that comes out of speech also – in fact, the whole area is fairly near to speech, isn't it? He says 'cannot' instead of 'can't'. He got that from books, not from speech. But most of it comes pretty directly from speech. And it has other features which make it like speech. He rather assumes that we're in his context. He invites us to accept an assumption that we know the sort of thing he's talking about, so he says, 'You see some funny people about these days.'

'Take that old man who lives down the corner.' Well, what old man? We've nothing leading up to him. He's come straight out of the boy's context and he's offering it to us to accept and assume the context, which is again like speech and which is again why I want to call it 'expressive'. The whole piece is expressive. This is not a case of expressive features in a piece which is out to do something else. This chap isn't trying to inform us, to tell us things he believes we want to know; he's simply sharing a slice of his experience with us, letting us into it, which is an expressive function. It's a way of being with him. It is also loosely structured. He moves to the old man, for example, and then back to school again. This loose structure is again typical of the expressive. The expressive is a term I take from the linguist Edward Sapir. He is usually called the father of American linguistics, but I think he deserves to be called the father of modern linguistics. Sapir says that in all language, two strands are interwoven inextricably, one an expressive pattern and one a referential pattern. Referential means you're talking about what's in the world and you are using your reference to what's in the world for useful purposes. You are informing people, instructing people, persuading people, and so on.

But the expressive bit of it. How does language get that? Sapir gives us one answer. He says that it is expressive because 'language is learned early and piecemeal, in constant association with the colour and the requirements of actual contexts' (Sapir, 1949, p. 10). In other words, we pick it up as we go. 'Early and piecemeal', and it never loses its ability to revive the actuality of these contexts with all their colours and all their requirements.

So I want to define expressive language as language close to the self: language that is not called upon to go very far away from the speaker. The prototype for linguists is the exclamation. You know, the noise you make when you drop the hammer on your toe. And if you are by yourself it's purely expressive. In other words, merely vents your feelings. If somebody else is there, then it is also a communication. It won't have any meaning unless a person can see the plight you're in and knows you, because we have different habits of exclamation; what might be a very mild exclamation for you might be a rather severe one for me. You need to know the person and the situation in order to get the full meaning of that communication. Well that's also true, in general, of the expressive. You need to know the speaker and the context.

Expressive language is giving signals about the speaker as well as signals about his topic. And so it is delivered in the assumption that the hearer is interested in the speaker as well as in the topic. In fact if I had to tie myself to one thing about the expressive I'd say that that was the most characteristic. It relies on an interest in the speaker as well as in the topic. It's relaxed and loosely structured because it follows the contours of the speaker's preoccupations. I sometimes take my wife for a drive, and I drive and she talks. And that talk is highly expressive. It's about anything that comes into her head. Things she sees from the car, things she remembers suddenly, things that she's forgotten in the kitchen and so on. It's highly expressive talk, loosely structured, only really communication to me because I am also in the context, because I know her and what has been happening around her. If I want to argue with her – or if she says something that I disagree with or if she says something I am curious about and want some information about – then her language is likely to move away from the expressive, further away from the person speaking and a bit nearer to the actualities of the world. Nearer to what Sapir calls the referential.

I'm saying all this about expressive because I do believe it's very important. I believe it has a very important function. Its function in one sense is to *be with*. To be with people. To explore the relationship. To extend the togetherness of situations. It's the language of all ordinary face-to-face speech. So it's our means of coming together with other people out of our essential separateness. But it's also the language in which we first-draft most of our important ideas. In other words, most of the important things that there are in the world were probably first discussed in expressive speech with somebody who was in the context. And if you put those two things together I think you'll see why I claim, in the third place, that it's the form of language by which most strongly we influence each other.

I was in New Orleans when Martin Luther King was shot, and of course the talk was everywhere. Talk on street corners and church porches, in bars, indoors. I really do believe that the quality of that talk, what it was able to achieve in influencing people's opinions, was a material factor in forming public opinion and hence the political outcome of the event. It's far more influential than sermons in church or printed political manifestos.

Expressive writing is primarily written-down speech, and that is, I think, why it is important as writing. Being written-down speech, it does something which I want to describe in two ways. First, it maintains the contact of the writing with the resources the writer has, resources which come from speech. We recruit and keep fit our linguistic resources, above all, through speech. So when we are using expressive language, we are writing in such a way as to maintain the closest contact with those resources. And then, saying that same thing a second way, expressive writing is also important because in it, we make sure the writer stays in the writing and doesn't disappear. We'll come back to that.

Nevertheless, writing, even expressive writing, is very different from speech and this is pretty obvious. In speech you have a face-to face situation. You have immediate feedback. When you are writing, you are left on your own. You have to work in a vacuum with no feedback. You have to imagine your audience and hold him fully in mind if you are to take his needs into account. What's written here and now is to be read there and then: some other time and some other place. I think we need to conjure up an audience for this rather lonely task, and this is one reason why I hold unorthodox views on the role of the teacher with regard to the child's writing. I think the teacher needs to extend to a child a stable audience. I think when a child is learning to write in the first stages, this business of meeting the needs of a reader is one of the real difficulties of coping with writing. The kind of encouragement the teacher can give – in other words, the extent to which the teacher is a good listener, a good reader – can make that easy for a child, and the stability of having the same reader from occasion to occasion is also, I think, very important to those stages.

And then there's the effect of the time lag. You write it here and now, and it's read elsewhere at some other time. How do you use that time lag? How do you use the time lag between the transmission and the reception? In speech, we usually trust the process of 'pushing the boat out'. Are we wrong in not trusting it also in writing? How far in writing ought we to have faith in the process you might call 'shaping at the point of utterance'? Or how far do you think this premeditation is something we should be much more deliberate about? We all know how expressive speech works; we all know about its importance for children. How in telling about what's been happening to them, for instance, in sharing their experiences, children are also shaping those experiences and therefore making them more accessible for their own learning. We don't learn from higgledy-piggledy events as they strike our senses; we learn from events as we interpret them, and one of the main ways of interpreting them is by talking about them – by giving them shape in language. And the incentive to do that is to share them with somebody else. Can this work with writing? Can the constant audience of the teacher and the even sharper shaping process that goes on when you write about experience: can this continue to serve for the child as the talk with his parents has served him in infancy?

Let me refer again to 'and glad of it'. We judged that to be ultimately – I judged that on your behalf – to be ultimately irrelevant. That is, writing as written-down speech won't go the whole way. Something else has to happen side by side with it.

I had this something else illustrated to me not too long ago when I was visiting a colleague of mine at home. I was shown a story which my colleague's wife had typed out at the dictation of their four-year-old boy. And the four-year-old boy's story included this sentence: 'The king went sadly home for he had nowhere else to go.' Well I was very interested in that from a four-year-old because, you see, 'for he had nowhere else to go' is not a speech form. He hadn't heard his parents say that. He hadn't used it in speech. It had come directly to him from the printed page. He hadn't read it but it had been read to him. In other words, he has done what the linguists would call internalised a form of the written language, and he's using it in an appropriate place. He's telling a story. He's using the storyteller's language as he had got it from the printed page by somebody's reading.

And that is the other process that has to go on alongside the written-down speech. As a child extends his reading, so he internalises more and more the patterns of the written language. I don't mean that globally – and I mean *many forms* of the written language appropriate to many different kinds of tasks. I think this process, once we understand it, needs to be gradual. I think we can easily short-circuit it if we're too deliberate about it. I don't believe in setting the written model for their writing. I believe in reading for reading's sake and the kind of internalisation that comes from reading for reading's sake will then articulate, interlink with the spoken resources. The linguistic resources which have in general been recruited at the spoken level. In other words I'm asking for a kind of metabolism. You know, language in any case is outside in the world, not in the child. He has to internalise it in order to speak. There is another internalising job when it comes to the written form. In both these cases, just as we internalise substances of the world and create our own bodies out of them by a process biologists call metabolism, so we need a metabolic process in internalising language. In other words it is highly selective and it depends upon internal structures already in existence. It's a personal job, a personal selection and internalising in terms of individual needs and interests. So I don't think we can hasten it. I think the way in which we treat reading in relation to writing sometimes is in danger of being too deliberate.

Reporting how she made oxygen was for Jacqueline a concern with the outside world. I'm suggesting that this sort of writing makes its best start in the expressive. Here's another little example. This is a ten-year-old country boy who lives in Suffolk.

> On Sunday I made some coal gas. I got a large peanut tin and punched a hole in the top. I filled it one-third full with small bits of coal. Nothing happened when I first put it on the fire, but after a while brown stuff came

out. It was gas. I immediately tried to light it, but it did not light. I tried to light it every five minutes. After fifteen minutes it lit. It lasted for eight minutes. My second try lasted one hour three minutes. Each time it did not turn to coke. The back of the tin was red hot.

Well, it's fairly near to speech but he's moving toward the language in which you would expect him to perform the kind of transaction he's after – giving us information. Pretty concrete. How about its shape? Well it simply takes the shape of his activities.

Here's a much later one and a very different one. Another stage in the journey. This is a 16-year-old black girl from a school in Connecticut.

When I first moved into my neighborhood twelve years ago it was a predominantly Jewish community. From the minute I moved in till just a few years ago I was an oddity looking for acceptance. I had no one in my neighborhood I could call a true friend. The air of prejudice hung so heavy in the air it choked the life out of the neighborhood. Slowly I watched the For Sale signs pop up, and gradually I watched most of the Jewish families move out. Until I was about eleven I never knew quite why. But when I was older I realized it was because of my family and the few other black families in the area. And that's why today there is a little hurt left in me from knowing that people can be so thick-headed and narrow-minded they would let false ideas force them to move out of their homes. Today I am fighting to keep myself from inflicting my hurt on someone else and trying not to let prejudice become a part of my life.

Attempting to do a job in the world but a much more advanced job at a much more abstract level. Much more exploratory. Much more a matter of theorising in order to solve her own problems.

Let me add very briefly that I believe the writing and the reading are complementary processes and we need both. We need to test out in writing what we can do with the written forms, what meaning we can derive from the written forms, what meaning we can communicate in the written forms. The written language forms a gateway to most further learning. . . .

But all that is only half the story. It's the more familiar half. I want to move on now to what I think is the less familiar half. And to do that I want to go back to a sort of beginning, a theoretical basis. I've already made brief reference to it. The most fundamental and universal kind of learning for human beings is learning from experience, which means bringing our past to bear upon our present. To do this we need to interpret, to shape, to represent experience. One way of representing, interpreting, and shaping experience is by talking about it. And we all do a great deal of it. Joseph Church, an American psychologist, has this to say about the process: 'The morning after the big dance, the telephone system is taxed while the matrons and adolescents exchange impressions until the event has been given verbal shape and so can enter into the corpus of their experience' (Church, 1961, p. 113). I'm sorry, I can't help smiling about that because he starts off like a human being and finishes like a psychologist, doesn't he? That last idea is the important one I'm after. There is such a thing as 'a corpus of experience' and talking does shape experience in such a way as to add to it – no doubt adding to what has in fact also been created largely by talk. There are, of course, many ways of representing the world to ourselves, and language is one of them.

Sapir suggested, many years ago, that we operate in the actual world not directly, but by means of – through the mediation of – a 'world picture', a representation of the world. Ernst Cassirer, a German philosopher mostly writing in America, in his book, *An essay on man* (1944), reports that, according to a German biologist, man is slower to react to an immediate change in the immediate environment than any other creature is, and he puts forward a hypothesis to explain it. He suggests that all creatures have a system of nerves carrying messages from the outside world into themselves and a system of nerves for carrying from themselves to the outside world their responses to those messages. And these two systems are linked together – the incoming stimulus and the outgoing response. But in man, for the first time, a third system is shunted across those two, and that's the symbolic system. A system of representation. So that man receives the signals from the outside world, builds them into his world picture – his representation from past experience of what the world is like – and responds, not directly to the incoming signals, but in the light of his total representation: he responds, in other words, to the incoming signals *as interpreted by the representation*. If that sounds a very involved process, I can think of a very simple example. If I say to you, as I might well, 'I thought I heard somebody coming upstairs,' I've expressed my response to an immediate change in the environment in terms heavily clothed in past experience. I think you'd find it very difficult to do it in a way that wasn't. We habitually take the signals in and interpret them in the light of our past experience of stairways, and people, and the world in general.

A representation lasts in time in a way events don't. So you can work on it. You can go back over experiences and work on them. Not only you but other people also. When the small boy comes home and tells his mum what's been happening in school, an important part of what he builds into his representation of his day in school is what his mother says as well as what he is saying. So we can affect each other's representations. You might say what I have been doing is to work upon (or try to work upon) your world picture in certain areas to do with schools and children and language.

Representing experience is a cumulative process. Looking back, our representation is a storehouse of past experience, selective of course, not total. But looking forward, that same storehouse is a body of expectations as to what may happen: a sheaf of expectations from which we can draw as appropriate in accordance with the stimulus that meets us. It's a cumulative process, but it's not like a snowball, rolling around gathering more snow on the outside. Because every new experience is liable to demand a change in the picture of the world as a whole. Mostly we can adjust in our stride. If an event is too unlike our expectations we have to respond as best we can, because events don't wait for us; but we are left, after it's over, with an undigested event, an undigested experience.

The expectations from which we draw, and which we put to the test in actual experience, are our hypotheses. And we modify our expectations in the light of what happens, just as the scientist puts his hypotheses to the test and modifies them in the light of what happens in the laboratory. So we are actively predicting experience at every moment in the light of this storehouse of past experience.

Let me draw a little picture of your world representation – the world as you have found it – a nice simple one – and then add an event, something happening to you at the moment.

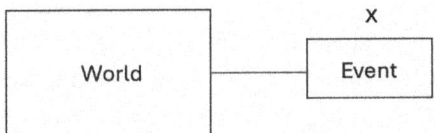

Figure 3.1.1

What's happening to you, you can only interpret in the light of your total representation: in other words the small square is subject to change in the light of what is in the large square. On the other hand, your total world representation is open to modification in the light of any new experience – that is, in the light of this (or any other) event. So the large square is also subject to change. Now while the event is happening, you are called upon to *participate* in it. For this reason your attention (represented by 'x' in my diagrams) will be focused upon changes to the smaller square: I have suggested that we can normally adjust to new experiences in the course of their happening. But if what happens is too unlike our expectations, then we are left, after the event is over, with an unmodified world representation and an undigested experience – still with a large square and a small square. But suppose the event is *not now happening*. Let me indicate the difference. In this next picture, the small square stands for an event which *has happened* and is being reconstructed in talk. And because it is not now happening, and we do not have to participate in it, we are free to concentrate upon changes in the total world representation, the large square.

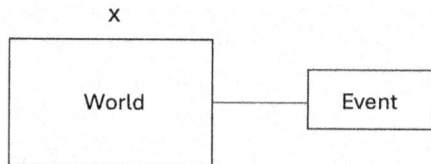

Figure 3.1.2

The difference of focus is very important: what we now have is a process of surveying the *total* in search of order and harmony and unity.

Actually, the whole scheme as I have depicted it is too simple, and I have very briefly to make it more complicated in the light of what sociologists would tell us. Now what the sociologists would point out, of course, is that I've spoken as though this were an *individual* matter, with only very cursory references to parents and other people. Sociologists will point out that the building of the world is to a great extent done cooperatively. The worlds we build are very like each other in many respects. So they would want to say we build by scanning, interpreting, acting *in* and acting *upon* situations. So that from joint action in encounters with other people we build a shared social world. I want to see that in two steps: take it first at a momentary level. In any encounter each member of the group interprets the situation in his way and acts in the light of that interpretation. To act, which includes speaking, of course, is to present oneself. So in this encounter, each member of this group is presenting himself. To act is also to *modify* the situation. But *interaction* means that these interpretations and self-presentations embodied in action are offered like pieces in a jigsaw, and it's the fitting together of the jigsaw that in fact confirms and modifies the individual interpretations and shapes the outcome of the encounter.

Expressive writing

And now, very briefly, look at that as a cumulative process. Day by day and year by year, we classify, further interpret, and store these interpretations and these self-presentations and so construct a social world and an individual personality within it. Thus, when sociologists look at us, the teachers in schools, what they see (and I'm quoting here a young British sociologist called Geoffrey Esland) – what they see is that 'the relationship between teachers and pupils is essentially a reality-sharing, world-building enterprise' (Esland, 1971, p. 72).

I want now to go back to the diagram and add a little to it. The two sides [of the diagram at Figure 3.1.3 below] represent two different relationships between *language* and *events*. On the left side, as we said, the events are actually happening, and the language constitutes a part of what is going on, a way of participating in events. Whenever we talk or write or read for some functional purpose – to get things done, to make things happen – we are using 'language in the role of participant'.

On the right-hand side, you will remember, the event is no longer happening: you are going back over it in talk. Therefore, for what I hope will be obvious reasons, I want to call that 'language in the role of spectator'.

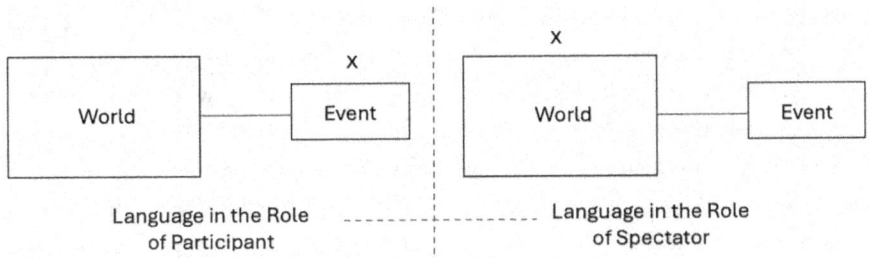

Figure 3.1.3

And in theory, at any rate, the distinction is clear. In the role of spectator we use language to reconstruct events, to talk about what is not now going on. However, it is not quite so easy as that. Suppose I invite you to be spectator of my past experience. I had a lovely weekend in New Orleans recently. Suppose I want to talk about it, in order to enjoy it again. I take up the role of spectator of those events for their own sake, for the pleasure of it. I might prevail upon you to listen and then you would take up the role of spectator of my past experience.

On the other hand, I might begin to tell you about my past experiences and after you had listened patiently in the role of spectator, you might suddenly find you were in the wrong role, because what I was doing was working up to asking you to lend me a fiver – working up to raising a loan. A hard-luck story. Well that's not the spectator role because that's participation. I am pursuing my practical purposes here, talking to make things happen – and so, participating in events. So even though I'm reconstructing past events, because they are the means to something I am now pursuing, they are not in the role of spectator.

We could contrast this with hospital talk. I don't know whether you've visited a hospital or been in a hospital, but you know on visiting day in hospitals the talk is all about operations, symptoms and illnesses and aches and pains. And all this is spectator-role talk. Going back over things in order to come to terms with them – to deal with as yet undigested events. On the other hand, in the doctor's consulting room, you may also reconstruct past experience and talk about your symptoms and your aches and your pains. That's quite different. You are contributing there to a diagnosis. Participant role. And if you got into the kind of vein you would use in the hospital, the doctor would soon recognise it and pull you out.

Another example: think of a party, and the party is over, and you and your fellow hosts are discussing the behaviour of your guests in order to discover who it could have been that left a ring on the wash basin. Well that's very helpful of you. It's very useful. You are doing part of the world's work. So you are in the participant role. On the other hand you'll probably find that the conversation soon drifts into another vein, and you find yourselves discussing the behaviour of your guests in order to *enjoy* their behaviour in a way you couldn't when they were still behaving. And that's pure spectator role.

We can take up the role of spectator of our own past experiences, and since you can of mine and I can of yours, we can become spectator of other people's experiences, real or unreal. Spectator of imagined experiences. Spectator of our own possible futures in our daydreams. So I'm including under this role of spectator a whole range of possibilities. In spectator role, we are free from the need to interact. Our attention is upon events that are not happening, interactions with people that are not now present. (We are, of course, in a situation and interacting with our listener. But we are minimising our interaction. We may offer him a drink as he listens to the story, but this is likely to be felt as an interruption to what we really are doing – which is to concern ourselves with events not now happening, for the sake of doing so.) Free then from the need to interact, we use that freedom, I suggest, first of all to pay attention to *forms* in a way that we don't when we participate. And the forms of language, particularly. . . .

We also use the participant role to evaluate. We bring onto the agenda of our talk with neighbours and other people a great deal of human experience by taking up the spectator role. I suggest that we take up the spectator role out of need – when

Expressive writing

we need to go back and come to terms with undigested experience. But we also take it up for fun and pleasure because we never cease to long for more lives than the one we've got. We've only got one life as participants. As spectators, countless lives are open to us. They are extensions of our own. And what is afoot when we are extending our experience into each other's as we gossip is above all an exploration of values. As I recount a story of events, I'm offering evaluations and I am looking to you listening to me to come back with your evaluations. I want to establish this as an important feature, because I believe we are dealing with a basic social satisfaction.[2]

I've suggested that in the spectator role we show a concern for the total world picture, a concern for the total context into which every experience has to be fitted. I've suggested that creating a world is to some extent a social process. Now the physical part of our world is very easy to corroborate. Corroboration that you have the same idea of this room as I do isn't going to be difficult. Where our world pictures are likely to be held vulnerable is not in the physical features, it's in the value system. It's in what we feel and believe about the world that we hold our world picture most privately and tentatively. So we're always offering evaluations to other people to see how they evaluate and in so doing are gaining the basic social satisfaction of having our value system, as it were, checked and calibrated against those of other people.

I now want to complete the diagram by adding a reference to the principal functions, or uses, of language, as we categorised them for the purposes of our research on writing.

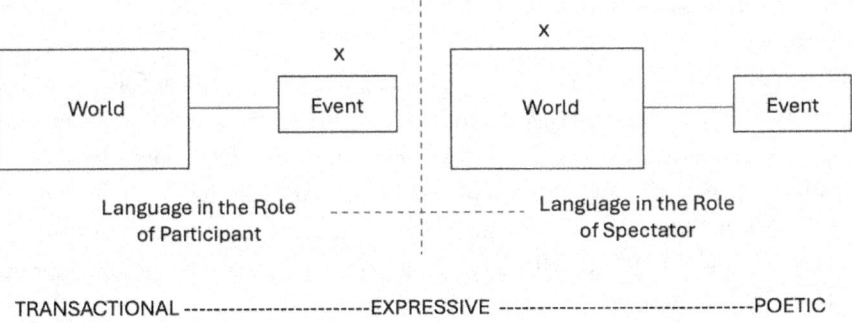

Figure 3.1.4

The middle term is one we've already talked about a good deal – the expressive function. Loosely structured, equally at home in the spectator role or the participant role – language close to the self. We saw Jacqueline attempting to meet the demands of a participant role, attempting to get something *done*. The kind of writing that fully meets such demands we labelled – for very obvious reasons – 'transactional'. It is important to see the line in the diagram as a continuous scale, a spectrum. We've already noticed that as the expressive moves towards the transactional, it has to make more explicit reference to the outside world. The personal features that are not relevant are omitted, and more of the context is filled in for somebody who is not in it already, not face to face sharing the same situations and events.

So those are the kinds of changes that go on as 'expressive' moves out to 'transactional'. I could say a lot more about the transactional, but I'm going to leave that, because the important things I want to discuss come on the other half of the diagram.

From the expressive to the poetic. In other words, language in the spectator role. Once again, as a piece of expressive writing changes to meet in full the demands of the spectator role, it changes from expressive writing to what I want to label 'poetic'. I don't mean rhymes. I don't mean meter. I don't mean poetry in the usual sense; poetry is certainly at the core of it, but is not the whole of it. By poetic I mean language as art – poetic in the original Greek sense, something made, a verbal object. So as we move from the expressive to the poetic, once more meeting the demands of a wider audience, once more language gets further away from self, but in a quite different way because for a quite different purpose. The personal features are given wider meaning as they enter into a very intricate complex organisation. Because the further you move along this scale towards the poetic, the greater is the attention paid to forms, to the organisation of form. The forms of language, but also the forms of events, the plot of the novel, the pattern of feelings – forms in general. So what you are doing is to create an artefact, a verbal object. And it's this refinement of organisation that gives personal features a kind of resonance by which they have meaning for an unknown audience. Transactional language is language that gets things done, language as a means. Poetic language is a construct, not a means but an end in itself. So language in the role of spectator is a spectrum that stretches, as far as the written language is concerned, from an intimate letter, a way of 'being with' someone, writing in the expressive, to literature: novels, poetry, drama.

I'm saying in part what has often enough been said before. It was said very elegantly by W.H. Auden about poetry:

> For poetry makes nothing happen: it survives
> In the valley of its saying where executives
> Would never want to tamper.

(Auden, 1950, p. 65)

Expressive writing

Poetry makes nothing happen. It's not transactional. One last point about that. I think perhaps I can make this clearer by contrasting the way we contextualise a piece of language, or make it our own. You know we have our own on-going purposes. If a piece of language is to mean anything to us at all we have somehow to incorporate it in those on-going purposes. In other words we have to contextualise it.

With transactional language, what goes on is *piecemeal* contextualisation. If you read a piece of transactional language – an article on a subject such as how to teach composition, or this piece of mine – then you take what you want from it and leave the rest. You pick a bit here, you leave all this because you don't accept it or you knew it already. You pick here, you pick there, you make new relations between those bits, and you make your own relations between those and what you already know and think. That is piecemeal contextualisation. What a writer of poetic language has to do at all cost is to avoid that piecemeal contextualisation. What he's after is contextualisation *as a whole*. In other words he wants to resist contextualisation until the poetic object has been built up by his reader. He wants a hard skin around it.

Of course we do respond to literature in this piecemeal fashion. I've heard children reading Yeats say, 'Oh, I didn't know Yeats was a spiritualist.' Or even, reading other poems, say, 'Oh, I didn't know there were camels in Tibet.' We do contextualise literature piecemeal. There is no reason why we shouldn't. But we do it knowing that we are not playing the game for which the poem is written. In order to do that we need to resist this piecemeal contextualisation. It doesn't matter whether there are really camels in Tibet – there are camels in Tibet in the poem and that's all that matters.

And yet, of course, we do in the end have to contextualise a piece of poetic writing. A novel can incorporate a message. What we must do is resist the piecemeal interpretation of that message because the message is embodied in the construct. When we have reconstructed the verbal construct, then we can make that our own – and I would call that global contextualisation.

I want to stress the importance of that spectrum from the expressive to the poetic. I think I can illustrate this with two pieces which represent, in a sense, poles. They're both expressive still, but they're both moving towards the poetic in very different ways. One was sent to us from Canada from the Jessie Katchem Primary School in Toronto. It was written by a boy who lived with his mother because the father had abandoned the two of them several months before. This is what he wrote:

> Once upon a time there was a little boy and he didn't have a mother or father. One day he was walking in the forest. He saw a rabbit. It led him to a house.

There was a book inside the house. He looked at the book and saw a pretty animal. It was called a 'horse'. He turned the page and saw a picture of a rabbit . . . a rabbit just like he had seen in the forest. He turned the page again and saw a cat. He thought of his mother and father, and when he was small and they had books for him and animals for him to play with. He thought about this and he started to cry.

While he was crying a lady said 'What's the matter boy.' He slowly looked around and saw his mother.

He said, 'Is it really you?'

'Yes, my son. I'm your mother.'

'Mother, mother . . . are you alive?'

'No child. This is the house that I was killed in.'

'Oh mother why are you here?'

'Because I came back to look for you.'

'Why mother? Why did you come back to look for me.'

'Because I miss you.'

'Where is father?'

'He is in the coffin that he was buried in. But don't talk about that now. How are you son? You're bigger . . . I'm glad to see you.'

'It's been a long time mother.'

While the boy and the mother were talking his father came into the room and said 'Hi son. How are you?'

'Fine,' said the boy, 'fine.'

Suddenly the mother and father came to life.

The boy was crying, and the mother and father were crying too. God suddenly gave them a miracle . . . to come to life. The boy looked at the mother and father and said, 'Oh Mother, oh Father.'

Well, spectator role taken from *need* – in order to repair as far as you can the fragmenting of your picture of the world, to come to terms with events. But as I said, the spectator role is not only used from need. We habitually take it up for much more commonplace and enjoyable reasons. Here's a very different example written by another boy. An 11-year-old boy called Malcolm in a school very near where I am working in London:

'Sir, can I have two pieces of paper?'

'Yes you can, Malcolm. What do you want it for?'

'To do a picture of a tiger, sir.'

'All right then, Malcolm.'

It took me two weeks to do that picture, but when he was finished he was Lord of the Jungle, he was magnificent. Lord of lords, Master of Masters.

The way I felt I just could not describe, but it was just the way Miss Harford felt. [Miss Harford was his English teacher.] Well, no one in this world could describe him, only someone out of this world could describe him. He was magnificent.

Poetry is a form of celebration. That is a celebration well within the expressive, but moving in the direction of poetry.

Everyone wants children to learn language to get things done, you know – even politicians and economists. If we as English teachers do not foster the kind of language which represents a concern for the total world picture, the total context into which every new experience that comes to a child has to be fitted, then I don't know who will.

I am going to finish very briefly by picking up one or two points. I've suggested that as there is a metabolism of the body, so there must be a metabolism of the mind in learning. A child must draw from the environment (which includes books and teachers) but draw selectively in accordance with the structure of his own personality. In other words, learning has an organic shape. Like a plant or a coral. As teachers we very often think of the shape of learning as though it were frost on the boughs we provide or barnacles on the bottom of our boats.

A child's learning has its own organic structure. Hence, the value of writing in the expressive, which is the language close to and most revealing of that individuality. Hence, also, the importance of individual work and work in small groups, and of the sea of talk on which all our school work should be floated.

Given these conditions I want to suggest that children learn to write above all by writing. This is an operational view of writing in school. The world about the child waits to be written about, so we haven't the need to go hunting around for exercises or dummy runs. We have to set up a working relationship between his language and his experience, and there is plenty there to write about. An operational view implies that we have our priorities. Of course we care about spelling and punctuation, but not more than we care about what the language is doing for the child.

Reading and writing and talking go hand in hand. And development comes from the gradual internalisation of the written forms so our standards, the standards we apply to their writing, must be such as to take care that we don't cut the writer out of the writing; or to put that another way, cut the writer off from his resources at the spoken level. Development comes in two main directions – towards the transactional and towards the poetic. And in either case, if we are successful, children will continue to write *as themselves* as they reach those two poles. Their explorations of the outer world demand the transactional; their explorations of the inner world demand the poetic, and the roots of it all remain in the expressive.

We don't often write anything that is merely communication. There's nearly always an element of 'finding out', of exploration. So it's a very common process for us to be able to read into our own writing something which we weren't fully aware of before we started to write. Writing can in fact be learning in the sense of discovery. But if we are to allow this to happen, we must give more credit than we often do to the process of shaping at the point of utterance and not inhibit the kind of discovery that can take place by insisting that children know exactly what they are going to say before they come to say it.

I want again to mention the importance of writing in the spectator role. Chaos is most painful in the area of values and beliefs. Therefore the harmonising, the order-seeking effects of writing and reading on the poetic end of the spectrum are highly educational, important processes.

And then finally the teacher as listener. We must be careful not to sacrifice to our roles as error spotters and improvers and correctors that of the teacher as listener and reader. I could sum it all up very simply. What is important is that children in school should write about what matters to them to someone who matters to them.

3.2 Functions and audiences in the development of writing

From *The development of writing abilities (11–18)*[3]

The excerpts which follow are from the first chapter of *The development of writing abilities (11–18)* (Britton et al., 1975). They describe the background to the research on the development of writing abilities in secondary-school students that Britton and his colleagues undertook between 1966 and 1975 (and to which Britton refers in 3.1 above). The approach that he and his team developed envisaged writers taking up a particular *function* of written language in relation to a specific *audience*.

The extensive empirical work was undertaken in two stages. The first was intended to test the validity of the approach. This involved the collection of 2,122 scripts from 63 schools of different types. These scripts covered the full range of the secondary-school age group (11–18). The scripts were drawn from different curriculum subjects and written in normal classroom conditions.

The second stage, the follow-up sampling, involved the participation of five schools in the London area across a period of four years. A first- and fourth- year class (Year 7 and Year 10 in today's parlance) were identified in each school, and a termly task agreed with collaborating teachers, designed to test out aspects of the team's approach. Examples of such tasks included imaginative story writing, a task inviting persuasion, and an exchange of writings between participating schools designed to sample writing for a peer-group audience.

The research's findings

With regard to *audience*, the researchers found that almost all (about 95%) of the writing pupils did was for the teacher, and that more than half of what they wrote for the teacher was writing from 'pupil to examiner'. ('Examiner' here refers to the teacher as assessor, marker and judge of pupils' work.)

Breaking these figures down further, it became clear that the great majority of writing in geography, history and science was for the 'teacher as examiner' – the percentages were 69%, 81% and 87% respectively; in English and religious education more of the writing was for the teacher as 'partner in dialogue' (65% and 64% respectively).

The disparity between the percentages quoted above for geography, history and science as against English and religious education (where the figures for 'teacher as examiner' were 18% and 22% respectively) was a finding which gave impetus to the language across the curriculum movement: the simple-to-state but hard-to-achieve idea that schools, and secondary schools in particular (because of their departmental structure), need to find common approaches (though not identical behaviours) across the staff of a school in key areas of language and learning. The situation in many secondary schools in the 1960s and 1970s was not merely that there were differences of approach; it was that those differences were mutually incoherent and contradictory, and therefore deeply confusing to the learner.

Britton and his colleagues of course agreed that teachers must assess. But they said that to confine children's writing almost exclusively to one audience, the teacher, and for that audience in three major curriculum subjects to act very largely in one role, that of examiner, is severely to constrain the role which writing should play in the learner's development.

The second group of categories by which Britton and his colleagues grouped writing was that of *function*: the purposes for and kinds of writing that secondary-school students undertake. The model the researchers proposed appears as Figure 3.1.4 on page 129 above. As may be seen there, it features a continuum:

transactional — expressive — poetic

Writing, the researchers said, begins with the expressive. Expressive writing is the written form of 'language close to the self'. It is the stem from which other kinds of writing flow. It is personal. The writer feels free to speculate, to tell anecdotes, to admit to feelings, to try out thoughts and ideas in a tentative way.

Transactional writing is the written form of 'language to get things done: to inform people (telling them what they need or want to know or what we think they ought to know), to advise or persuade or instruct people'. Factual truth has a high value in transactional writing.

Poetic writing is not confined to poetry. 'Poetic writing uses language as an art medium.' It is any kind of writing where the imagination is active, for example in the writing of fictional stories.

The researchers found that the majority of the writing they had collected (about two thirds) was located towards the transactional end of the continuum. Once this average proportion was broken down by subject, differences were sharp: 34% of writing in English was transactional, while the figures for geography, history, religious education and science were 88%, 88%, 57% and 92% respectively. The kinds of transactional writing students were required to do were overwhelmingly those of low-level factual report and the generalised re-presentation of previously given information. There was very little theorising or dialogue of ideas or advocacy or argument.

Britton and his colleagues were anxious to make it clear that they were not in any sense 'against' transactional writing. They were, however, concerned that the kinds of transactional writing young people were doing largely excluded those requiring a measure of independent thought. And when they combined their findings about the function of most pupils' writing with those about the audience for most pupils' writing, it became clear that what we have called 'low-level factual report and the generalised re-presentation of previously given information', written by the pupil for the teacher as examiner, was easily the commonest kind of writing that pupils were doing in school.

Underlying the taxonomies of audience and function, Britton's broader theory of participant and spectator roles distinguished between 'acting on the world by means of the accumulated representation of experience, and acting on the representation itself'. The movement from expressive language towards the transactional or the poetic depended on this distinction.

The categories of function and audience which Britton and his colleagues proposed did not intend to deny that other systems of categorisation, such as those of genre, might also offer insights – as indeed they have done, subsequently. But the value of the approach the research team took, with its concentration on the centrality of learning and with Britton's argument for the developmental importance of expressive language, has repeatedly been demonstrated in the years since the research was published. And the use of the taxonomies to survey the writing choices made available in school, and in curriculum subjects, has remained a lasting contribution.

We classify at our peril. Experiments have shown (Tajfel and Wilkes, 1960) that even the lightest touch of the classifier's hand is likely to induce us to see members of a class as more alike than they actually are, and items from different classes as less alike than they actually are. And when our business is to do more than merely look, these errors may develop, in the course of our dealings, into something quite substantial. Yet, in the present state of our knowledge about the way we perceive differences and similarities, the process of classifying seems an essential stage on the way to understanding our environment, or indeed responding to it even in more practical ways: if we see somebody throw something at us we may well spend the split second wondering what category of missile it is – as well as ducking! In handling the objects of our world or relating to the people in it, we must classify as far as we can go, and one reason for an inadequate response is a failure to go far enough: if burning petrol and burning brushwood are simply 'fires' to us, we may use the wrong kind of extinguisher, and are only lucky if we don't.

It is easy to classify fires or missiles because we already possess a knowledge of the different categories which are available. There is, however, no satisfactory way of classifying pieces of writing. The serious consequences of this were brought home to the authors when, in a previous piece of work (The Schools Council, 1966), we undertook to experiment in ways of marking General Certificate of Education compositions. In the first place, we needed to build up over the course of a year a general assessment of a pupil's ability as a writer. We knew we wanted an 'all-round' picture of his ability, but what kinds of task should we include? Writing a memo is different from writing a sonnet; writing a love letter is different from writing a letter to *The Times*. Again, writing about bombs is different from writing about combs is different from writing about tombs – and so we might go on. What was to constitute a relevant difference between one task and another? In other words, a naïve global sense of the ability to write needed to be broken down into distinct and comprehensive categories of task. We did the best we could – worked by hunch to produce something a little more adequate than the time-honoured textbook categories of narrative, descriptive, expository and argumentative. We arrived at eight assorted tasks which acted, so to speak, as landmarks but certainly did not attempt to map out the field (The Schools Council, 1966, pp. 35–38). . . .

Of course, we hoped that any categories we devised for writing would be useful not only to researchers and examiners but also to teachers, particularly since it is probably in school that the global view of writing has its most insidious and powerful effects. Many teachers, we suggest, entertain the belief that an English teacher has only to teach pupils 'to write' and the skill they learn will be effective in any lesson and in any kind of writing task. As a result, it seems to us, a learning process properly the responsibility of teachers of all subjects is left to the English teacher alone, and the inevitable failures are blamed upon him. We would urge against this theory the belief that children learn to write largely *by writing* and that it is misguided to expect them to 'practise' in one lesson what they will actively employ in another: but that, of course, is a belief that rests on the assumption that writing cannot be regarded globally.

It is our intention in the present research to describe stages in the development of writing abilities. Clearly, therefore, a major part of the work will lie in finding satisfactory means of classifying writings according to the nature of the task and the nature of the demands made upon the writer; and, as far as possible, a way of classifying that is both systematic and illuminating in the light it sheds upon the writing process itself.

***

The relation between speech and writing

It seemed to us that one very promising way into our investigation lay in considering the relationship between speech and writing – how the two processes differed and how they were alike.

Speech is constantly on the move, and the problem of all who have studied it has been to find ways of classifying the circumstances and directions of its moves. We drew on Sapir's (1949) theory of the essentially expressive nature of all speech and the way in which it moves to a greater explicitness at the expense of its expressive features when the need to communicate increases. Expressive language signals the self, reflects not only the ebb and flow of a speaker's thought and feeling, but also his assumptions of shared contexts of meaning, and of a relationship of trust with his listener. He does not therefore need to be particularly explicit until he finds his listener does not understand or accept what has been said. Then the demands of the situation will cause the speaker to become more explicit, possibly more formal, and thereby edit out some of the expressive features of his utterance in order to communicate more fully.

We extended Sapir's notion of this movement of the expressive to include movement in an opposite direction from the referential or communicative – towards what we have called the *poetic*. Here the demands of shaping an utterance into a wrought verbal construct, such as a story or a poem, modify the expressive language no less than the demands of the communicative, but in very different ways.

We thus arrived at a dynamic three-term scale (communicative–expressive–poetic) which might be used to distinguish very broadly one utterance from another across the whole range. It seemed to us to have important theoretical implications, but in practical terms it was still too broad to be adequate as a tool of analysis for our purposes.

In Sapir's notion of expressive speech being modified according to the demands of situations, we found a most important link between speech and writing. The writing of young children is often very like written down speech, and some writings by mature writers also have expressive features that make them seem nearer to speech than to writing. Clearly the degree of difference between speech and writing will vary a great deal, partly according to the demands of the situation (contrast a personal letter, for instance, with a history essay or a sociological article), and partly according to social conventions and the level of sophistication or personal taste of the writer. Expressive language interested us particularly, both because it represented some overlap between speech and writing, and because, looked at developmentally, it seemed to be the mode in which young children chiefly write. Its relationship to thinking, moreover, seems particularly direct and this suggests its importance as a mode of learning at any stage. It appears to be the means by which the new is tentatively explored, thoughts are half uttered, attitudes half expressed, the rest being left to be picked up by the listener, or reader, who is willing to take the unexpressed on trust. Its use is not, of course, always exploratory, but exploratory situations seem to call for it. Thus, a study of the expressive elements in writing has been a continuing thread in our work.

The work of Piaget and Vygotsky on inner speech has made a valuable contribution to our understanding of the way thought, speaking and writing interrelate; George Mead's (1934) concept of the process by which we internalise a 'generalised other' we have found helpful in relating a speaker's processes to a writer's. There are of course striking differences in the effect of context: writing is solitary, premeditated and a sustained act of imagination; there is no direct listener and no contemporaneous feedback as in speech. Something has constantly to be envisaged and a flow of words kept going.

Vygotsky has observed that writing is remote from the purposes of the child, and children have somehow to acquire a sense of what it is for and what it is like, if they are to learn to do it. Little work[4] seems to have been done in tracing a young child's developing sense of the conventions governing the uses of writing. A child of three and a half in a nursery school kept asking her teacher for 'the handbag story'; what she wanted was for the teacher to turn out the contents of her handbag, identifying each object and saying what it was for. Older children would be likely to have learnt not to call this string of items 'a story'. Somewhere along the line, by experience rather than by definition, we acquire a notion of the differing forms of written language that serve differing purposes; and some of these modes will for a long time remain, in Vygotsky's words, 'far from the purposes of the child'.

Arriving at a multi-dimensional model

... We have said that much of the aid we derived from existing research came from work on speech, and in our search for a shifting-focus model for written language Jakobson's (1960) notion of a hierarchy of speech functions was an important influence on our thinking. He identifies features common to any speech situation and suggests that function consists of a focus upon one of these features. Since any utterance may shift in focus from one feature to another, he brings in the notion of a 'hierarchy of functions' present in any utterance: that is to say he envisages the possibility of determining a dominant function in any utterance.

When a speaker's focus is on himself (the *addressor*) his speech will be, in Jakobson's terms, *emotive*: Dell Hymes (1968), however, suggests the term *expressive* for this function and this certainly accords better with the notions we have taken from Sapir. When a speaker shifts his focus towards his listener (the *addressee*) or his topic (the *context*) his utterance is likely to move into the *conative* or *referential* respectively: again, when his focus is on the *message* (that is, on the exact words and their interrelationships), this represents a move into the *poetic*. . . .

Hymes, in developing Jakobson's views, suggests that this model can at present be no more than a preliminary outline: 'as a guide for fieldwork, its concern should be for scope and flexibility.' He points out that actual situations are far more complex than Jakobson's model might imply; this model, however, was important to us because it provided a dynamic classification for speech functions which might be adapted and applied to written utterances.

In adapting the model, we had to determine whether a particular piece of writing could be ascribed *as a whole* to a particular function, or whether there were functional shifts of focus within a sustained written utterance comparable to those we had observed in tape recordings and transcripts of conversation. Our experience of reading the scripts many times suggested that the first alternative was correct, and the subsequent history of the project bears out our contention. There is ample evidence to suggest that a writer sets out to do one thing in a way speakers seldom do: in other words, that one of the differences between speech and writing lies in the sustained attitude that a writer takes up with regard to features in the situation – a stance which, in favourable circumstances, he maintains to the end of his written utterance.

We were interested in exploring the relationships between the seven broad types of function suggested by Hymes. Our conception of the expressive function as the 'matrix' from which a writer moves in one of two opposite directions (towards the *transactional*[5] or the *poetic*), according to the demands of different situations and his own response to them, provided the basic structure of our model, but it needed to be extended and refined to cover differences within the transactional and the poetic. In tackling this problem we became interested in James Moffett's (1968) scale of abstraction: his 'I/It' scale of varying relations between a speaker and his topic. Moffett's notion of 'distance' is on the one hand temporal; for instance, we may experience an event and comment upon it while it is happening, or, at one remove of distance, we may report it. This temporal move enables us to distance the event in other ways: by relating it, for example, to other events, experiences or ideas; by comparing it with similar events, classifying it, introducing relevant reminiscences or items of historical context. At a further remove we may theorise about the event or the classification of it and use this speculation to produce other hypotheses. . . .

It will be seen that our notion of expressive writing moving on occasion towards, or into, the poetic enabled us to dispense with the terms 'personal' and 'creative' writing: and our other spectrum, from expressive to transactional, covers in a more precise way the difference between personal and impersonal writing of an informative kind.

3.3 What writers have in common
'Shaping at the point of utterance'[6]

In this published talk (1982a), Britton's voice is in relaxed speaking mode, proposing, speculating and carrying forward an implicit argument – for the piece was a contribution to a book about the rhetorical tradition in writing. As he proceeds, it becomes clear that he is sceptical about this approach to the teaching of writing – an established way of framing writing pedagogy in America and Canada at that time (the 1980s). He calls up evidence both from established writers (most notably in the extended passage by Heinrich Von Kleist), and also from primary classrooms to argue that there is something much more fundamental than planning, revision and drafting to the process of writing, and that is the ability to tune in to the movements of thinking and hear 'an inner voice dictating'.

Britton suggests that this 'spontaneous shaping', which can be observed in both speech and writing, is the process whereby we discover our meanings through language. And it is the need, above all, to *share* our meanings which encourages us to go further and to clarify them for a reader or an audience.

Britton's view of writing is inextricably linked to reading at all ages and stages. In reading we are always, to some degree, observing what the writer is doing; in writing we are always drawing on what we have learned from reading. The authors we learn from are constantly providing what Margaret Meek Spencer called 'untaught lessons'; we learn from them the tunes and patterns of language that become part of our inner resources. Authors are probably more aware than anyone of the value of listening to that 'inner voice dictating' and of the way in which it can surprise us or lead us to a discovery. Britton makes clear that in experienced writers 'the act of writing becomes itself a contemplative act revealing further coherence and fresh pattern'.

He points to the obvious fact that initially children draw principally on the linguistic resources of speech, and then increasingly – depending on their experience – on those of the books and stories that have been read to them and that they are beginning to read themselves. He speaks of young writers shuttling between the general resources of speech and 'internalised forms of written language'. Drawing on the work of Michael Polanyi, he stresses that, while writers are obviously always 'subsidiarily' aware of words and structures, their prime focus is (or should be) on the meanings they want to convey. 'To focus on the words would be to inhibit the handling of meaning by writer or reader.' This laconic statement is a devastating rebuke to much practice in early literacy education.

As in many other texts, Britton is aware of more than one continuum: a continuum that links reading and writing; a continuum that connects novice writing to the work of experienced authors; and a continuum with personal storying at one end and established works of literature at the other. He shows us what all writers have in common, and in doing so takes 'literature' out of a special compartment and presents it as the fullest development of story and song.

The two words 'spontaneity' and 'invention' as we ordinarily use them must surely have something in common: an element of surprise, not only for those who encounter and respond to the act or expression, but also for those who originate it. I want to suggest here that rhetoricians, in their current concern for successive drafts and revision processes in composing, may be underestimating the importance of 'shaping at the point of utterance', or the value of spontaneous inventiveness. It is my claim, in fact, that a better understanding of how a writer shapes at the point of utterance might make a major contribution to our understanding of invention in rhetoric.

In all normal speech we do, almost of necessity, shape as we utter. Syntactically, we launch into a sentence and hope somehow to reach closure. We had a Director at the Institute of Education where I once worked who was a very powerful speaker, but also a great 'um'-er and 'ah'-er. As you listened to him it would go something like this: 'It seems to me, Mr Chairman – ah – in spite of the difficulties Professor X has raised – ah – that what we most need – ah – in the present circumstances – ah – and – ah – at this moment in time – ah – in some way to bring to a conclusion this intolerably long sentence.' Listening, we could tell precisely at what point he foresaw his total structure, the point at which he 'took it on the run'.

What is not so easily demonstrated is that the shaping as we speak applies not only to syntactic but also to semantic choices. When we start to speak, we push the boat out and trust it will come to shore somewhere – not *anywhere*, which would be tantamount to losing our way, but somewhere that constitutes a stage on a purposeful journey. To embark on a conversational utterance is to take on a certain responsibility, to stake a claim that calls for justification: and perhaps it is the social pressure on the speaker to justify his claim that gives talk an edge over silent brooding as a problem-solving procedure. Heinrich Von Kleist, the early 19th-century German writer, puts this point boldly in an essay he called 'On the gradual fabrication of thought while speaking':

> Whenever you seek to know something and cannot find it out by meditation, I would advise you to talk it over with the first person you meet. He need not be especially brilliant, and I do not suggest that you *question* him, no: *tell* him about it. . . . Often, while at my desk working, I search for the best approach to some involved problem. I usually stare into my lamp, the point of optimum brightness, while striving with utmost concentration to enlighten myself. . . . And the remarkable thing is that if I talk about it with my sister, who is working in the same room, I suddenly realize things which hours of brooding had perhaps been unable to yield. . . . Because I do start with some sort of dark notion remotely related to what I am looking for, my mind, if it has set out boldly enough, and being pressed to complete what it has begun, shapes that muddled area into a form of new-minted clarity, even while my talking progresses.
>
> (Von Kleist, 1951, p. 42)

As teachers, we are likely to have similar evidence from much nearer home: how often have we had a student come to us with his problem, and in the course of verbalising what that problem is reach a solution with no help from us.

Then what about writing? First, it must be said that students of invention in writing cannot afford to rule out of court evidence regarding invention in speech: there must be some carry-over from expression in the one medium to expression in the other. Shaping at the point of utterance is familiar enough in the way young children will spin their yarns to entertain an adult who is willing to provide an audience. (A ten-minute tape-recorded performance by a five-year-old boy winds up: 'So he had ten thousand pounds, so everyone loved him in the world. He buy – he buyed a very fast racing car, he buyed a magic wand, he buyed everything he loved, and that's the end of my story what I told you.' A five-year-old sense of closure!) There is ample evidence that spontaneous invention of this kind survives, and may even appear to profit from, the process of dictating, where parent or teacher writes down what a child composes orally. That it is seriously inhibited by the slowing down of production when the child produces his own written script is undeniable. But it is my argument that successful writers adapt that inventiveness and continue to rely on it rather than switching to some different mode of operating. Once a writer's words appear on the page, I believe they act primarily as a stimulus to *continuing* – to further writing, that is – and not primarily as a stimulus to *re*-writing. Our experiments in writing without being able to see what we had written suggested that the movements of the pen capture the movement of our thinking, and it is a serious obstacle to further composition not to be able to re-read, to get 'into the tramlines' again. An eight-year-old Newcastle schoolboy wrote about his own writing processes: 'It just comes into your head, it's not like thinking, it's just there. When you get stuck you just read it through and the next bit is there, it just comes to you.' I think many teachers might regard the outcome of such a process as mere 'fluency', mere verbal facility, and not the sort of writing they want to encourage. It is my argument that highly effective writing may be produced in just that spontaneous manner, and that the best treatment for empty verbalism will rarely be a course of successive draft making.

'It just comes into your head, it's not like thinking': it seems that Barrett Mandel (1978) would agree with the eight-year-old, for he calls his recent article on writing, 'Losing one's mind: learning to read, write and edit'. I quote his views here because they are in part an attempt to make room for the process of shaping at the point of utterance. He sets out the three steps that occur in his own writing process: '(1) I have an idea about something I want to write; (2) I write whatever I write; (3) I notice what I have written, judge it, and edit it, either a lot or a little.' And his claim is that the relationship between (1) and (2) is not one of cause and effect; 'rather, step one *precedes* writing and establishes a frame of mind in which writing is likely to occur.' 'It is the act of writing that produces the discoveries,' he claims, and, by way of explanation, 'words flow from a pen, not from a mind; they appear on the page through the massive co-ordination of a tremendous number of motor processes. . . . More accurately, I *become* my pen; my entire organism becomes an extension of this writing implement. Consciousness is focused at the point of the pen.'

So far, so good, but since Mandel goes on to approve of his colleague, Janet Emig's, description of writing as 'a form of cognition', it seems to me a little perverse to propose (by his title, 'Losing one's mind . . .') a mindless form of cognition. 'Freeing one's mind' would be more appropriate, the freedom being that of ranging across the full spectrum of mental activity from the autistic pole to the reality-adjusted pole, as Peter McKellar (1957, p. 5) has described it. Or, as we might speculatively describe it today, right brain and left brain in intimate collaboration.

I want to associate spontaneous shaping, whether in speech or writing, with the moment-by-moment interpretative process by which we make sense of what is happening around us; to see each as an instance of the pattern-forming propensity of a person's mental processes. Thus, when we come to write, what is delivered to the pen is in part already shaped, stamped with the image of our own ways of perceiving. But the intention to *share*, inherent in spontaneous utterance, sets up a demand for further shaping.

Can we go deeper than this: penetrate beyond the process of drawing upon our own store of interpreted experience? Perl and Egendorf (1979) believe we must if we are to provide a full account of writing behaviour. In an article they call 'The process of creative discovery' they speak of a new line of philosophical enquiry, the 'philosophy of experiencing', and quote from the writings of Eugene Gendlin (1962). 'Many thinkers since Kant,' they suggest, 'have claimed that all valid thought and expression are rooted in the wider realm of pre-representational experience.' 'Experiencing', or pre-representational experience, 'consists of continuously unfolding orders rather than finished products'; in Gendlin's words, it is 'the felt apperceptive mass to which we can inwardly point.' It is fluid, global, charged with implicit meanings which we alter when by expressing them we make them explicit.

D.W. Harding, psychologist and literary critic, explores a similar distinction in his book *Experience into words*:

> The emergence of words or images as part of our total state of being is an obscure process, and their relation to the non-verbal is difficult to specify.... The words we choose (or accept as the best we can find at the moment) may obliterate or slightly obscure or distort fine features of the non-verbal background of thinking.... A great deal of speaking and writing involves the effort to be a little more faithful to the non-verbal background of language than an over-ready acceptance of ready-made terms and phrases will permit.
>
> (Harding, 1963, pp. 170–172)

Perl and Egendorf comment on that effort as they observe it in their students: 'When closely observed, students appear to write by shuttling back and forth from their sense of what they wanted to say to the words on the page, and back to address what is available to them inwardly.' This is in essence the process they call 'retrospective structuring', and its near inevitability might be suggested by comparing writing with carving: the sculptor with chisel in hand must both cut and observe the effect of his cut before going on. But retrospective structuring needs to be accompanied by what the authors call 'projective structuring', shaping the material in such a way that the writer's meaning carries over to the intended reader. It is in this aspect of writing that 'discovery', or shaping at the point of utterance, tends to break down: a mistaken sense of a reader's expectations may obstruct or weaken the 'sense of what they wanted to say' – or, in Harding's terms, 'obliterate fine features of the non-verbal background of thinking'. Observing unskilled writers, Perl and Egendorf comment: 'What seems particularly unskilled about the way these students write is that *they apply prematurely a set of rigid critical rules for editing* to their written products.' 'Prematurely' might be taken to mean at first draft rather than at second or third, but I think this does less than justice to the authors' meaning. Minor editing – for spelling, for example – is better left, we can agree, to a re-reading stage. What is at issue here is a more important point: that too restricted a sense of a reader's expectations may result in 'projective structuring' coming to dominate the shaping at the point of utterance, to the exclusion or severe restriction of the 'retrospective structuring', the search for a meaning that in its expression satisfies the writer.

Such a conclusion would gain general support from a neat little study by Mike Rose (1978), a study he calls 'Rigid rules, inflexible plans and the stifling of writing'. A case study of five fluent writers and five with 'writer's block' leads him to conclude that 'the non-blockers operate with fluid, easily modified, even easily discarded rules and plans, that are often expressed with a vagueness that could almost be interpreted as ignorance. There lies the irony. The students that offer the least precise rules and plans have the least trouble composing.'

What I have suggested, then, is that shaping at the point of utterance involves, first, drawing upon interpreted experience, the results of our moment-by-moment shaping of the data of the senses and the continued further assimilation of that material in search of coherence and pattern (the fruits of our contemplative moments); and, secondly, that it seems to involve by some means getting behind this to a more direct apperception of the felt quality of 'experiencing' in some instance or instances; by which means the act of writing becomes itself a contemplative act revealing further coherence and fresh pattern. Its power to do so may depend in part upon the writer's counterpart of the social pressure that listeners exert on a speaker, though in this case, clearly, the writer himself is, in the course of the writing, the channel through which that pressure is applied.

I must now add the much more obvious point that in the initial stages of learning to write a child must draw upon linguistic resources gathered principally through speaking and listening, and apply those resources to the new task of writing. Some children, however, will also be familiar with some forms of the written language derived from stories that have been read to them. A four-year-old, for example, dictated a fairy story of his own composition in which he said, 'The king went sadly home, for he had nowhere else to go', a use of 'for' that can hardly have been learnt from listening to speech. Thus, the early writer shuttles between internalised forms of the written language and his general resources recruited through speech: that he should maintain access to the latter is important if he is to embark on the use of writing to fulfil a range of different purposes. His progress as a writer depends thereafter, to a considerable degree, on his increasing familiarity with forms of the written language, the enlargement of his stock of 'internalised' written forms through reading and *being read to*. (The process of recreating the rhythms of the written language from his own reading must derive from that apprenticeship to an adult's reading.) To put it simply, if rather crudely, I see the developed writing process as one of hearing an inner voice dictating forms of the written language appropriate to the task in hand.

If it is to work this way, we must suppose that there exists some kind of *pre-setting mechanism* which, once set up, continues to affect production throughout a given task. The difficulties many writers feel in 'finding a way in' or in 'finding one's own voice' in a particular piece of writing, as well as the familiar routine of running through what has been written in order to move on, seem to me to supply a little evidence in favour of such a 'pre-setting mechanism'. Beyond that I can offer only hints and nudges. There is, for example, the phenomenon of metric composition. Read aloud a passage in galloping iambics and most listeners are enabled to compose spontaneously in that rhythm; young children's facility in picking up pig-Latin or dog-Latin is probably another example of the same sort of process. And by way of explanation, there is Kenneth Lashley's (1961, p. 194) longstanding notion of a 'determining tendency' in human behaviour:

> The cortex must be regarded as a great network of reverbatory circuits constantly active. A new stimulus reaching such a system does not excite an isolated reflex path, but must produce widespread changes in the pattern of excitation throughout a whole system of already interacting neurons.

Such a determining tendency, he argues, is related to an individual's *intention*. In this and other respects the notion parallels Michael Polanyi's (1969, p. 146) description of focal and subsidiary awareness. Applying that to the writing process, a writer is subsidiarily aware of the words and structures he is employing and focally aware of an emergent meaning, the meaning he intends to formulate and convey. And it is the focal awareness that guides and directs the use made of the means, of which he is subsidiarily aware. In similar fashion, a reader's attention is not focused upon the printed marks: he attends *from* them to the emerging meaning. To focus on the words would be to inhibit the handling of meaning by writer or reader. 'By concentrating on his fingers,' says Polanyi, 'a pianist can paralyse himself; the motions of his fingers no longer bear then on the music performed, they have lost their meaning.'

Painting in oils, where one pigment may be used to obliterate another, is a very different process from painting in watercolours, where the initial process must capture immediately as much as possible of the painter's vision. Do modes of discourse differ in production as sharply as that? And does our present concern with pre-planning, successive drafting and revision suggest that in taking oil painting as our model for writing we may be underestimating the value of 'shaping at the point of utterance' and hence cutting off what might prove the most effective approach to an understanding of rhetorical invention?

Acknowledgements

I am grateful to Geoffrey Summerfield of New York University and Frank Smith of the University of Victoria who introduced me to the articles by Heinrich Von Kleist and Kenneth Lashley respectively.

Notes

1. The source of this text is a lecture given in 1972, reprinted in Britton (1982b), pp. 94–111.
2. 'For an explanation of this and other important ideas I have drawn upon here, see Harding (1937).' Britton's note.
3. The source of this text is Britton et al. (1975), pp. 1–3, 10–12, 13–15.
4. 'But see A.N. Applebee, "The spectator role: theoretical and developmental studies of ideas about and responses to literature, with special reference to four age levels" [PhD thesis, 1973, University of London]'. Britton's note.
5. 'We abandoned the commonly used term "communicative" because, in a sense, any use of language may be said to imply some kind of communication. We use instead "transactional", as a self-explanatory term in utterances where some transaction is involved, such as informing, recording, instructing, convincing, etc.' Britton's note.
6. The source of this text is a talk given in 1980, reprinted in Britton (1982a), pp. 139–145.

References

Auden, W.H. (1950). *Collected shorter poems, 1930–1944*. London: Faber and Faber.
Britton, J. (1982a). 'Shaping at the point of utterance' [1980], in Pradl, G. (ed.), *Prospect and retrospect: Selected essays of James Britton*. London and Monclair, NJ: Heinemann Educational and Boynton/Cook, pp. 139–145.
Britton, J. (1982b). 'Writing to learn and learning to write' [1972], in Pradl, G. (ed.), *Prospect and retrospect: Selected essays of James Britton*. London and Monclair, NJ: Heinemann Educational and Boynton/Cook, pp. 94–111.
Britton, J., Burgess, T., Martin, N., McLeod, A. and Rosen, H. (1975). *The development of writing abilities (11–18)*. London and Basingstoke: Macmillan.
Cassirer, E. (1944). *An essay on man*. New Haven, CT: Yale University Press.
Church, J. (1961). *Language and the discovery of reality*. New York: Random House.
Esland, G. (1971). 'Teaching and learning as the organisation of knowledge', in Young, M. (ed.), *Knowledge and control*. London: Collier-Macmillan.
Gendlin, E. (1962). *Experiencing and the creation of meaning*. Toronto: The Free Press.
Harding, D. (1963). *Experience into words*. London: Chatto and Windus.
Hymes, D. (1968). 'The ethnography of speaking', in Fishman, J. (ed.), *Readings in the sociology of language*. The Hague: Mouton Publishers.
Jakobson, R. (1960). 'Linguistics and poetics', in Sebeok, T. (ed.), *Style in language*. Cambridge, MA: MIT Press.
Lashley, K. (1961). 'The problem of serial order in behavior', in Saporta, S. (ed.), *Psycholinguistics: A book of readings*. New York: Holt, Rinehart and Winston.

London Association for the Teaching of English (1950). 'The meaning and marking of imaginative composition'. *New Era*, 31 (7), 1950, pp. 137–143.

London Association for the Teaching of English (1960). *And when you are young: Prose and verse by young writers, 5–18*. London: The Joint Council for Education through Art.

Mandel, B. (1978). 'Losing one's mind: Learning to write and edit'. *College Composition and Communication*, December 1978, pp. 363–365.

McKellar, P. (1957). *Imagination and thinking*. London: Cohen and West.

Mead, G. (1934). *Mind, self and society*. Chicago, IL: University of Chicago Press.

Moffett, J. (1968). *Teaching the universe of discourse*. Portsmouth, NH: Boynton/Cook.

Perl, S. and Egendorf, A. (1979). 'The process of creative discovery: Theory, research and implications for teaching', in McQuade, D. (ed.), *Linguistics, stylistics and the teaching of composition*. Akron, OH: Department of English, University of Akron, pp. 121–127.

Polanyi, M. (1969). *Knowing and being*. London: Routledge and Kegan Paul.

Rose, M. (1978). 'Rigid rules, inflexible plans, and the stifling of writing: A cognitivist analysis of writer's block'. Department of English unpublished paper. Los Angeles, CA: University of California.

Sapir, E. (1949). *Culture, language, and personality*. Berkeley and Los Angeles, CA: University of California Press.

The Schools Council (1966). *Multiple marking of English compositions: An account of an experiment conducted by J.N. Britton, N.C. Martin, H. Rosen*. Schools Council Examinations Bulletin 12. London: Her Majesty's Stationery Office.

Tajfel, H. and Wilkes, A. (1960). 'Effects of a classification on judgments of length'. *Bulletin of the British Psychological Society*, 41, A10–A11.

Von Kleist, H. (1951). 'On the gradual construction of thoughts during speech'. Trans. M. Hamburger. Broadcast on the Third Programme, BBC, 12 January 1951. *German Life and Letters* 5 (1), pp. 42–46. https://onlinelibrary.wiley.com/doi/10.1111/j.1468-0483.1951.tb01029.x

SECTION 4

Teachers and research

Enquiry in its broadest sense occupied Britton throughout his professional life. His formal investigations included studies of response to poetry, imaginative composition, multiple marking and the development of writing abilities. Alongside his considered and developed projects were also explorations conducted in more informal ways, through his reading of research by others, notes and observations and recordings, and examples culled from classrooms and from daily life. It is a characteristic of the voice that Britton brought to English teaching that he draws on insights from all these sources.

Britton joined the English department at the University of London Institute of Education at a time when educational enquiry was mainly shaped by traditions of philosophy, psychology and, more recently, sociology: the 'educational disciplines', as these were termed. In his writings, he respected the framing of the search for truth in these traditions, and he was aware also of the importance of research for educational practice and political choice. He saw, though, that his hopes for English teaching, and his concentration on developing practice to support young people's learning, required particular sorts of concentration. The turn to language's role in learning in the work that followed was always accompanied by his own reflection on young people and what could be learned from interactions with them; and it was always tested in collaboration with teachers as participants in the design and practice of his research.

Britton's earliest, formal enquiries in his MA degree (1952) were already characteristic. He approached his work on the development of literary judgement with a different sort of interest from the then prevalent concerns. Much practice at that time, supported by certificated examinations, had taken the new criticism of I.A. Richards (1929) to imply the acquisition of literary judgement through a practical concentration on this in the classroom. Britton took a different path. He qualified too simple an emphasis on training and instruction by focusing on readers' experience and by asking how young people's literary judgements develop over time.

He explored these issues through a study that drew on the research methods of psychology. The starting point was key: the question to be asked. The aim was then to provide a basis from which to influence educational opinion through a well-judged, experimental design, involving sampling and statistical analysis. The skills in this continued to be characteristic of Britton's formal research. They figured in due course in investigations into the marking of compositions and in the major work on the development of writing abilities, which has been illustrated in the previous section.

The pieces that follow in this section reflect Britton's further thinking about the interaction between research and the work of teachers. The impetus arises jointly from his research collaboration with the Schools Council and from his on-going engagement with teachers and their pupils' learning. In its relatively brief existence (1964–84), Schools Council initiatives and funding contributed considerably to developments in English teaching.

Britton's 'A note on teaching, research and "development"' (1982b), originally written in 1969 for colleagues on the Schools Council English committee, reflects that background. He is seeking to ensure a considered notion of 'development' in his colleagues' understandings about research and in their hopes for its impact in classrooms. We may add that this project also required some delicacy on Britton's part, since he needed to mediate between the understandings of teachers, policy makers and researchers.

In 'A quiet form of research', written in the course of an active retirement and published in 1983, Britton develops ideas about research as an activity. He explores the interrelation of teaching and research, differentiating research in the social sciences, and in education, from research methods appropriate to the physical sciences. In a manner that recalls his earlier 'Note. . .', he rejects the conventional model of research as an activity conducted elsewhere and then applied in classrooms. Instead, he juxtaposes teaching, development and research as 'interrelated modes of enquiry, sources of knowledge on a widening range of applicability'.

In 'Vygotsky's contribution to pedagogical theory' (1987) Britton acknowledges his intellectual debt to Vygotsky: a debt even greater than that to any of the other significant figures, from a wide diversity of disciplines, on whose work his own thinking and writing drew. He shows how his understanding of Vygotsky's work has developed since his first encounter with it; and he shows the relevance of Vygotsky's insights to teachers and learners in contemporary classrooms many decades after the research of which those insights were the fruit.

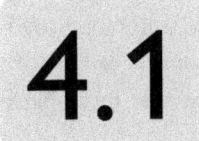 4.1 'A note on teaching, research and "development"'[1]

In this brief piece, Britton leads our understandings as readers first through an account of representation addressed principally to teachers, and then on to the processes of 'development' which research must pass through as teachers make their journey to 'discovery of a different order'. The metaphor of the repeated journey beautifully conveys the process of 'development', the travel made by teachers from the starting points offered by research findings, as they re-work these in the continually renewing activity of the classroom.

It is interesting to see Britton, towards the end of the piece, looking to extend his argument towards the recently formed teachers' centres. The emergence of these centres, the ambitions of the Schools Council and the tone of Britton's paper reflect a precious period of partnership between schools, stakeholders, policymakers and academics in a joint concern for taking public education forward.

Perhaps we don't want to know

To risk a sweeping generalisation, it seems to me that the attitude to research of teachers in England differs from that of teachers in America: and that each attitude has its inherent strengths and weaknesses. American teachers, as a result no doubt of their training, are more sophisticated readers of research reports, attach more importance to new findings, and are liable, I suspect, to make a too direct application of such findings to their practice as teachers. Teachers in England are less sophisticated in the language of educational research, expect much less in the way of assistance from this quarter, and are often suspicious of any advice that does not originate from classroom experience, or at the least confirm them along the lines of the convictions they have derived from their own experience. What is admirable about such self-confidence I need not underline: its weakness lies in the fact that as teachers we may be charged with attempting to hoist ourselves up by our own bootstraps. What linguists, psychologists, sociologists and philosophers can explain or suggest about the nature of human behaviour *ought* in some way to be available to us as an aid to our intuitive practice of the art of teaching.

Knowing and doing

Our experience is a constant succession of confrontations; and what is meant by a 'confrontation' could hardly be more vividly illustrated than by thinking of a teacher facing his class. In order to act responsibly in any situation we must interpret what confronts us, and this involves *representing it to ourselves*. We are able to make such a representation because we are not new-born into each confrontation but can draw upon past experience: that is to say, upon our store of representations of previous encounters with the world. This we may do badly or well: to do it well means, obviously, to represent as fully and faithfully as possible what is there. A principal reason for doing it badly is that we fall back on something ready-made: a formulation of a past situation is brought in to serve, with little or no adaptation, as a representation of the present. (This may result in our acting *irresponsibly*, as the psychologist George Kelly [1963] has pointed out: we shirk response to what is actually there by applying some ill-fitting ready-made formulation such as a school rule or a stereotyped status-image.)

What we *do* in any situation, then, is done in the light of the representation we make: and that representation is made in the light of what we perceive and what we *know*. Parts of this knowledge will be unsystematic and loosely formulated, as for example recognising that it is John Smith we are talking to and recalling a few random facts about John Smith's home circumstances: other parts of it will be highly systematic – as for example knowing the details of a psychologist's coherent analysis of the stages of mental development; or, to take a very different but not necessarily irrelevant case, knowing the structure of a Shakespeare sonnet in relation to the metrical principles that govern English verse forms. Our systematic knowledge, the fruits of our past thinking, the fruits of our past looking (and listening etc.), and – more mysteriously still – the fruits of our past intuitions, imaginings, feelings: all these are frames of reference in the light of which we represent to ourselves the constantly changing situations that confront us.

Putting it crudely, it is the continual reformulation of what we know in the light of what we perceive that matters; and the hardening of what we know into a formula that we apply ready-made instead of reformulating – that is the danger. Thus, our most powerful ideas are relatively general, relatively unformulated starting points from which we constantly reformulate.

Research and teaching

Research findings are things we can *know* which could have a bearing on what we *do* when we teach. And 'development' should be the name we give to the process of bringing this kind of knowing into relationship with this kind of doing. But how does it work?

The conclusions reached by a research team working in controlled situations cannot be directly apprehended and applied by teachers working in conditions where every variable is actively varying. For the teacher to reformulate from the general starting point to meet particular circumstances is in this instance a dangerous impossibility. The research team may step out of their quarters into the schools in order to produce materials that embody certain of their findings – a kit for the job, so to speak. For the teachers who work with the members of the team in the classroom this may be a very valuable kind of development work: it may enable them, that is to say, to modify their own insights in the light of the fresh thinking and so have at their disposal new knowledge that will enable them to represent more faithfully and more fully what confronts them in the classroom. But if the kit produced is then regarded as a means of persuading teachers to apply the research findings without undergoing the modification of insights – a means in other words of teaching better than they know – then clearly the stage that is essentially what we mean by 'development' has been omitted.

For development is a two-way process: the practitioner does not merely *apply*; he must reformulate from the general starting points supplied by the research and arrive at new ends – new not only to him, but new in the sense that they are not a part of the research findings, being a discovery of a different order. The value of the research lies in supplying the starting point for many such discoveries; the value of each discovery is limited to the successful solution of this particular problem at this particular time; but the power of the teacher to make that journey and make it again – there above all lies the value of the whole enterprise.

If there is to be a kit, then, something we can call 'development' must go with it. Obviously there are not enough research workers to go round the schools working in turn with the teachers – even those who would welcome the opportunity. What then can we imply?

Teachers' centres

I think there are implications here for those who plan educational research. A development aspect built into a research project from an early stage could act as a check upon the relevance of the enquiry and the operational value of the starting points it might provide: the nature of the enquiry in its details might be 'corrected' by such a monitoring process.

Clearly there are important implications for in-service training and initial training of teachers. But the implications I wish finally to pursue here are those for teachers' centres. The 'do it yourself' spirit that still makes the notion of teachers' centres an attractive one could, it seems to me, generate the kind of situation which provides the most fruitful point of application for the expert – the research worker and the theoretician: that makes possible, in fact, the development process as we have described it.

It will take time. The 'do it yourself' impetus dies out if, after a while, nothing much seems to have happened. In other words, the pooling of experience makes the right beginning but needs to lead into a more clearly defined enquiry – a committed attempt on the part of a group to make corporate discoveries. A measure of success in this is likely to lead the group to set itself more ambitious tasks, and at the point where the difficulties of achieving them seem insurmountable this is the situation in which an experienced worker in a similar area may in fact find his most profitable audience. Again, the process is two-way: the expert's knowledge can speak to the group in answer to questions they have already asked themselves: and the reformulating of his findings in the terms of their insights comes as an extension from that centre.

The most active field of research relevant to education today is probably that of language. The need for development work among English teachers is therefore particularly urgent. The need is urgent but the process cannot be hurried.

4.2 'A quiet form of research'[2]

This article moves easily between Britton's own trajectory as teacher and researcher, the work of scholars in other disciplines, and research by teachers in schools. The article resonates with what had by this time become a tradition of enquiry in English teaching, begun with the formation of the London Association for the Teaching of English in the immediate post-war years. The concept of 'development' that Britton introduces draws on this tradition and on the value placed on teachers building their own understandings and contributing their insight.

The balance of his final position is characteristic. He acknowledges the interplay of three strands of educational enquiry: teaching as heuristic, development appropriately understood, and basic research. It is a vision of collaborative endeavour, coupled with a recognition, as he puts it elsewhere, that 'what the teacher can't do in the classroom can't be achieved by any other means'. We may note the contrast with the mandating of curriculum which has followed since, alongside the 'frameworks' and Ofsted curriculum reviews through which teachers' work has subsequently been regulated.

Yes, I think things are moving, we are making some progress, and there are signs of a widening realisation that research methods appropriate to the physical sciences are not the best model for research in the social sciences. The most recent doctoral thesis on an educational topic that has come my way is a case study of a writing course, and the writer, Nancy Jones of the University of Iowa, outlines her perspective this way.

> The validity of laws about natural phenomena – that, for example, H_2O freezes at 32 degrees Fahrenheit, or that testosterone has a direct role in

> maintaining the accessory sex organs in male rats, requires that studies which support them be capable of replication. It is one thing to do that with inanimate objects like water or animate objects like rats whose breeding and environment can be extensively controlled and manipulated so as to minimize differences among them. It is quite another thing, of course, and finally impossible, ethically and politically, to do that with people.
>
> (Jones, 1982, p. 10)

Coming at things from another angle, Cindy Ray of Pioneer Valley Regional School in Massachusetts opens a proposal for a research project in her own classroom: 'Research is not primarily a process of proving something, but primarily a process of discovery and learning,' and adds, 'This view of research is tremendously liberating, for it allows classroom teachers to take seriously the ordinary business of their lives as teachers.'

When younger members of our profession give us a lead in this direction, I am optimistic about the future of educational research.

In the physical sciences, routine research may be seen to *accumulate*. As the monographs on a particular topic fill more and more of the shelf, our secure knowledge of the topic grows. Gaps may be revealed, demanding further research, and these are likely in time to be filled. While, as Karl Popper (1976) has shown, proof of these findings is never possible, yet the chance of disproof becomes ever more remote, and at each stage we act on what we believe.

Experience shows that what accrues in the social sciences is not like this. Contradictory findings abound; what is true of one individual or group of individuals in one context proves inapplicable to others in other contexts. Teachers, from their own experience, are very aware of this phenomenon: what works with one group fails with another. Any generalisations we attempt to make must, therefore, be made in the light of *context* in the broadest sense of that word, and in the final analysis we have to recognise that the context of any human action is so complex as to be experimentally uncontrollable. Common sense – the kind that comes from the experience of living in any family – has taught us all to behave in the implicit light of this truth. We come, paradoxically, to expect the unexpected of people.

Once again, we act in the light of what we believe to be the case, but the mode of appraisal, the criteria for believing,, will be different from the criteria we apply in the physical sciences. Limiting our concern to what Thomas Kuhn (1962) has called 'normal' scientific activity, we should expect the criteria for acceptance to change as we move from the physical to the social sciences, from demonstration by empirical evidence to logical reasonableness, and explanatory power and compatibility with experience. In Popper's terms, falsification by empirical procedures gives way to falsification by critical procedures.

> The conscious adoption of the critical method becomes the main instrument of growth. . . . The critical method, though it will use certain tests wherever possible, and preferably practical tests, can be generalized into what I describe as a critical or rational attitude. . . . I tried to argue that this critical attitude of reasonableness should be extended as far as possible.
> (Popper, 1976, pp. 115–116)

It should be clear that there is no argument here for the uncritical acceptance of findings in the social sciences or for lack of rigour in the modes of inquiry. As far as educational research is concerned, I think a lack of rigour shows itself most blatantly when experimental programmes or procedures that can profitably be *described* are in fact *prescribed*. I remember one enthusiastic researcher who, in a prestigious conference, expressed the hope that 'by this time next year' his thoroughly researched social-studies programme would be in use in every school in the state. To think in this way is to ignore totally the teaching/learning context – the minutiae of behaviour of a particular teacher in moment-by-moment interaction with a particular group of students in a particular school and locality on a particular occasion. However well a programme may have been researched, it can achieve its objectives only as a result of the full participation of both students and teachers.

If research is seen primarily as a process of discovery, then the day-to-day work of a teacher comes under the term *teachers as researchers*. It cannot be said too often that effective teaching depends upon the concern of every teacher for the *rationale* by which he or she works. Teaching consists of interactive behaviour, and it is the teacher's share in this behaviour that most concerns us. In the course of interacting with individuals and classes, a teacher must make a hundred and one decisions in every session – off-the-cuff decisions that can only reliably come from inner conviction, that is to say by consistently applying an ever-developing rationale. This requires that every lesson should be for the teacher an inquiry, some further discovery, a quiet form of research, and that time to reflect, draw inferences, and plan further inquiry is also essential.

I believe the notion that teaching is interactive and not uni-directional has been with us long enough for us to realise that what the teacher does not achieve in the classroom cannot be achieved by anybody else – by a department head, a principal, the writers of statutory guidelines, or anybody else. It was for this reason that, in opening the International Conference in Sydney on 'English in the Eighties' [see 5.3 below], I was rash enough to suggest that in moving into the eighties we were initiating 'the decade of the classroom teacher' (Britton, 1982a).

'Teachers as researchers': yet if this enterprise is not to miscarry, we must be clear what we mean by research. Nancy Jones develops her perspective by saying:

> It becomes easy to forget what a very basic – even mundane – thing research is, at first and at last. To some extent we engage in it every day, and we certainly do whenever we investigate, inquire, or look at something again with the aim of obtaining more information and knowledge, or discovering something about it. Research is not, by and large, an esoteric experience, and empirical research . . . certainly is not. . . . It is not in touch with super-human spheres but is the product of human thought and activity, therefore subject to misdirection and error.
>
> (Jones, 1982, p. 9)

I think it is useful to demystify research in this way – to see what is common to deliberate research projects and our day-to-day judgments, but I think we then need to establish the level of applicability of what we discover, or, in George Kelly's terms, 'the range of convenience' of the constructs we discern.

Kelly (1963) would certainly support us in the demystification, for he conceives of all of us as essentially scientists in our ordinary mode of operating. Every significant piece of behaviour is, for him, an experiment. As human beings, we meet every new situation armed with expectations derived from past experience or, more accurately, derived from our interpretations of past experience. We face the new, therefore, not only with knowledge drawn from the past but also with developed tendencies to interpret in certain ways. It is in submitting these to the test of fresh experience – that is, in having our expectations and modes of interpreting either confirmed or modified – that the learning, the discovery, takes place. It is always open to us, of course, to ignore differences between what we expect and what takes place – and we may have powerful reasons for doing so – and then the learning does not take place. We act and decide on what we believe to be the case, even when those beliefs fly in the face of evidence. And we remain personally responsible for what we know and believe, whether it be a presentiment that something is about to fall on our head or a conviction that a cooperative classroom is more effective than a competitive one.

As researchers, then, and as teachers and as human beings, we are in the business of learning by experiment. Let me pursue the question of establishing the level of applicability of our findings. In a remarkable collection of classroom investigations carried out by teachers in one inner-London comprehensive school, John Richmond analysed the speech and writing of a number of Jamaican teenagers. Here are two findings from his analysis.

> Pat is obviously in considerable confusion about the use of speech marks. They appear where they're not wanted, they don't appear where they are wanted. . . . The English speech mark system is tedious and pedantic, of course. . . . However, stuck with our system as we are, the setting-out and marking of speech was the second major area which Pat and I might fruitfully work on in her fourth year [Year 10].
>
> I believe the following things to be true: (a) The nature of speech has a major effect on the nature of writing. (b) A great deal of writing is done in school, maybe too much. (c) If children sense confusion and contradiction around their language, they are likely to use it less well than if they sense approval and security around it. (d) On the other hand, crisis sometimes spawns beauty. (e) It is not a coincidence that poverty, nonstandard dialects and alienation from school are often to be found in the same area.
>
> (Eyers and Richmond [eds], 1982, pp. 147–148, 117)

The detailed recording and analysis of data in this account lend support to both sets of conclusions, yet clearly the use to be made of what is discovered differs widely from the first example to the second. The finding in the first instance is one I can make no direct use of because I am not Pat's teacher.

I think educational inquiry can take three forms in relation to the uses to which the findings may be put. The first is an integral part of *teaching* itself, and provided we recognise the heuristic nature of teaching, its essential grounding in inquiry, we need give it no other name. For the second, I would revive a word that has perhaps fallen into disuse – the word *development* in the special sense it has when partnered with the word *research*. Linked in this way, *research* has been used to describe the discovery of something that might, directly or indirectly, be applied to assist the practitioner, and *development* to describe the process of helping practitioners to discover the research and apply it to their own situations and practice. Whenever researchers in education are tempted to embody their discoveries in *teacher-proof kits* (and some funding agencies seem to see this as cost-effective), a stress on the necessity of the development phase becomes paramount.

The third variety, what I have called *research*, might be distinguished by calling it *basic research*. What is important to point out is that all three varieties may be pursued in schools. If my judgment of the evidence offered by John Richmond for his broad conclusions in the second example above is a just one, all three may be carried out by the teachers in the schools.

Teaching is something we *do*; research findings are something we come to *know*; development is the process by which we bring this kind of knowing into relation with this kind of doing. Development uses a research finding as its starting point and proceeds to the formulation of fresh hypotheses, asking new questions and arriving at new ends. The value of a piece of research from a practical point of view lies in supplying starting points for a range and variety of such enterprises, and I have no doubt the most effective way of carrying out such research is by means of a team project involving researchers *and* teachers at all stages from the earliest planning to the interpretation of findings.

But as teachers we have to draw also on research that is not all educational. The legitimate ends of researchers in the social sciences may have nothing to do with schools or education and yet may provide understandings from which we build our rationale for teaching. As Michael Halliday has pointed out:

> A child doesn't need to know any linguistics in order to use language to learn; but a teacher needs to know some linguistics if he wants to understand how the process takes place – or what is going wrong when it doesn't.
> (Halliday, 1981, p. 11)

He goes on to show how closely linguistic research and *development* may be interlinked:

> Applied linguistics is not a separate domain; it is the principles and practice that come from an understanding of language. Adopting these principles and practices provides, in turn, a way in to understanding language. In this perspective you look for models of language that neutralize the difference between theory and application; in the light of which, research and development in language education become one process rather than two.
> (Halliday, 1981, p. 11)

'The ordinary business of our lives as teachers' may indeed, as Cindy Ray surmised, 'be taken seriously.'

I have looked at teaching, development, and research as interrelated modes of inquiry, sources of knowledge on a widening range of applicability. But the implications of my title cover a wider span yet, seeing knowledge itself as a form of inquiry. Here is the title in its setting, a paragraph from Michael Polanyi's *Knowing and being*:

> Knowledge is an activity which would be better described as a process of knowing. Indeed, as the scientist goes on enquiring into yet uncomprehended experiences, so do those who accept his discoveries as established knowledge keep applying this to ever-changing situations, developing it each time a step further. Research is an intensely dynamic enquiring, while knowledge is a more quiet research. Both are ever on the move, according to similar principles, towards a deeper understanding of what is already known.
>
> (Polanyi, 1969, p. 132)

Knowing, then, is to be seen as a form of doing. There is no simple sense in which we *apply* our knowledge in the way we apply a poultice to a swelling. In any confrontation, what we know must be reformulated in the light of what we perceive and our knowledge is thus for ever on the move.

The point of maximum effect of the educational system on the child is in the classroom. The nature of the school as a community within a community can enormously help or hinder what goes on in the classroom and have its own effect in other less dominant ways. If the eighties are to be the decade of the classroom teacher and realise the full potential of interactive teaching and learning, teachers will need all the help we can give them, whoever we are – researchers, administrators, trustees, parents – or, of course, schoolchildren.

4.3 The community of the classroom

'Vygotsky's contribution to pedagogical theory'[3]

The third text in this section reflects both Britton's continuing exploration of ideas and the importance he attached to work with teachers. The article appeared in the research journal of the National Association for the Teaching of English, *English in Education*. In it, Britton offers both an introduction to Vygotsky's work and an extension of his own earlier reading of Vygotsky's research in the latter's *Thought and language* (1962) in the light of new Vygotsky texts made available through the publication of *Mind in society* (Vygotsky, 1978).

Britton neatly summarises Vygotsky's re-working of Piaget's account of egocentric speech and the investigation of the planes of speaking and thinking in the final chapter of *Thought and language*. He then revisits these key findings in the light of his revised awareness of Vygotsky's central contention: 'the claim that human consciousness is achieved by the internalisation of shared social behaviour'.

Subsequent work on Vygotsky's writings, especially by one of the present editors (Barrs, 2022), has shown that the 1962 translation of *Thought and language* was not, as Britton writes, 'of the whole work' – far from it; and Barrs and others have detailed important criticisms of the editing and preparation of the texts made available in *Mind in society*. But the 1962 book was still a revelation to English readers, and the first indications of the scale of Vygotsky's wider work, including his concentration on the social origins of consciousness, were made available through *Mind in society*; Britton's article reflects this new awareness and his response.

The article provides a powerful and moving introduction to a thinker central to Britton's own development, shuttling between a beautiful exposition of ideas and a review of implications for the classroom, in a manner so characteristic of Britton's writing. It is also a reminder of Britton's commitment to reading and re-rereading, demonstrating the continued refining of his perspectives in his on-going consideration of young people's thinking and of the part that language plays in it.

The story of Vygotsky's influence on educational thinking in the West is a fantastic one – it reads, as they say, like a fairy story. A young Russian intellectual – in the first instance a student of literature – at the age of 38 writes a book on the relation of language to thought. Having previously worked on the ideas with colleagues for some ten years, he finishes the manuscript off in haste, a race against tuberculosis, and dies before it is published. Two years after its publication the book, *Thought and language*, is suppressed by the Soviet authorities and remains so for 20 years – though not before the substance of a magnificent last chapter, presented as a paper at an American conference, finds its way – in English – onto the pages of a psychological journal. A long silence is finally broken when, in 1962, 28 years after its original appearance, scholars in Cambridge, Massachusetts produce an English translation of the whole work and Bruner is on hand to write the introduction.

But that is hardly more than the beginning of the story. Perhaps as an effect of the 'Cold War', recognition of the significance of Vygotsky's work is slow to develop: seminal works in language acquisition and development continue to be published with slight reference, or none, to his ideas – and surprisingly enough, particularly so in America. Cambridge (Mass.), however, continued to take the lead: in 1971 MIT Press brought out an English translation of a collection of Vygotsky's early writings on literary texts under the title *The psychology of art*. And in 1978 four American editors, working with A.R. Luria, Vygotsky's close colleague, disciple and friend (and in turn his successor in Moscow), produced an edited translation of seminal work by Vygotsky and gave it the title *Mind in society*. Finally, there has this year appeared a revised and re-edited translation of *Thought and language* from MIT Press.

In his introduction to the original Russian edition of *Thought and language*, Vygotsky had written, 'we fully realize the inevitable imperfections of this study, which is no more than a first step in a new direction'. In which direction? Vygotsky has this answer: 'Our findings point the way to a new theory of consciousness' – and he goes on to indicate four aspects of the work that are *novel*, and – consequently – 'in need of further careful checking'. I have the sense here of someone embarking on an idea he knows he cannot himself carry through to a conclusion.

His four discoveries, to state them as briefly as I can, are these:

1. Word meanings evolve during childhood: it cannot be assumed that when a child uses a word he means by it what we as adult speakers would mean.
2. While accepting Piaget's theory of the growth of *spontaneous concepts* – ideas arrived at by inference from (or evidenced by) our own experiences, Vygotsky adds the notion of *non-spontaneous concepts* – ideas taken over from other people (notably teachers) – taken over as problems needing solution, or as 'empty categories', so to speak, which need time to find embodiment in our own experience and ground themselves in our own knowledge base. Vygotsky sees this as a two-way movement, 'upward' of spontaneous concepts, 'downward' of non-spontaneous concepts, each mode facilitating the other – and the joint operation being characteristic of human learning.
3. Vygotsky believed that mastery of the written language – learning to read-and-write – had a profound effect upon the achievement of abstract thinking. The *constancy* of the written language, grafted, so to speak, upon the *immediacy* of the spoken language, enables a speaker to *reflect* upon meanings and by doing so acquire a new level of control, a critical awareness of his/her own thought processes.
4. Speech in infancy, Vygotsky claimed, is the direct antecedent of thinking at a later stage. When children discover that it is helpful to speak aloud about what they are doing, they begin to employ what Vygotsky termed 'speech for oneself'; and thereafter speech takes on a dual function and, in due course, develops differentially; conversation becomes more effective as *communication*, while monologue or 'running commentary' (speech for oneself) changes in what is virtually the opposite direction. That is to say, in conversation children extend their control of the grammatical structures of the spoken language and increase their resources of conventional word meanings. In their monologues, on the contrary, they exploit the fact that they are talking to themselves by using as it were 'note form' – skeletal or abbreviated structures that would mean little to one who did not already share the speaker's thoughts – and *personal, idiosyncratic* word meanings: pet words, inventions, portmanteau terms, rich in meaning for the originator but minimally endorsed by convention.

Vygotsky observed these changes in the speech of children from about three years old to about seven – changes that set up a marked difference between their conversational mode and their use of 'speech for oneself'. On the strength of these observations he speculated that, rather than 'withering away' as Piaget had suggested, speech for oneself became internalised and continued to operate as the genesis of thought, perhaps moving through the stages of *inner speech* to *verbal thinking* and thence to the most elusive stage of all – thought itself.

By this account, then, we *think* by handling 'post-language symbols' – forms that began as speech but which have been successively freed from the constraints of the grammar of the spoken language and from the constraints of conventional, public word meanings. It is this freedom that characterises the fluidity of thought – and accounts for the necessity of *imposing organisation* upon our thoughts when we want to communicate them.

It was a brilliant insight on Vygotsky's part to realise that when speech for oneself becomes internalised it is in large part because the child, in handling the freer forms of speech that constitute that mode, begins to be capable of carrying out mental operations more subtle than anything he or she can put into words. I think we can become aware of the reciprocal process when as we listen to discussion we engender some response – a question to be asked or a comment we want to make – and have a clear sense that the process of moving from the fluid operation of thought units to the utterance of rule-governed 'public' speech using conventional word meanings is one that may demand strenuous mental effort on our part.

When *Mind in society* appeared in 1978, a review by Stephen Toulmin (1978) in the *New York Review of Books* underlined Vygotsky's concern with consciousness. He saw Vygotsky as denying on the one hand that human consciousness can be regarded as simply an effect of the genes, of *nature*, or on the other hand as an effect of environment – of *nurture*, claiming that both influences must interact in the creation of mind in the individual. He gave his review the title 'The Mozart of psychology' (nominating Luria in consequence as 'The Beethoven') and suggested that Western psychology urgently needed to take on the broader perspective that Vygotsky had initiated.

It is in this work that Vygotsky's central contention becomes clear – the claim that *human consciousness is achieved by the internalisation of shared social behaviour.* A series of 'temporary connections' is made by the individual within the individual life-span; each link makes possible further links, each operation begins with external *observable social behaviour* – an exposed segment, as it were, of what is to become inner behaviour. Thus is indicated, surely, a new emphasis upon the observation and study of childhood activities for the light they throw upon later behaviours not open to observation.

But social behaviour implies interaction within a group whose activities have been shaped to cultural patterns. The relationship between individual development and the evolution of society is a complex one, not a matter of mere recapitulation or parallelism. The familiar story[4] of the psychologist Kellogg (Kellogg and Kellogg, 1933) and his chimpanzee comes to mind: the chimpanzee had acted as companion to Kellogg's infant son and for a period of years both creatures developed, so to speak, in tandem – able to share each other's activities – but only up to the point where the boy learned to speak: the young Kellogg is today, I believe, himself a scientist; the chimpanzee remains – a chimpanzee! In the historical development from animal to man, the acquisition of language is a watershed: in the development of the individual child from birth to three or four years, the acquisition of language is a watershed.

Speech, that begins as a shared social activity on the part of the child and becomes a principal means of the mental regulation and refinement of his individual behaviour – this is the prime example of Vygotsky's theory of internalisation to achieve consciousness. He gives us a further striking example when he claims that make-believe play in early childhood constitutes the earliest, and at that time only available, form of *imagination*. It is nearer the truth, he says, to claim that imagination in adolescence and later is 'make-believe play without action' than it is to claim that make-believe play in young children is 'imagination in action'.

The implications of these ideas for pedagogy are, of course, enormous. If speech in childhood lays the foundations for a lifetime of thinking, how can we continue to prize a silent classroom? And if shared social behaviour (of many kinds, verbal and non-verbal) is seen as the source of learning, we must revise the traditional view of the teacher's role. The teacher can no longer act as the 'middle-man' in all learning – as it becomes clear that education is *an effect of community*. Bruner, in a recent book, devoted a chapter to Vygotsky's ideas, and in a later chapter makes this comment:

> Some years ago I wrote some very insistent articles about the importance of discovery learning. . . . What I am proposing here is an extension of that idea, or better, a completion. My model of the child in those days was very much in the tradition of the solo child mastering the world by representing it to himself in his own terms. In the intervening years I have come increasingly to recognize that most learning in most settings is a communal activity, a sharing of the culture. It is not just that the child must make his knowledge his own, but that he must make it his own in a community of those who share his sense of belonging to a culture. It is this that leads me to emphasize not only discovery and invention but the importance of negotiating and sharing – in a word, of joint culture-creating as an object

of schooling and as an appropriate step *en route* to becoming a member of the adult society in which one lives out one's life.

(Bruner, 1986, p. 127)

The notion that shared social behaviour is the beginning stage of learning throws responsibility upon those who interact socially with the growing child. By interacting in such a way that their awareness of approaches to skilled behaviour, their awareness of snags and obstacles to such behaviour, are made available to learners, they are in fact (in Vygotsky's terms) *lending consciousness* to those learners and enabling them to perform in this relationship tasks they could not achieve if left to themselves. Again in Vygotsky's terms, this is to open up for the learner 'the zone of proximal development' – an area of ability for which one's previous achievements have prepared one, but which awaits assisted performance for its realisation. That assistance may take the form of teacher-student interaction, or peer tutoring, or group activity – as well, of course, as in the give and take of social cooperation in and out of school.

Viewed thus broadly, we might add that a learner by taking part in rule-governed social behaviour may pick up the rules by means hardly distinguishable from the processes by which they were first socially derived – and by which they continue to be amended. On the other hand, along may come the traditional teacher and – with the best intentions, trying to be helpful – set out to observe the behaviour, analyse to codify the rules and teach the outcome as a recipe. Yes, this may sometimes be helpful, but as consistent pedagogy it is manifestly counter-productive.

Taking 'community' in a micro sense, it is likely that we all live in a number of communities. As teachers we are responsible for one of those – the classroom. It is clear we have a choice: we can operate so as to make that as rich an interactive learning community as we can, or we may continue to treat it as a captive audience for whatever instruction we choose to offer.

Wherever Vygotsky's voice can be heard, perhaps that choice constitutes a zone of proximal development for many of us.

Notes

1. The source of this text is an unpublished paper written in 1969, reprinted as Britton (1982b), pp. 149–152.
2. The source of this text is Britton (1983), pp. 89–92.
3. The source of this text is Britton (1987), pp. 22–26.
4. In fact, husband and wife Winthrop and Luella Kellogg both participated in the psychological experiment, bringing a female chimpanzee up alongside their infant son, as the dual authorship of their book suggests. Britton was wrong to write in 1987 that their son Donald was then a scientist. He died by suicide in 1973, a few months after the death of both his parents.

References

Barrs, M. (2022). *Vygotsky the teacher*. Abingdon, Oxon and New York, NY: Routledge.
Britton, J. (1952). 'An enquiry into changes of opinion, on the part of adult readers, with regard to certain poems, and the reasons underlying these changes.' MA in Education, University of London.
Britton. J. (1982a). 'English teaching: Prospect and retrospect' [1980], in Pradl, G. (ed.), *Prospect and retrospect: Selected essays of James Britton*. London and Monclair, NJ: Heinemann Educational and Boynton/Cook, pp. 201–215.
Britton. J. (1982b). 'A note on teaching, research and "development"' [1969], in Pradl, G. (ed.), *Prospect and retrospect: Selected essays of James Britton*. London and Monclair, NJ: Heinemann Educational and Boynton/Cook, pp. 149–152.
Britton, J. (1983). 'A quiet form of research'. *The English Journal*, 72(4), April 1983, pp. 89–92.
Britton, J. (1987). 'Vygotsky's contribution to pedagogical theory'. *English in Education*, 21(3), pp. 22–26.
Bruner, J. (1986). *Actual minds, possible worlds*. Cambridge, MA: Harvard University Press.
Eyers, S. and Richmond, J. (eds) (1982). *Becoming our own experts*. London: The Talk Workshop Group. Available online at www.becomingourownexperts.org.
Halliday, M. (1981). Interview in *The English Magazine*, Summer 1981.
Jones, N. (1982). 'Design, discovery and development in a freshman writing course'. Dissertation, University of Iowa.
Kellogg, W. and Kellogg, L. (1933). *The ape and the child*. New York: McGraw Hill.
Kelly, G. (1963). *A theory of personality: The psychology of personal constructs*. New York: Norton.
Kuhn, T. (1962). *The structure of scientific revolutions*. Chicago, IL: University of Chicago Press.
Polanyi, M. (1969). *Knowing and being*. London: Routledge and Kegan Paul.
Popper, K. (1976). *Unended quest*. London: Fontana.

Richards, I. (1929). *Practical criticism: A study of literary judgment*. London: Kegan Paul.

Toulmin, S. (1978). 'The Mozart of psychology'. *New York Review of Books*, 28 September, pp. 51–57.

Vygotsky, L. (1962). *Thought and language* [1934]. Trans. E. Haufmann and G. Vakar. Cambridge, MA: MIT Press.

Vygotsky, L. (1971). *The psychology of art* [1925]. Cambridge, MA: MIT Press.

Vygotsky, L. (1978). *Mind in society*. Cole, M., John-Steiner, V., Scribner, S. and Souberman, E. (eds). Cambridge, MA: Harvard University Press.

SECTION 5
A certain idea of English

This section brings together a number of Britton's arguments about the teaching of English. They stretch in time and range from his early intervention in what is usually known as the Dartmouth Seminar (1966), through reflections on literature written late in life in *Literature in its place* (1993), to a moving address made to an international conference on the teaching of English in 1980, where Britton offers his retrospect across the decades, and shares his prospect for times ahead. We finish the section with a group of present-day student teachers discussing Britton's work.

Britton's talk at Dartmouth, the earliest of these pieces, makes an argument against defining English in terms of different kinds of knowledge. The piece has a continuing relevance for its demolition of the strategy of looking to a specific content as a means of formulating English work in school, and for the directness with which Britton's own alternative position is stated. He makes his case through an insistence on an operational approach to language as providing the rationale for English teachers' responsibilities; and goes on to suggest 'that the area in which English operates is that of personal experience'. His summary, added at the closing of his talk, offers one of the sharpest and most forthright statements of the position he had reached at this point in his work.

> One, we learn language by using it. By that I mean operations and not dummy runs. Two, we learn to live by using language. . . . Thirdly, in English lessons the area of operations is that of personal experience; and that is the nearest I can go to finding a substance which I would call, 'This is English.' . . . Fourthly, insofar as study of language aids the practice anywhere in the curriculum, not simply in the area of English concerns, that also is the responsibility of the English teacher.

It is interesting to set this powerful argument offered at a key point in the development of post-war English teaching beside the meditative reflection on the place of literature in human development in the second piece in this section. This is the final chapter of *Literature in its place*, published in 1993. Both pieces are informed by insights from the philosophical base of Britton's thinking, with its perception of the role of language in experience. His final reckoning with the place of literature returns to his reading of Vygotskyan thought. He draws on the exploration of feeling and cognition in Vygotsky's *Thought and language* (1962), especially in the final chapter of that work.

Britton's interest in literature had from the first explored alternatives to the critical analysis that was becoming increasingly influential in his initial years of teaching. What he took from I.A. Richards was not the Leavisite emphasis on literary judgement, but the stress on the interdependence of intellect and feeling in works of literature. As Britton's work developed, he focused on the seeds of imagination in the language and thinking of young children. In this chapter, granddaughters replace the daughters in his earlier discussions of *Thought and language*. Following their lead, he dwells, together with Vygotsky's striking argument, on the internalisation of play as sourcing the powers of imagination in adult thought.

Britton emphasised the everyday ordinariness of process in his thinking about literature – the combination of imagination and intellect and feeling in gossip and in story as well as their deployment in more sophisticated work. He concludes his chapter by referring to his concept of spectator-role activities and sets this understanding of the place of literature alongside the university-promoted enterprise of determining a literary canon. He argues that we do not need to limit or exclude. 'We like what we like,' he comments, 'and that may at one and the same time include a Shakespeare sonnet, a limerick, a current magazine story, a best-selling novel – meeting different aspects of our immediate concerns without setting up in competition.' It is a perception that draws on the place that literature has had for him, in his own rich engagement across a lifetime.

One outcome from the seminar at Dartmouth was the formation of IFTE, the International Federation for the Teaching of English, which in due course added the participation of Canada and Australia to the link established between the UK and the US. Britton played a prominent role in these developments and led the organisation of the second international conference in 1971. He was lead speaker at the third international conference held in Sydney, Australia in 1980, and a part of his opening address forms the third piece here. His speech at this conference is a celebration of what had been achieved in English teaching from those first early days, looking back before the war. It is also in part a personal farewell. The piece is included here as an indication of Britton's continued interest in English teaching and of the regard in which his work was widely held.

We have given this section the title 'A certain view of English'. This is in part to indicate our sense that the arguments that Britton brought to English teaching are drawn from and provide a view: a view of possibility. The section offers glimpses: the potential of an operational approach to language; a focus on what young people are making of their reality as the central area of concern for English teaching; a stress on the activities of the spectator role; a rationale based in recognition of the resources of young people; the irreplaceable awareness and support of teachers.

Re-reading Britton's work today offers a new urgency to hopes for collaboration between politicians, stakeholders, administrators and teachers in taking public education forward. For reasons that will be obvious, we conclude the section and this reader with an account of today's student teachers engaging with the work of Britton: an ending, and a beginning.

5.1 The scope of English

'What is English?'[1]

The first text in this section, 'What is English?' (Britton, 1966), was given in that year as a presentation to an Anglo-American audience at the conference usually known as the Dartmouth Seminar. The piece provides an overview of Britton's thinking at that point about English teaching, drawing on his own theoretical synthesis and setting a tone for conference discussions that was widely taken up.

By way of background, the Dartmouth Seminar, officially the Anglo-American Conference on the Teaching and Learning of English, was a joint initiative of the American National Council of Teachers of English (NCTE) and the newly formed British National Association for the Teaching of English (NATE). Representatives of both associations met for a month at Dartmouth College, New Hampshire, to discuss the principles of English teaching and consider new initiatives. As well as Britton, British delegates included Frank Whitehead, Douglas Barnes, Geoffrey Summerfield, John Dixon, Harold Rosen and David Holbrook. Different views and lines of thought existed, of course, within both sets of representatives. But it is generally held that the two sides drew on different backgrounds and came with somewhat different aims and expectations: the Americans with concerns for defining English as a discipline, an organised body of knowledge with its own integrity, the British more concerned with the classroom teaching of English and with principles of practice. The opening paper by Professor Kitzhaber and Britton's paper in response represent, to some extent, two moves initiating the dialogue that followed.

Kitzhaber had offered a tripartite framework – English as a discipline based in knowledge about language, literary knowledge, and the skills of communication. This way of representing English and its 'knowledge base' is familiar to English teachers across the world: with variations, it continues to be how English has been parcelled up, and how its different areas of interest have been conceptualised.

Britton asks interesting questions about each of these three elements, but he goes on to develop a more general reservation. He takes issue with the 'out there' question, the starting point that English is a 'something' we could come to know, together with 'the very large assumption that if we find out what it is, it follows that this is what the English teacher should be teaching'. Rather than asking, 'What is English?', he proposes, we should instead be asking, 'What ought English teachers to be doing?'.

From informal accounts by members, the move was transformative in enabling and directing discussions at Dartmouth. It is a move that continues to offer a challenge to the more recent promotion of 'knowledge-rich' curricula.

The major part of Britton's paper is premised on the priority of his preferred question. Having criticised reference to 'communication skills' as 'altogether to underestimate the importance of language', he continues with an account of his own view of language and its use in representing the world, adding his distinction between participant and spectator roles. Such ideas would not have been well known at the time, especially to his American audience. A particular interest of this piece is the manner in which Britton shapes the presentation of his position to meet this context, with some anticipation of possible criticisms from academic colleagues.

There is an illuminating comment on the notions of 'structure' and the 'structuring of experience', clarifying the interplay between experience already structured though language and the structuring undertaken by the language user through the activity of thinking and learning. As Britton remarks, 'We learn from experience, but not the meaningless flux of sense impressions. We learn from experience as it is structured – as it is shaped. And the primary means of shaping experience is language – our own language and other people's language.'

It follows from this picture of language and experience that what English teachers should be doing is actively encouraging the use of language with the resources presently at their disposal. Britton acknowledges teachers' responsibility for enabling young people to develop their capacity to use language effectively, but the development of language is not an end in itself. As he puts it, 'By that I don't mean that we resign responsibility to improving efficiency, but the substantive thing is the use of the language to learn.' The notion of 'practice', still an important word in educational discussion, is ambiguous, especially in relation to using language. By 'practice', he insists, in a telling contrast, 'I want to mean operations not dummy runs.'

'How to improve language proficiency?' and 'How, on what, and where should language operate?' – Britton finishes with these two questions. Both could seem quite close to Kitzhaber's 'skills of communication', but they have behind them an altogether different understanding of the part that language plays in young people's lives, of the ambition and potential of this role, and of the means through which resources in the use of language are acquired.

Britton is bringing to the question 'What is English?' the fruits of his reading and research. Behind his account of language lie his explorations of Sapir, Cassirer, Langer and Vygotsky, and his personal synthesis constructed from many sources. In his paper, he is drawing on this synthesis and negotiating with the different but familiar response to describing the territory of English teaching offered by Professor Kitzhaber. His paper presents his own line of thinking, geared to the occasion, and shaped by his awareness of different responses likely to be present in his audience. In insisting that English as a school subject involves a continuing engagement with and reshaping of experience, Britton offers a challenge to the many more recent attempts to define a more narrowly circumscribed knowledge base.

Although I am not one for formalities, I feel there is a courtesy involved in thanking Professor Kitzhaber for his paper, for the very determined way in which he has struggled to open the question, or, perhaps, struggled to keep the question open. It has been part of what I have done in reading his paper to pursue the lengthening shadow of his own special interest – such as he has quoted somebody as putting it – to find what his stand itself would be upon the topic that he is laying before us. And, I have no apology for the fact that what will come out in the end from what I want to say will be the lengthening shadow of somebody else's special interest.

The problem is no less than an attempt to identify, as stated by Professor Kitzhaber in his paper, essential organising principles for English. His method has been to examine the subject English itself within the terms of his experience of it – English as it goes on in his experience. I want to make my first comment very clearly that it seems to me that English is itself an element in a larger structure – a larger structure of education. I can see no possibility of defining English, or, if that is putting it too strongly, I can see no useful way of defining it without considering its place in the total structure. English as a subject in the university is paralleled by psycholinguistics, by anthropology, by biochemistry, by many other subjects which have their respectable place in the university curricula. But until somebody comes to look at their possible contribution into a larger structure, their possible place in the larger structure, one can say nothing useful about them as teaching subjects.

Professor Kitzhaber recognises this fact on his first page. But, I think, he sidesteps it by putting the blame on public opinion. In other words, the educator may have views about it, but public opinion allows those views to come into practice. Now, it seems to me that public opinion can allow a course of action to take place or disallow it. It can't justify or refute its value as education. For this reason, I think the question may need dividing. I don't want to come down sharp on this, but I want to suggest that possibly this question we are facing may have to be divided in the end. We may have to ask, 'What is English in the university?', 'What is English in the schools?' I'll leave it at that at the moment, although obviously you could subdivide there if you wanted to. Or possibly even subdivide in some other way: 'What is English for the college-bound student?', 'What is English for the terminal student?' I think anyone searching for a unifying organising principle would be very loath to accept this division and would try to find some formulations which subsumed the various kinds corresponding to those divisions, but they might have to give up in the end. I should be very loath to accept the second of those divisions and I think if we found ourselves at a later stage in our discussions as a group proposing that, I should want to bring strong arguments in favour of the first division, of university/school, rather than the division between the total career of those going to the university and the career of those who are not.

I hope I am not misreading between the lines, but in trying to pursue this lengthening shadow, it seems to me the underlying assumptions of Professor Kitzhaber's paper suggest that English is:

1. a body of knowledge called grammar
2. a body of knowledge called literature
3. the skills of communication.

This may be unfair to the paper. I may have put it much more sharply than he would want to do, but . . . certainly Professor Kitzhaber himself, in his final section, refers to the skills of communication as a possible unifying idea. I think I would suppose also that of these three, the skills of communication perhaps are less important in Professor Kitzhaber's view.

Now, there certainly exists a body of knowledge about English language – both a grammatical body of knowledge and other kinds of linguistic bodies of knowledge. There also exists a body of knowledge psychologically speaking, sociologically speaking, and anthropologically speaking. If we need to consider these, we must look at their educational claims per se, their claims in their own rights to be a part of a child's schooling. Is there a body of knowledge called literature? And, here I think, is a major question. Certainly, there is a body of knowledge *about* literature – there is an historical body of knowledge, there is a critical body of knowledge. I would gather from the papers, if not only from my colleagues from the United Kingdom, that there would be a strong view to resist the idea that literature itself can be regarded as a body of knowledge. Those of us who have taught in schools, in England anyway, have only to think of the difference between knowing *Julius Caesar* for an examination and whatever we may feel *Julius Caesar* is meant for. They seem to be two quite different things.

Third are the skills of communication. Now, I feel to formulate this as 'the skills of communication' is altogether to underestimate the importance of language. In other words, there are respectable bodies of facts and theories from sociologists and psychologists which establish the function of language as something much more than is suggested by 'the skills of communication'. In bringing this element into the English syllabus, we have to take account of those more general facts about language. This is fully set out in James Moffett's [1966] paper. The Newsom Report (Central Committee on Education, 1963), which we brought copies of, has made a strong impression on teachers in England in recent years and one of its major points is that it is indeed very difficult to separate the educational from the social objectives.

In the latter part of the paper, Professor Kitzhaber goes on to ask whether any part could be the unifying principle – the organising central principle. I must say I thought his comments on the shortcomings and pitfalls in common practice in attempting to put these into practice are extremely helpful. What I think lies behind it in the end is what I might call the Oregon Trident. We have in fact an idea of literature as cultural heritage, knowledge about language on humane grounds, and thirdly skills and knowledge of rhetoric. So that we have two 'out there' components and a third component which is partly a process, an activity, a skill and partly 'out there'. By 'out there,' I mean that the question itself, 'What is English?' is an 'out there' question. It assumes that English is something and it makes the very large assumption that if we find out what it is, it follows that this is what the English teacher should be teaching. Now, this seems to me to be a very big assumption for the setting of this paper and for the paper itself to make. The answer is in consistent terms – in terms of 'out there' commodities. I strongly suggest that in order to avoid reification we need to rephrase the question and not say, 'What is English?', but ask more simply, 'What ought English teachers to be doing?' 'What ought teachers of English in the university, the school, etc., to be doing?'

On that basis, I want to lengthen my own shadow, or rather the shadow of my own special interest. I think we need first to ask, 'What is the function of language – the function of the mother tongue in education?' – and putting it into its larger structure – its larger context, 'What is the function of the mother tongue in learning?'... What we want, it seems to me, is an operational view of language – an operational view of the teaching of the mother tongue. Then, of course, it is open to you if you want to say 'What is English?', 'Well, at least it is not an operational view in the teaching of the mother tongue.' Edward Sapir discovered, or rather formulated, this for us a long while ago: 'It is best to admit that language is primarily a vocal actualization of the tendency to see realities symbolically' (Mandelbaum [ed.], 1949, p. 15). And he explains this: '... actualization in terms of vocal expression of the tendency to master reality not by direct and *ad hoc* handling of that element, but by the reduction of experience to a familiar form' (p. 14). Now, this is of the same stable ... as Cassirer's (1944) statement comparing man to the animals on the basis of the fact that man has a third system shunted across his two systems. The animals have the effector and receptor systems; man has a third system, the symbolic system, shunted across the two. Crudely and oversimplified, it all adds up to this: we use language to represent the world (and ourselves in the world) to ourselves, and from then onwards we act in the real world by the light of, with the aid of, in the terms of, that representation. Well, if we represent the world to ourselves in language and then operate in accordance with that representation there are two kinds of activity open to us. One, we may do just that – we may operate in the real world by means of representation. Secondly, this is a point that I think has been missed, we may also act directly upon the representation itself. We may improvise upon the picture of the world we built up from experience in all kinds of ways and to suit all kinds of purposes – and we habitually do. I should like to establish a distinction between the two situations as far as the use of language is concerned, saying that we can use language to operate in the real world – call that the role of participant – and we can also act directly upon the representation in language – call that the role of spectator. It seems to me that this is a fundamental distinction of use in our discussion. We have seen it confused – the small child who goes to the school's matinee and calls out, 'Look out guvner, he's behind ya,' is not able to save the hero. It is in the nature of the distinction that he is using participant language in a situation which is a spectator situation. By saying spectator, I do not mean uninvolved; the participant is somebody who is participating in the world's affairs and getting things done. So we use language in these two roles and in both of them we are structuring or we are shaping experience. I used the word 'structuring' and David Holbrook didn't like it but I still want to use it. You can call structuring experience 'jargon' if you like – but on the other hand, it is of great value in this sense that if you look up 'structure' in the Oxford dictionary, you will find that it has, as a noun, two senses: one, the shape that we find that is there and that we perceive; and two, the shape that we have given to something. Put both of those into the verb – and I want to suggest that in using language to shape experience we are not only finding shape, but that we are giving shape. And, to distinguish the two is very difficult.

We learn from experience, but not the meaningless flux of sense impressions. We learn from experience as it is structured – as it is shaped. And, the primary means of shaping experience is language – our own language and other people's language. The best example, I think, of this is to think of the young child whose curiosity goes in all directions and whose curiosity in all directions is served by his speech, and who then comes to school. Now, Frank Whitehead suggests that at school we primarily want to improve the efficiency of the child's use of his mother tongue. Yes, I want to go a step further and say 'Yes' emphatically to that. But, more than that, learning lies in the actual operation of language. So we are not simply concerned to improve the efficiency of the process, we are concerned to use the process at whatever stage of efficiency he may be at. By that I don't mean that we resign responsibility to improving efficiency, but the substantive thing is the use of the language to learn, whatever its state of efficiency may be. And, that is what I was meaning by an operational view of language. A simple example: whenever a student writes effectively, he does two things. He copes with experience he has been writing about by shaping it in words, and the writing may be the act of perceiving the shape of experience – not the evidence that it has been perceived, but the act of perceiving it. Whenever a student writes successfully he shapes the experience and he also gets a bit better at doing so next time. Whenever he successfully reads something which has tested his ability, strains his ability, he has coped with experience with the assistance of the author. He has shaped experience – entered into and altered and shaped experience – and has also improved his skill, his ability to read difficult passages. Now, we have consistently given our attention to the second of these and ignored the first of these. That is what I mean by the substantive operational value of language in learning. We confuse it in our word 'practice' which we can use with two meanings. By practice, I want to mean operations and not dummy runs.

So, for us there are two problems, it seems to me. One is how to improve language proficiency and the second is how, on what, and where should language operate. Let me take the more orthodox of these questions first. How to improve the language proficiency of a child? Well, I believe – and it is clear from many of the other papers that we have been reading – that we learn to write by writing, learn to speak by speaking, etc., etc. But, we have to ask after that, 'To what extent does language study aid practice?' This is a major question. I don't think it can be settled by discussion but I think knowledge of any research there may be and also the commissioning of further research is probably essential in order to get an answer to this question. To what extent can the study of language aid in its operation? . . .

Secondly then, the latter, the unorthodox question, 'On what should language operate – in what areas of experience?' Here I am treading on very difficult ground, I know, but let me return to the small child whose curiosity goes in all directions, who goes to school where socially acquired areas of knowledge and concern are carved out of his curiosity and pursued in different parts of the curriculum. In his science lessons, history lessons, geography lessons certain areas of his curiosity continue to be explored with the aid of language. I know that science is more than a body of scientific facts, but let us begin with it as a body of scientific facts, which leads to the systems, which lead to philosophies in the end, etc. What about English lessons then? I think there is a clue to the area of operations in English lessons in what actually goes on in English lessons in England. On both sides of the Atlantic the two major emphases, I would say, have been upon literature, and upon writing – creative writing, personal writing, whatever you like to call it. These are not answers. It seems to me that these are clues to where the answer might lie. I suggest that the area in which language operates in English lessons is that of personal experience, in other words, relations with other people, the identity of the individual – the relation between the ego and the environment, however you like to phrase it. Personal experience is a very difficult term to use, but if you consider that to be a human person, you have a feeling concomitant in your experience, and that the socially derived bodies of fact, etc., are concerned primarily to exclude that – not from their processes, but from their end results – then I think you can see that personal experience has a quality which is not to be found in other areas. This seems to me to be the area of operations for language in English lessons. We could dig out of this area socially derived bodies of public fact – sociologists do so and psychologists do so and anthropologists do so, and so on. For the moment, we don't do very much of this in schools; we operate by another method. We operate by what I call the spectator role, not the participant role. In other words, we use literature. After all, the themes of literature are the human themes; they are the relationships between man and his environment; and not every type of relationship, but only the relationships in which the human quality or the emotional relationship is a part of what is afoot. Just very briefly on that. The importance of this area isn't simply its intrinsic importance, but this is also the area in which, in fact, all knowledge must come together for the individual. It is, in fact, the integrating area for all public knowledge. My mother used to make jam tarts and she used to roll out the pastry and I remember this very well – I can still feel what it is like to do it, although I have never done it since. She used to roll out the pastry and then she took a glass and cut out a jam tart, then cut out another jam tart. Well, we have cut out geography, and we have cut out history, and we have cut out science. What do we cut out for English? I suggest we don't. I suggest that is what is left. That is the rest of it.

Summary

One, we learn language by using it. By that I mean operations and not dummy runs. Two, we learn to live by using language. I would like to defend myself against the progressive labels, or should I say the criticisms Professor Kitzhaber very rightly attaches to some results of progressive education. By learning to live, I don't mean learning to use a telephone; I might mean learning to write a sonata or a novel or govern a country. By using language we learn to live. Thirdly, in English lessons the area of operations is that of personal experience; and that is the nearest I can go to finding a substance which I would call, 'This is English.' In other words, if I look for the substance of the teaching of English, this is where I would find it, in my view. Fourthly, insofar as study of language aids the practice anywhere in the curriculum, not simply in the area of English concerns, that also is the responsibility of the English teacher.

What I have omitted is a part answer to the question that I thought we might have to frame. I have not faced up to the obvious bifurcations of this study which will necessarily take place as it gets more advanced. I mean there is clearly an intrinsic value in the study of language at university level. We must ask whether it has intrinsic value also at an earlier state in education. Again, how far at university level will literature be a specialised historical or critical study and will it in any respects be a continuation of the process I have described in referring to schools – the structuring of personal experience as a means of learning to live?

Finally, on this vexed question of articulation of the subject, experience is cumulative and growth is sequential; we have to face the possibility that we may not be able to go further than that. Perhaps we can only program to provide the circumstances most favourable to the experiences and the growth of individuals and of groups.

In facing such a possibility, we may be helped by a remark made by George Kelly when he lectured in London recently:

Man does not always think logically. Some take this as a serious misfortune. But I doubt that it is. If there is a misfortune, I think it more likely resides in the fact that, so far, the canons of logic have failed to capture all the ingenuities of man, and perhaps also in the fact that so many men have abandoned their ingenuities in order to think 'logically' and irresponsibly. For each of us the exercise of ingenuity leads him directly to a confrontation with his personal responsibility for what happens. But, of course, he can avoid the distressing confrontation if, through conformity to rules, he can make it appear that he has displaced the responsibility to the natural order of the universe.[2]

5.2 'Literature in its place'[3]

Literature in its place (Britton, 1993) comprises a set of meditations written late in life on the place that literature has occupied in Britton's own life as thinker, reader and poet, together with conclusions about its place in human life more generally; and by extension, we may add, its place in English teaching. Some of the most arresting passages are, as here, the insights that he draws from his relations with young people, or from reflections on their work. The chapter that follows (also called 'Literature in its place') takes us from the make-believe of grandchildren, through an account linking an article by Michael Oakeshott with Vygotskyan thought, to a discussion of more recent gender-based understandings of literature, reading and writing. He concludes with hopes for a mode of reading – 'a highroad that stretches the length of a lifetime', as it has done for Britton himself.

[Earlier in this book], I began to speak of the 'anatomy of human experience', and I traced its beginning in the early interaction of a child with an adult, arriving at common understandings before speech could communicate them. And then, in the course of months, the interchange of meanings becomes possible, all in enacted make-believe play.

Michael Oakeshott writes in *The voice of poetry in the conversation of mankind* (1959) that that voice can be recovered by any of us who can recall our first uses of speech in infancy.

> Everybody's young days [he tells us] are a dream, a delightful insanity, a miraculous confusion of poetry and practical activity in which nothing has a fixed shape and nothing has a fixed price. . . . We speak an heroic language

of our own invention, not merely because we are incompetent in our handling of symbols, but because we are moved not by the desire to communicate but by the delight of utterance.

(p. 61)

The delight of utterance certainly brings to mind my younger grandchild as she was a few years ago. You see her here at twenty-two months of age, talking with her mother, Alison, and my wife (whom she knows as Danny):

A: (to Lucy) What's your name?
L: Kathy.
D: Katherine?
A: Is it really Kathy?
L: No.
A: What's your name really?
L: Sheila.
A: It's *not* Sheila! What's your real name?
L: Lucy.
A: Yes!
D: What's mummy's name – do you know that?
L: Yes. Chocolate!
A: Chocolate? I'm not called chocolate. What's my name? What's mummy's name?
L: Alison.

At 22 months, trying out the possibles – alternatives to the actual – must be delightful; but very soon more fully imagined alternatives will constitute the delight of utterance as Oakeshott understood it. Lucy approaches that when, two and a half years later, she begins, very properly, 'Once upon a time there was a little dog called Lucy . . . and . . . he won and they went into a dairy and there they had a nice time . . .' (I suppose the 'word that means me' must acquire a very special significance to a child – the word that the keepers of the child's world may utter in praise or blame, to love or to reject – and that one can hardly expect a sensible child to hear dispassionately.)

Lucy was not a great storyteller; her interests seemed at this stage to be in how things *worked* – what made them tick, what you could *do* with them. It was Laurie, my elder granddaughter, who explored the whole range of what is possible when delight of utterance takes precedence over the informative function. Take, for instance, the language of her make-believe situation at the age of four years one month [see 1.3]. She is playing the role of mother and I am her child: 'Now it's time for the little darlings to go to sleep,' she begins; and after a suitable pause she ends with 'Morning!' A couple of months later, Laurie plays a concert of roles – impersonations of authoritative figures in a succession of scenes, 'I'm the mummy,' 'I'm the school teacher,' 'Now I've got to be your mummy coming home.'

This first enactive, imaginative mode of speech is certainly something we may often observe. I see three- or four-year-olds walking down the street, leaning outwards from their grasp of an adult's hand and doing what I can only call 'holding forth'. That they should be encouraged to do so by the way we listen and respond seems to me crucial, a way of sharing their life space and the role that language plays in their early experience. It's likely that at this early age children find it easier to manipulate verbal responses to experience than they do to adapt their behaviour in relation to the people and objects that feature in their environment.

It seems to me important to realise that the language in which we make these verbal responses establishes the mode in which, throughout our lives, in talk, in reading and writing, we engage with the imagined experiences offered to us in literature.

When Michael Oakeshott wrote of the voice of poetry in the conversation of mankind, he made it clear that that voice must cover imaginative constructions – not only those of poets, but those of writers whose purposes were, broadly speaking, literary, and also works of art produced by painters, potters, sculptors, and other creative makers. That same breadth of purpose marks what Vygotsky wrote of in *The psychology of art* (1971). While his illustrative examples are all taken from the verbal arts, he makes references from time to time to other symbolic modes. He stresses above all the educative purposes of art: 'From the most ancient times art has always been regarded as a means of education, that is, as a long range program for changing our behaviour and our organism' (p. 253). The effects of art take their time; they are no quick fix. Vygotsky calls it a delayed reaction: indeed, 'Art is the organization of our future behaviour. It is a requirement that may never be fulfilled but that forces us to strive beyond our life toward all that lies beyond it' (p. 253). It is, I think, a mistaken pragmatism that underrates the effect of a dream or a vision upon our sense of reality.

The language of literature, Vygotsky suggests, represents the merging of conscious and subconscious processes. 'In our minds there exists a continuous, lively and dynamic connection between the two areas' – and this is recognisable both in the language of literature and in the language of children's make-believe play.

'Literature in its place'

It follows that works of art enable subconscious processes to be given social expression, and by this means contribute to the mores of our society. He suggests that the rhetorical means by which this is achieved is in setting up formal constraints that modify the anticipated effects of the content – the events narrated. 'The form,' he suggests, 'is not a shell which covers the substance. On the contrary, it is an active principle by which the material is processed and, occasionally, overcome in its most involved, but also most elementary properties' (Vygotsky, 1971, pp. 145–146). A plain, unvarnished factual account of events might, for example, be frightening to a listener; on the other hand, the way the story is told might so underplay the fearful aspects – its 'elementary properties' – that the whole situation no longer seems threatening.

The example Vygotsky gives of such a reversal refers to a short story by the Russian writer Bunin; the material consists of the association between a young woman student and a guards officer. It is an account of an infatuation that ends in the girl's suicide. But the form in which the story is told – its round-aboutness, its broken-time sequences, its omissions – 'processes the material', softening, sweetening its effect. It might be helpful to think of the way the musical form of a song will differ from the grammatical structures of the words that are sung. The difference lies in the ends or purposes of the music. Whereas the meaning of the words might be seen as a straight line from unfamiliarity to familiarity, from ignorance to understanding, the form of the song, Vygotsky suggests, 'can be graphically represented as a curve around a straight line' (Vygotsky, 1971, p. 148). The author sets it out in his way, Vygotsky says, in order to 'undo life's turbidity and transform it into a crystal transparency. He did this to make life's events unreal, to transform water into wine, as always happens in any real work of art' (p. 154).

We certainly expect of a work of literature that it will embody an evaluation of experience and will not merely record the circumstances, the events and encounters of life as we live it. The culture of any society consists in the evolving accumulation of such evaluations. In Vygotsky's account, effective form is a constant; the reversal, in a full sense (as he applied it to Bunin's short story), will be occasional and not universal. A work of literature may indeed distil the truth of a general sentiment – something of the 'all in each of everyman', as Coleridge has it. It is by means of the individual responses, whether to the events of our lives or to works of art – and art-like works – that cultural mores are determined. Vygotsky for that reason believes that any explanation of the nature of responses must begin by tackling the problem areas of *emotion* and *imagination*.

He does so himself in his final work, *Thought and language* (1962), published only after his death. The book was suppressed two years later and remained so for

20 years. It is in this book that he states his belief that *intellect* and *emotion* must be seen in close relation to each other. This is a view that we as teachers learned from I.A. Richards in *How to read a page* (1942). Richards suggests that a reader's mind should focus on 'awareness of interdependence . . . to see that our sense of the hanging together allows no severance of head and heart – no neutral intellect fighting against the motives which make up its activity' (p. 240). Similarly, for Vygotsky, intellect and emotion meet at the immediate level of word meaning. Analysis, he believes, 'demonstrates the existence of a dynamic system of meaning in which the affective and the intellectual unite. It shows that every idea contains a transmuted affective attitude towards the bit of reality to which it refers' (Vygotsky, 1962, p. 8). The expression of any idea, that is to say, has in it an element that represents the way we feel about it.

An individual's ability to handle word meanings is thus seen to be an index of personality that throws light upon intellectual, social, and affective characteristics. *Thought and language* examines the ways in which an individual child sets about developing the use of word meanings that reflect the understandings of adult members of the community into which he is born. Vygotsky concludes that thought and language 'reflect reality in a way different from perception' and form the 'key to the nature of human consciousness'. 'Words play a central part not only in the development of thought but in the historical growth of consciousness as a whole. A word is a microcosm of human consciousness' (Vygotsky, 1962, p. 153).

The words we have used in speaking, in writing, in thinking about the world we live in, present an ordered awareness as close to the truth of our existence as we can master. Learning to use word meanings in ways current among adults in a society is a process that takes time – and may in fact never be satisfactorily achieved by many of its members. Progress depends on building stage by stage. A striking early example of this fact relates to the power of *imagination*. At the earliest stage, children must rehearse in active play the scene that strikes their fancy; if they do not enact – rehearse perhaps – a make-believe performance, there is no imagined construction. But at a later stage, make-believe play that is rehearsed in the mind, make-believe without action, becomes possible – and the power of imagination is born (Vygotsky, 1978, p. 93).

In his work on the psychology of art, Vygotsky illustrated broad general concerns, but with a focus upon fable, short story and tragedy. In earlier chapters [of this book], I have referred to narrative – spoken and written – enactment and drama, argument, poetry and novels; and using the term loosely, I have included all of these save argument under the name of *literature*. The term is one we are used to in many contexts – from its early appearance relating to folk tales and fairy tales, through leisure reading at all stages, to examination work in high school, and through to a major role in academia, where it is often given one of a wide range of particular, and sometimes even contradictory, definitions.

The forms of writing, reading, and talking that make up the material of this study have been, somewhat scantily perhaps, defined as utterances in the role of spectator. Their everyday uses take the form of familiar chat – exchanging views and news – about the weather, our states of body and mind, about neighbours, family, friends. But there is always something more than just information in our words uttered as spectators. There is always in some degree an indication of how we feel about someone or something; our words carry . . . the pluses and minuses of our verdicts upon the world. They share characteristics of works of art as Vygotsky defined them: they have aesthetic value – they may be either works of art or, at a less intense or finished level, they might be called art-like. But as we know, it takes a writer and a reader to constitute a work in the verbal arts – and anything we offer in this way has a putative existence.

Focussing on what is offered – and I am thinking at the moment principally of something written by a child – what is offered has what might be seen as an inbuilt *direction*. It is likely to be going somewhere, because the writer's approval of her/his own work goes with it, and we learn from experience that what satisfies him/her today is likely to lead to further demands the next time. This is a movement of change by which a writer builds a highway of past satisfactions. And the message for us as teachers is that we should not discourage early enthusiasms because they are art-like in what may seem to us crude ways. It is up to us to recall that they travel the road we ourselves set out upon.

The treatment of works of literature that originates in the universities, but permeates activities at many levels, is governed by the concept of the literary canon. Every new work submits to the process of seeking a place in that hierarchy; and old works are manoeuvred up or down in the order as opinions change with regard to them. Of course, individual likes and dislikes obtain, but there is also a sense in which a fairly reliable social order also exists. It will fluctuate as works gain or lose esteem and it will show variations from social group to social group, but recognition of the standing of particular works is likely to be some part of the social and academic context in which they are regarded and discussed. My argument here is that no such place-seeking and place-holding procedure need limit the movements of change open to spectator-role artifacts; we like what we like, and that may at one and the same time include a Shakespeare sonnet, a limerick, a current magazine story, a best-selling novel – meeting different aspects of our immediate concerns without setting up in competition.

Such a view finds strong support among critics who fight for adequate recognition of women writers and working-class writers. The authors of *Re-writing English: cultural politics of gender and class* (Batsleer et al., 1985) claim that the literary canon consists not simply of a series of recommendations but of a hierarchy 'whose value derives not from any intrinsic properties but from the fact that they necessitate a continuous process of comparative placing and opposition' (p. 29). The ordering of a 'literary ideology' becomes the basis of grades in school examinations, in degree results, and in the career possibilities open to academics. F.R. Leavis and his fellow writers in *Scrutiny* are seen as prime upholders of the literary checklist and condemned for their elitism and their intolerance of what they judge as 'mass civilization'. On the other hand, the Schools Council, sponsored by the Ministry of Education, appears to the writers of *Re-writing English* as useful in loosening the stranglehold of the university-based schools examinations boards and so creating freedom to experiment in the curricula of some state schools. What is recommended by these critics is then a much broader conception of what is suitable reading matter in high schools and what kinds of writing should be encouraged – and clearly this includes much greater tolerance for expressive and conversational styles.

American concerns in this field focus more directly on awareness of gender, whether in the student, the teacher or the writer. In her essay 'Gender issues and the teaching of writing' (1992a), Nancy McCracken sets up distinctions between what is essentially 'masculine' and what is essentially 'feminine' in conception, while she is careful not to attribute either role to a person. She cites evidence showing how classroom discussion relies mainly on contributions from boys, in part, no doubt, because there are strong cultural pressures against women's voices being heard too frequently. Masculine talk is seen as speaking in order to *be right* – to put someone else in the wrong – 'machine-gun language' (McCracken, 1992a, p. 170) it has been called. A woman's role in life is seen as that of nurturer – and this suggests that women are likely to find greater difficulty in acquiring the 'academic goals of rationality, critical thinking and autonomy' (p. 171). Educators must find ways of helping women to apply their 'central ways of knowing – care, concern, connection' (p. 171).

McCracken quotes sociolinguistic accounts of differences observed between men and women in their modes of conversing: when men talk together they handle mainly safe, public topics and proceed in a kind of one-upmanship rivalry. When women talk, they tend to deal with unresolved, open and often private topics, and they do so by collaborative inquiry (p. 173).

Applying such observations to the teaching of writing, McCracken believes that students would profit by keeping a journal in which they share their concerns with fellow students. She stresses the need to encourage use of a range of models beyond the customary critical or expository essay; women's ways of thinking find expression in a wide variety of forms and represent powerful alternative modes of intellect. She concludes that 'where we listened only for major and minor premises, we must now listen also for truth statements shaped into different patterns, e.g. metaphors and parallel narratives', and she names the 'non-academic, but central, modes of Celebration, Lament, and Puzzlement' (McCracken, 1992a, p. 180).

In a further essay, 'Re-gendering the reading of literature' (1992b), McCracken wants us to see that school reading has mostly been defined by what boys do, and this has been mistakenly established as the sole reading position allowed to girls. This is necessary, she says, because both girls and boys grow up reading as boys. Until recent years the stories read in schools have largely been the work of male writers, and most of us have modelled our reading habits upon the critical approaches expected of men. While stories by women have become more plentiful in books and magazines, English teachers brought up in university departments dedicated to the literary canon find themselves in difficulty when faced with new works in unfamiliar modes. They need to make a fresh approach to these texts, subordinating all they learned in academic circles about ways of treating the eternal themes to the conclusions arrived at by shared reading and discussion. And in such discussions, what we have learned from experience, both our cognitive responses to events and the tacit dimensions of our beliefs and expectations, are the final arbiters that control the conclusion. I think we should remind ourselves of Keats's definition of 'negative capability' in a letter to his brother and sister-in-law (December 21, 1817): 'that is, when a man is capable of being in uncertainties, mysteries, doubts, without any irritable reaching after fact and reason.' The way it feels to the reader, what it does for him/her, may yield a more lasting influence than any critical analysis aimed at advocating what is often regarded as an expert interpretation.

Where the exercise of the imagination is concerned, we may well ask what agency can claim the right to oversee individual preferences. Politicians of all parties, authoritarian powers in education, in industry, in society at large, may claim such a right and annex the power to enforce it; and the more unequal a society is in the distribution of its wealth, its resources, and its employment opportunities, the greater will be the constraints upon the imaginative activities within the society at large. The 'conversation of mankind' that Oakeshott envisaged was a free exchange of many voices, and prominent among them were the voices of poetry, the 'delight of utterance'.

It seems to me that what above all else is required in education is that girls and boys, men and women, who have learned to read in men's ways, should learn to read also in women's ways – open to the demands of caring and connecting, of playing the believing game as they approach possible new sources of imagined or recorded experience. McCracken concludes her chapter by saying: 'Only as we add literature written from multiple perspectives and teach ourselves and our students to read as both men and women will we start to reap the individual and cultural benefits long attributed to the reading of literature' (1992b, p. 20).

I envisage a mode of reading that promotes 'care, concern, and connection' – one that could become a central mode of response to spectator-role offerings throughout the range from fairy stories to Shakespeare and the whole academically accepted literature, including the kind of children's offerings that form stepping stones on the high road of their imaginative satisfactions – a high road that stretches the length of a lifetime.

And that brings me to the end of this particular journey; I finish it in the company of Laurie, my elder grandchild. A week or two after her fourteenth birthday I asked her to come and talk with me about what she liked to read, a matter which I had previously had no opportunity to discuss directly with her. Our conversation ended like this:

Me: What's your latest, then?
L: My latest? Oh I've just started on a Daphne du Maurier. I can't quite remember what it's called – the tea blowers, or something like that – and that's something to do with glass-blowing – a glass-blowing family or something – and that's as well – and Dad being a glass-blower . . . I think I find I like books where slightly – where I can believe slightly they have something to do with me – maybe 'cos – most of the books I've mentioned are somehow something to do with me, connected to me, if you know what I mean – books I can relate to.

'Books I can relate to': in the role of spectator we create a life of the mind, we read *ourselves*. The range is enormous – the books (as Laurie knows) we can relate to, the stories we tell, the experiences we exchange, the dreams we dream. We learn from them, directly and indirectly, gathering knowledge of the world, past, present, predicted – contemplating what has been and what *might* have been, and inventing the impossible.

Shakespeare's *A midsummer night's dream* ends with the celebration of Theseus's wedding to his Amazon bride, Hippolyta. Theseus chooses to see a play prepared by the 'hard-handed men that work in Athens here'; but Hippolyta doesn't seem to fancy the idea. Theseus tells her it is all a matter of using your imagination.

> The best in this kind are but shadows, and the worst
>   Are no worse, if imagination mend them.

Imagination – the ability to perceive what is conveyed by tacit powers, in a succession of sounds to hear music, as Coleridge reminds us, and in the sounds of words to hear images that reflect our unspoken judgments of reality.

5.3 Autobiographical coda

From 'English teaching: retrospect and prospect'[4]

Britton gave the lecture from which the following extracts are taken as the opening address at the Third International Conference on the Teaching of English, in Sydney, Australia, in August 1980. His concern is with both retrospect and prospect. As retrospect, he offers a personal review of 50 years, from his own beginning as an English teacher through the decades that have followed. His tracing of events couples English teaching with wider public movements and acknowledges that there is room for doubt as well as confidence. But at a conference which has brought together teachers of English from across the world, there is also cause for optimism. The importance of the piece is in its vision, its awareness of a view of learning and classrooms that his audience will share, in its hopes for 'a decade of the teacher': a prospect for a future that might lie ahead.

... I set up shop as an English teacher in a state secondary school 50 years ago next month. The year before I began, in 1929, there was published an official report on *The teaching of English in the elementary schools of London* [Board of Education, 1929]. A curious document. Among other recommendations it warned teachers to 'draw a sharp distinction between the language of the home and the street and the language the school is trying to achieve'. And it went so far as to suggest that teachers should not set children to talk or write about their homes or neighbourhoods, because that would be inviting them to use the wrong language. (Some of you have heard me refer to that before – how can I but repeat myself when I talk so much?)

There are plenty of teachers in our various countries who still operate a 'fresh start policy' for language in their classrooms. But we have made some advances in 50 years: no official statement would dare to put forward so linguistically naïve and ignorant a view today. Thirty years of intensive study of the way children acquire language in infancy – thirty years of watching and listening to children – have taught us a lesson we shall not forget.

'Watching and listening' – it is only in more recent years that we have begun to realise how language behaviour builds on earlier non-verbal behaviour: how cooperative routines set up between infant and adult, mostly in the form of play, increasingly generate *meaning* for the infant; and how early language comes in to highlight meanings already established in this way. Thereafter, language has a crucial role to play, enriching and extending cooperative behaviour, cumulatively reaping the harvest of earlier understandings, organising memory into narrative form, vastly increasing in scope and accessibility the body of expectations with which the child will meet every new event. Here is learning indeed, a model for all subsequent learning: using language to make sense of the world gives the child – Hey presto! – a mastery of language. It is our task as teachers to build on that learning, to enrich and extend it, to harness it ever more closely to ever more complex modes of experience.

This challenge has never been greater than it is today in the multicultural classrooms we are facing. Wayne O'Neil, American linguist, broke into a learned discussion once to say:

> I think that any book that comes out of this conference ought to make it perfectly clear that all of what we talk about is for naught if in fact American education is going to proceed to be exactly what it has been, a way of drawing people away from their roots and cultures rather than a way of increasing their activity within those groups and cultures.
>
> (Kavanagh and Mattingly, 1972, p. 156)

I know no more promising way of increasing such activity within subcultural groups than by cherishing and nourishing the speech of the home and the neighbourhood and by helping it to find the kind of expression, in story, poem, play, which can communicate the spirit of the subculture to a multicultural audience. That nourishing means, of course, that we can no longer limit our concern for literature to a concern for any canon, be it classical or national. Standard English? Yes, that's on the agenda too, seen essentially as the written language in which information is stored and made available.

In the '30s we knew nothing about language learning in infancy. Such studies as existed were locked away in fat, unreadable psychology manuals. Clearly, our educational bosses were no wiser than we were, on the evidence of the 1929 report I have referred to. And that fixes my baseline.

The '40s, among other events we have tended to forget, saw the teenage revolution. Young people gained, once and for all, a kind of independence (which, like the age of puberty, grows earlier every year). New attitudes to authority emerged: a teacher's authority could no longer be assumed but had to be earned, patiently and sometimes painfully. Martin Buber understood this very well: he spoke of the period as 'the time of the crumbling of bonds' and saw, in consequence, that the teacher could no longer represent 'the ambassador of history to this intruder, the child', but 'faces the child as individual to individual' (Buber, 1947, pp. 93–94).

If I have laboured this point, it is because it is so consistently forgotten by certain critics of enlightened educational policies today – including some of those who urge us 'back to basics': nothing is more sadly futile than a belief that we can put the clock back.

The '50s I find difficult to recall in any clear focus. Perhaps that is because it was a decade of spadework; teachers in their classrooms patiently tackling the task of working out new methods of teaching and learning appropriate to the new relationships, the individual-to-individual stance of teacher to child. For the new relationships demanded a new conception of the learning process itself, a move from a uni-directional to an interactive view.

In England, I believe one important aspect of this movement was the increasing influence of primary-school teachers on their secondary-school colleagues. The secondary-school subject specialist is more prone to seeing learning as a uni-directional process – something proceeding from teacher to pupil – than is the primary-school teacher who must see himself as a facilitator of learning in all areas of the curriculum.

I do not imply that the problems of the secondary school can all be solved by applying the successful experience of primary-school teachers – indeed some of the problems posed by attempting this rapprochement seem as far away from solution today as ever. But the recognition that learning is always an interactive process is a crucial first step: its implications – that talking and writing may be modes of learning, that a curriculum must be negotiable, that in-school and out-of-school learning should be inseparable parts of one pattern – the working out of these implications constitutes an area of active innovation in secondary schools today.

These were the ideas that blossomed in the '60s, a heady and dangerous decade. I see it as a 'grand processional' from the Dartmouth Seminar in America [1966] to the Bullock Report in England [Department of Education and Science, 1975]. It was heady to have ideas that had germinated in quiet processes and small circles suddenly come out into the open; and dangerous in the way that an institutionalised orthodoxy is always dangerous. The new orthodoxy was no exception: the grand processional swept into its wake many who were more in the swim than in the know, and they did much to supply ammunition to the critics, the nostalgic admirers of education in the 'good old days'. The term 'child-centred education' came to be widely used, and it seems to me a highly ambiguous and even misleading term. Interactive learning (like the cooperative ploys of infant and adult) is a *joint* undertaking. Vygotsky (1978), urging the social and cultural nature of learning, has put this very clearly, showing how operations and calculations originally carried out overtly in joint activity with an adult become internalised with the help of inner speech and so shape the child's consciousness. 'Adult- and child-centred' seems a more accurate description of the kind of education we have in mind, appropriate to an interactive view of learning, and highlighting the crucial role of language, in its many modes, as the principal instrument of interaction.

It is easy, I think, to characterise the '70s: it is the 'age of anxiety'. You remember that Auden wrote a 'Baroque eclogue' with that title epitomising the years of the Second World War. But his definition of anxiety in that poem seems to me to fit exactly the mood of the '70s: 'their vision shrinks as their dreams darken'. A world recession creating basic uncertainty about the future – the darkening of our dreams; and with that a shrinking of perspectives, a limiting of the number of factors we are prepared to take account of in making a judgment. In educational terms, this means a 'back to basics' policy ('rationalisation', as some administrators interpret the term), and, in England, the anti-progressive views of the Black Papers.

With this shrinking of perspectives, my grand processional has been re-christened 'the decadent '60s'. The writers of the Black Papers, as I have suggested, draw ammunition from practices based on a laissez-faire philosophy and other instances of the work of bandwagon progressives. I think there is an urgent need for thorough study of the highly complex structure of the open classroom, the highly complex demands of interactive learning and negotiated curricula. And for that reason I welcome two recent studies produced by your National Working Party on the role of language in learning, *Negotiating the curriculum* and *Literacy around the workbench*.

What we have learned must be preserved, even when it seems like a soft sell in a hard market. We have learned that mastery of language comes with its purposeful use and that attempts to teach the bare skills by practice exercises is bound to fail. It is the user's own intention that releases the powers of mastery: any practice will help only in so far as it feeds directly into a mainstream of activity that is purposeful.

Put at its broadest, we master language by using it to make the most of our lives.

★ ★ ★

If this were not an assembly but a more convivial occasion, I should ask you now, with 'English in the '80s' in mind, to raise your glasses and drink a toast to the *decade of the teacher*. As we have developed our view of learning as interactive, and that of the curriculum as negotiable; as we have recognised the dramatic effect of intentions upon performance, by teachers as well as by students; as it has become clear that teaching consists of moment-by-moment interactive behaviour, behaviour that can only spring from inner conviction – I think we are, perhaps for the first time, ready to admit that what the teacher can't do in the classroom can't be achieved by any other means. Not the 'grand processional' then, not the 'age of anxiety', but the 'age of the classroom teacher'.

No, I do not mean that nobody else matters, nobody else can help. I think there are great opportunities for people like me – in professional development, initial and in-service training, whatever you call it – provided we see that interactive learning applies to teachers as well as to those they teach; provided we see our role as helping them to theorise from their own experience, and build their own rationale and their own body of convictions. For it is when they are actively theorising from their own experience that they can, selectively, take and use other people's experiences and other people's theories.

I see a vital role for administrators, once it is realised that they are teacher supporters rather than building superintendents or systems analysts – and teacher support means helping teachers to learn as well as helping them to teach.

Walking down Euston Road ten days ago, I was thinking about this occasion and wondering whether 'the age of the classroom teacher' was altogether too optimistic an idea to be realistic. Then I saw, outside Friends' House (the Quaker headquarters), a poster which seemed to me as I read it to be putting my thoughts into words. It contained a quotation from Rufus Jones, an American Quaker in the early years of this century: 'I pin my hopes to quiet processes and small circles in which vital and transforming events take place.'

Moving into the '80s, into rough waters with plenty of problems educational, social and political, I am not pessimistic. I pin my hopes to quiet processes and small circles in which I believe I shall see, if I'm still alive at the end, vital and transforming events taking place.

5.4 Today's student teachers reading and discussing Britton

We close with an account of student teachers discussing Britton, put together from their reports of what transpired. We introduce the context more fully in what follows, and other than our thanks to the students taking part and our record of the value and interest provided by their work, there is no need for further introduction.

In the summer of 2022, students on the Secondary English PGCE at the Institute of Education, University College London, were invited to read 'Talking to learn', Britton's chapter in *Language, the learner and the school* (Barnes, Britton and Torbe, 1986), extracts from which form 2.4 above. They then discussed the chapter in seminar groups. These were students nearing the end of their pre-service programme: the seminars took place on the day after the end of their second (and final) school placement. What follows is an attempt to provide a flavour of the varied conversations that took place in these seminars.

The students read Britton in the light of their recent school experiences. Anita[5] suggested that this was a validating piece for her to read at the end of the course, because it provided a justification for a noisy classroom. Anita's first placement had been in a school where collaborative talk could flourish; her second school, on the other hand, had insisted on tightly controlled classroom routines and on a pedagogic model that assumed the one-way transmission of knowledge from teacher to student. Rosa and Hana commented on how the issues explored felt completely up-to-date – and loved the view of education as humane, as the enabling of students to understand and to ask questions. Reacting to the reductive prescriptivism that they had encountered on their placements, both read Britton as offering hope of a different way of being a teacher. Athena liked Britton's idea that we use talk to refine our value systems, and also pointed out that it is through talk that we as teachers learn about our students' value systems. She reflected on a difficult discussion in a Year 10 class she had recently taught that had revealed the prevalence of deeply sexist attitudes among the boys. This opened up a conversation about how a teacher might respond to such moments, and to wider exploration of what counts as acceptable talk in the classroom and of the criteria that might be used.

There was interest in Britton's use of extensive transcripts of student talk. Anna expressed surprise at how contemporary it all felt – the rhythm of the students' interactions and the language they used. Some had found it hard to follow these conversations – and there was the suggestion that it would have helped if Britton had given pseudonyms for the speakers. Others, though, welcomed the length of the transcripts: they felt that this enabled them, as readers, to weigh up the evidence for themselves, and to gain a sense of the development of the conversations over time. (As Beth put it, 'You could get the story of *Moby-Dick* in a summary but it's not the same as reading it!') Hana's group became engaged in a discussion about rice: her (Somali) version being different from Ayyub and Fateha's south Asian versions, and from Sapphyre's (Nigerian-heritage) defence of jollof rice. In effect, they were enacting the kind of conversation that they had been reading about.

Chloë commented on the kind of talk that is represented in 'Talking to learn'. She knew a lot about the school where her partner worked, and she recognised that its practice and its valorisation of talk placed it at the progressive end of the current spectrum of schooling; but, she said, their version of talk was one closely controlled, in organisation, in tone, in content, by the teacher – it's not the sort of conversation enacted by the girls in the first transcript in Britton's chapter. For Judith, the inclusion of this transcript, 'where they are talking about their home and what goes on there' poses questions about English as a subject or discipline: 'It's almost, like, saying is this English? It's like saying is Harold Pinter a playwright, or is Samuel Beckett a playwright? Is that English? And the whole idea that there is a defined destination, knowledge is in the subject, it's just a fallacy.' The argument that Judith is beginning to make here involves a rejection of current versions of 'knowledge-rich' curricula, in which English is reduced to forms of propositional knowledge that can be easily taught and tested, on the grounds that such models fail to take account of the affective and aesthetic dimensions of the experience of literary texts. At the same time, in seeing the transcript as analogous to a script by Beckett or Pinter, Judith echoes Britton's interest in language in the spectator role, and thus in seeing a continuum between everyday and literary language. What follows from this, for Judith as for Britton, is the imperative to remain attentive to what students say – to treat such talk as seriously as a literary text.

Consideration of the transcripts prompted students to return to Britton's starting point, the challenge of identifying how learning happens. Talking about the danger of planning and teaching as if learning were reducible to a linear process, with predetermined outcomes and goals, Maya wondered if what was learnt 'along the road' might be just as valuable, 'and actually, you might end up somewhere completely different'. While she accepted the teacher's responsibility to guide the shared exploration of a text, she worried about the tendency to enforce a single interpretation on students.

Fatima focused on Britton's questioning of what was on- or off-topic, of how difficult it is, in reality, to make sharp distinctions between what is relevant and what is not, on the importance of deferring judgement on this. And she touched on the issue of time – the importance of allowing time for the conversation to develop, as well as the time that it takes to build pedagogic relationships. Chloë, too, was struck by the final part of the chapter, with its emphasis on relationships as a precondition of the kind of talk that might enable learning, and its understanding that trust was something that had to be earned by the teacher. Reflecting on her journey through the PGCE year, she recognised the stages that Britton describes that a teacher has to go through to get to a place where the kind of talk among peers that is so productive can be enabled.

The conversations around 'Talking to learn' enabled the student teachers to think differently about their classroom experiences, to view them, and their own formation as teachers, their values and commitments, in a new light. One might even say that what was enacted in the seminars was the kind of dialogic relationship between research and practice that Britton envisaged in his 'A note on teaching, research and "development"' (4.1 above) (Britton, 1982b).

Notes

1. The source of this text is Britton (1966).
2. The editors have not been able to trace the source of this reference.
3. The source of this text is Chapter 7 of Britton (1993), pp. 81–92.
4. The source of this text is Britton (1982a), reprinted from the original lecture given in 1980.
5. Students' names have been replaced with culturally appropriate pseudonyms.

References

Barnes, D., Britton, J. and Torbe, M. (1986). *Language, the learner and the school* (3rd edition). Harmondsworth: Penguin Books.

Batsleer, J., Davis, T., O'Rourke, R. and Weedon, C. (1985). *Re-writing English: Cultural politics of gender and class*. London and New York, NY: Methuen.

Board of Education (1929). *General report on the teaching of English in London elementary schools, 1925*. London: His Majesty's Stationery Office.

Britton, J. (1966). 'What is English?' Working papers of the Anglo-American Conference on the Teaching and Learning of English (Dartmouth College, Hanover, New Hampshire, 20 August to 16 September 1966). Available at https://files.eric.ed.gov/fulltext/ED082201.pdf.

Britton, J. (1982a). 'English teaching: retrospect and prospect' [1980], in Pradl, G. (ed.), *Prospect and retrospect: Selected essays of James Britton*. London and Monclair, NJ: Heinemann Educational and Boynton/Cook, pp. 201–215.

Britton. J. (1982b). 'A note on teaching, research and "development"' [1969], in Pradl, G. (ed.), *Prospect and retrospect: Selected essays of James Britton*. London and Monclair, NJ: Heinemann Educational and Boynton/Cook, pp. 149–152.

Britton, J. (1993). *Literature in its place*. Portsmouth, NH: Boynton/Cook.

Buber, M. (1947). *Between man and man*. London: Routledge and Kegan Paul.

Cassirer, E. (1944). *An essay on man*. New Haven, CT: Yale University Press.

Central Advisory Committee for Education (1963). *Half our future* (the Newsom Report). London: Ministry of Education.

Department of Education and Science (1975). *A language for life* (the Bullock Report). London: Her Majesty's Stationery Office.

Kavanagh, J. and Mattingly, I. (eds) (1972). *Language by ear and by eye: The relationships between speech and reading*. Cambridge, MA: MIT Press.

Mandelbaum, D. (ed.) (1949). *Culture, language and personality: Selected essays of Edward Sapir*. Berkeley, CA: University of California Press.

McCracken, N. (1992a). 'Gender issues and the teaching of writing', in McCracken, N. and Appleby, B. (eds), *Gender issues and the teaching of English*. Portsmouth, NH: Boynton/Cook.

McCracken, N. (1992b). 'Re-gendering the reading of literature', in McCracken, N. and Appleby, B. (eds), *Gender issues and the teaching of English*. Portsmouth, NH: Boynton/Cook.

Moffett, J. (1966). 'A structural curriculum in English'. *Harvard Educational Review*, 36(1), pp. 17–28.

Oakshott, M. (1959). *The voice of poetry in the conversation of mankind*. London: Bowes and Bowes.

Richards, I. (1942). *How to read a page*. New York, NY: Norton.

Vygotsky, L. (1962). *Thought and language* [1934]. Trans. E. Haufmann and G. Vakar. Cambridge, MA: MIT Press.

Vygotsky, L. (1971). *The psychology of art* [1925]. Cambridge, MA: MIT Press.

Vygotsky, L. (1978). *Mind in society*. Cole, M., John-Steiner, V., Scribner, S. and Souberman, E. (eds). Cambridge, MA: Harvard University Press.

Index

Titles in *italics* or inverted commas are writings by Britton unless otherwise indicated. A letter n following a page number indicates a reference in the notes.

abstract thinking 168
action, talk in support of 22, 24, 25, 26, 27
active learning 7, 12, 55
Advanced level (A-level) examinations 4
agency of children 7, 12
'anatomy of human experience — the role of inner speech, The' 38–47
Anglo-American Conference on the Teaching and Learning of English (Dartmouth Seminar) (1966) 6, 175, 178–187, 200
'Animula' (Eliot) 45
anticipation, as component of learning 101
Applebee, A. 35, 36, 151n4
art, works of 37, 45, 190, 191, 193
art-like works 191, 193
assessment *see* evaluation (assessment)
Assessment of Performance Unit 78
Auden, W.H. 130, 201
audience, written language 6, 10, 11, 114, 135–136, 137
authority, teacher's 106–107
awareness, focal and subsidiary 36, 144, 150

'back to basics' policy 200, 201
Barnes, D. 6, 51, 83, 107, 178
Barrs, M. 166
basic research 159, 163–164
Batsleer, J. 194
behaviour, and language 66

behavioural psychology of learning and language acquisition 5
'being told' 65, 70, 72, 75
'best practice' 12
Black Papers 52, 53, 65, 72, 73, 76, 82, 201
Blair, T. 53
Board of Education 56–57, 198
Boyson, R. 79
Bruner, J. 34, 167, 170–171
Buber, M. 106, 200
Bullock Report (1975) 6, 8, 51, 53, 71, 72, 73–74, 76, 78, 200; Chapter 4 'Language and learning' 65–70, 72, 75
Bunin, I. 191
Butler, R.A. 4

Callaghan, J., Ruskin College speech (1976) 52–53
Cassidy, F. 58
Cassirer, E. 78, 124, 180, 183
Cazden, C. 80
Central Advisory Council for Education (England) 52, 73, 182
Certificate of Secondary Education (CSE) 4, 6, 113, 114
'child-centred' education 72, 201
Chomsky, N. 68
Chukovsky, K. 45
Church, J. 124
classics, teaching of the 5

Index

cognition 8, 146, 176; *see also* thought/thinking
cognitive psychology of learning and language acquisition 5
Coleridge, S.T. 191, 197
collaborative talk 84, 85, 203
common-sense concepts 72, 76, 77, 101
communication 25; skills of 178, 179, 180, 181, 182
community 170–171
comprehensive schools 4, 5, 52, 65
conative speech 141
concept development 35, 168
confrontations 156
consciousness 166, 167, 169–170, 171, 192, 201; nature/nurture and 169; social origins of 166, 169–170
context, and applicability of research findings 160, 161
contextualisation of language 130–131
cooperative talk 51, 62
critical method in research 161
Critical Quarterly (journal) 52
critical reading 10
Crosland, A. 52
CSE *see* Certificate of Secondary Education
cultural psychology 5–6
curriculum 4, 106; hidden 108–109; 'knowledge-rich' 179, 204; mandated 159; National Curriculum 53; negotiated 108, 201, 202; 'output' model of 108

Dartmouth Seminar (1966) 6, 175, 178–187, 200
Department of Education and Science, *A language for life see* Bullock Report
determining tendency 149–150
development, and research 154, 155, 157, 158, 159, 163, 164
development of writing abilities (11–18), The 6, 114–115, 135–142
Dewey, J. 53, 81
dialect 55, 58, 60–61
disciplinary view of English 178, 181–182
discovery/discovering 39, 143, 148; learning by 70, 74, 170; research as process of 160, 161
discursive symbolism 37
Dixon, J. 178

drama 38, 54, 130, 192
drawing 29, 30; speech 30, 31–32

Education Act (1944) 4
Egendorf, A. 147–148
egocentric speech 25, 26, 27, 28, 166
Eliot, T.S. 45
Emig, J. 146
emotion 191; and intellect, interdependence of 192; *see also* feeling
emotional development, and language 8
emotive speech 141
engagement 101–102
English on the anvil 2
English as a discipline 178, 181–182
English in Education (journal) 166
'English teaching: retrospect and prospect' 198–202
Enquiry into Reading and the Teaching of English *see* Bullock Report
Esland, G. 127
evaluation, and meaning, interrelationship between 47
evaluation (assessment) 71, 72–73, 74, 78–79, 80–81; *see also* marking
examinations, public *see* public examinations
exclamation 119
expectations 36, 66, 67, 125, 126, 148, 162, 195, 199
experience 78, 175, 185; corpus of 124; interpretation of 7, 65, 66–67, 124, 126, 148, 162; language and shaping/structuring of 124, 176, 179, 180, 183–184, 186; learning from 124, 179, 184; pre-representational 147; reflection on 8, 10, 11; representation of 67, 69, 124–127, 137, 156; sharing of 11
Experience into words (Harding) 147
experiencing 147, 148
expertise 106–107
expressive language 6, 77–78, 84, 114, 119–120; expressive talk (speech) 72, 77, 78, 84, 85, 98–99, 101, 102, 106, 120, 121, 139, 140, 141; expressive writing 10–11, 72, 76, 77–78, 84, 101, 116–134, 136, 137, 140, 142; as language close to the self 119
Eyers, S. 163

Index

fantasy 8
feeling 6, 8, 62, 84, 99, 109, 176; *see also* emotion
'finding out for oneself' 65, 70, 72, 75
flight-path of my words, The 4
focal awareness 36, 144, 150
form, organisation of 130
Freud, S. 45
function, written language 6, 10, 11, 114, 135, 136, 137, 141–142

GCSE *see* General Certificate of Secondary Education
'Gender issues and the teaching of writing' (McCracken) 194–195
gender-based understandings of literature, reading and writing 188, 194–196
gendered language 14
Gendlin, E. 147
General Certificate of Secondary Education (GCSE) 4
General report on the teaching of English in London elementary schools, 1925 (Board of Education) 56–57, 198
generalised representation of experience 67, 69
generational differences in language use 59
geography, writing in 136, 137
gesture 33
Gibbons, S. 3
gossip 10, 11, 176
Gove, M. 53
government intervention 53
grammar 5, 52, 58, 68, 181
grammar schools 4–5
Graves, D. 35
'Great Debate' in English education 52–53, 74
group discussion 69, 75
guidance, as heart of teaching 81
Gurrey, P. 2
Gusdorf, G. 46, 66

Halliday, M. 164
Harding, D.W. 147, 148
Hargreaves, D. 107
Heath, S. 102
heuristic function of language 65, 70, 74
heuristic nature of teaching 159, 163

hidden curriculum 108–109
history: learning in 78; writing in 136, 137
Holbrook, D. 178, 183
home language 17, 19–28, 51, 54–55, 57, 198, 199
How to read a page (Richards) 192
Howe, M. 75–76
Huxley, A. 47
Hymes, D. 141, 142
hypotheses 125; language of 69; scientific 76–77, 106

IFTE *see* International Federation for the Teaching of English
imagination 38, 44–45, 170, 176, 190, 191, 192, 195, 197
imaginative writing 5
independent learning 108, 109
informative writing 77, 142
inner speech 8, 17, 18, 27, 28, 43, 46, 47, 63, 140, 169, 201
intellect, and emotion/feeling, interdependence of 176, 192
intention 150
intentions of the learner 72; effect on performance 29, 32, 202; evaluation and 80–81
interaction 39, 40–42, 171; and teaching 161–162
interactive view of learning 107–108, 109, 200, 201, 202
internalised forms of language 122, 134, 144, 149, 169, 170
International Conference on the Teaching of English (1980) 161–162, 175, 176–177, 198–202
International Federation for the Teaching of English (IFTE) 6–7, 176–177
interpretation, of experience 7, 65, 66–67, 124, 126, 148, 162
invention 170; in writing 144, 145–146

Jakobson, R. 141
Jones, N. 159–160, 162
Jones, R. 202
judgement: development of 10; literary 153–154, 176; shared, and marking 6, 114

Kavanagh, J. 199
Keats, J. 195
Kellogg, W. and Kellogg, L. 170
Kelly, G. 76, 156, 162, 186–187
Kitzhaber, A.R. 178, 180, 181, 182, 186
knowing 165; and doing 156–157; knowledge as process of 101
knowledge: as form of inquiry 163; language and generation of 66, 69, 70; as process of knowing 101
'knowledge base' of English 178–179, 181–182
'knowledge-rich' curricula 179, 204
Kuhn, T. 160

Langer, S. 6, 37, 180
language: acceptable forms of 58–59; acceptance of differences in use of 59, 60; across the curriculum 6, 51, 136; and behaviour 66; behavioural psychology of 5; changes in 59; cognitive psychology of 5; conative 141; contextualisation of 130–131; and emotional development 8; expressive *see* expressive language; and first-hand experience 61; 'fresh start' policy 55, 56–57, 59, 198; gendered 14; and generalised representations of experience 67, 69; and generation of knowledge 66, 69, 70, 72; generational differences in use of 59; heuristic function of 65, 70, 74; home 17, 19–25, 51, 54–55, 198, 199; of hypothesis 69; and inner representation 67; internalised forms of 122, 134, 144, 149, 169, 170; and learning 5, 12, 51; operational view of 1, 5, 7–9, 52, 54, 56, 57–58, 117, 133–134, 175, 177, 179–180, 183, 184–185, 186; in participant role *see* participant role; poetic use of 6, 116, 130, 131, 134, 136, 137, 139, 141; practising 54, 56; referential 119, 120, 141; and representation of experience 67, 69, 124–127, 137, 156; rules of 67–68, 69; and shaping/ structuring of experience 124, 176, 179, 180, 183–184, 186; in spectator role *see* spectator role; and thought/thinking 5, 7, 8, 68;

transactional *see* transactional language; written *see* writing/ written language; *see also* speech; talk
'Language in the British primary school' 51, 53, 71–82
Language, the learner and the school (Barnes, Britton and Torbe) 51; 'Talking to learn' 83–110, 203–205
Language and learning 3, 5, 7–8, 17, 51; 'Learning to speak' 19–28; 'Now that you go to school' 54–64
language for life, A (DES) *see* Bullock Report
'Language performance' (Assessment of Performance Unit) 78
language proficiency 179, 184–185
Lashley, K. 149
LATE *see* London Association for the Teaching of English
learning 7, 8; active 7, 12, 55; affective and social dimensions of 84; anticipation as component of 101; assessing quality of 73; behavioural psychology of 5; cognitive psychology of 5; as coming to know 99, 110; cooperative talk and 51, 62; by discovery 70, 74, 170; disorderliness of 83–110; as evolutionary process 56; from experience 124, 179, 184; and group discussion 69; in history 78; independent 108, 109; interactive view of 107–108, 109, 200, 201, 202; and language 5, 12, 51; lifelong 54, 56; by listening 70, 74, 75; as necessary precondition for instruction 8; by reading 70, 74, 75; research as process of 160; rote learning 78, 85; school, as building upon learning of infancy 54, 55–56; by talking 54, 56, 70, 72, 74, 75, 107–108; to talk by talking 54, 56; to write by writing 117; by writing 70, 74, 75–76
'Learning to speak' 19–28
Leavis, F.R. 5, 194
lexical relationships 68
life and work of Britton 1–13
lifelong learning 54, 56
linguistics 12, 164

Index

listening 62, 65, 70, 85, 107; adult/teacher as listener 8, 107, 108, 115, 121, 134; learning by 70, 74, 75; and spoken language 8; to stories 34
literacy 6, 9, 29–37, 52, 65, 66, 71, 74
literary canon 52, 193–194
literary judgement 153–154, 176
literary knowledge 178
literary study 11, 12
literature 38, 45–47, 144, 176, 181, 182, 185, 190, 191, 192–193; gender-based understandings of 188, 194–196; intellect and feeling, interdependence of in 176; 'socially relevant' 52; teaching of 9–10
Literature in its place 3, 8, 38–47, 175, 176, 188–197
London Association for the Teaching of English (LATE) 2–3, 5, 6, 17, 51, 83, 113, 159
Luria, A. 5, 8, 17, 43, 54, 66, 167, 169

make-believe (pretend) play 8, 10, 17, 29, 30, 31, 33, 34, 38, 41–42, 43–44, 45, 170, 188, 190, 192
managerial role of teachers 107
Mandel, B. 146
Mandelbaum, D. 183
manipulative play 33–34, 36
marking 80, 81, 113–114; multiple 113–114; preoccupation with 73; validity of shared judgement over individual 6, 114
Martin, N. 2, 3, 6, 113
Marxism and the philosophy of language (Volosinov) 46–47
Mattingly, I. 199
McCracken, N. 194–195, 196
McKellar, P. 147
Mead, G. 140
meaning 7, 8, 41, 46–47, 115, 123, 143, 144, 150, 199; and evaluation, interrelationship of 47; negotiation of 102; sharing of 143; word 168, 192
meaning and marking of imaginative composition, The (LATE) 3, 113
memory, visual 67
Meneghello, L. 55, 60–61, 62
metric composition 149

midsummer nights's dream, A, (Shakespeare) 196–197
Mind in Society (Vygotsky) 41, 44, 101, 166, 169, 201
Moffett, J. 63, 142, 182
Monday Club 73
monologue 22, 25, 26, 27, 42, 43; *see also* running commentaries
Morgan's Junior English Grammar 2
multicultural classroom 199
Multiple marking of English compositions (Schools Council) 6, 113

National Association for the Teaching of English (NATE) 6, 166, 178
National Council of Teachers of English (NCTE) 116, 178
National Curriculum 53
National Foundation for Educational Research (NFER) 65
nature/nurture and consciousness 169
negative capability 195
negotiated curriculum 108, 201, 202
new literary criticism 5, 153
New York Review of Books 169
Newsom Report (1963) 182
non-spontaneous concepts 168
'note on teaching, research and "development", A' 154, 155–158, 205
'Now that you go to school' 54–64
nursery rhymes 45

Oakeshott, M. 188–189, 190, 195
observation 39; scientific 77
Ofsted 53, 159
O'Neil, W. 199
operational view of language 1, 5, 7–9, 52, 54, 56, 57–58, 117, 133–134, 175, 177, 179–180, 183, 184–185, 186
oracy 6
Ordinary level (O-level) examinations 4, 113; composition papers 114; importance of topic in 114; multiple marking 113–114
'output' model of curriculum 108

participant role 116, 137, 179, 183; in talk 62, 63, 127–128; in writing 9, 10, 114
perception 37

Index

performance targets 12
Perl, S. 147–148
philosophy 12, 153, 156
phonics 52
Piaget, J. 25, 26, 45, 140, 166, 168
pictorial representation 33, 34
play 8, 176, 199; make-believe (pretend) 8, 10, 17, 29, 30, 31, 33, 34, 38, 41–42, 43–44, 45, 170, 188, 190, 192; manipulative 33–34, 36
Play, dreams and imitation in childhood (Piaget) 45
Plowden Report (1967) 52, 71, 73, 74
poetic use of language 6, 116, 130, 131, 134, 136, 137, 139, 141, 142
poetry 5, 10, 130, 133, 192, 195
Polanyi, M. 36, 84, 101, 144, 150, 165
political context 52–53, 65–66
Popper, K. 76–77, 160, 161
Pradl, G. 71
'Prehistory of the development of written language' (Vygotsky) 29
presentational symbolism 37
pretend play *see* make-believe (pretend) play
progressive education 72, 73, 74, 186
psychology 12, 153, 154, 156; behavioural 5; cognitive 5; cultural 5–6
psychology of art, The (Vygotsky) 45, 167, 190–191, 192
public examinations 4; *see also* Advanced level (A-level) examinations; Certificate of Secondary Education (CSE); General Certificate of Secondary Education (GCSE); Ordinary level (O-level) examinations

'quiet form of research, A' 154, 159–165

Ray, C. 160, 164
'Re-gendering the reading of literature' (McCracken) 195, 196
Re-writing English: cultural politics of gender and class (Batsleer et al.) 194
reading 9, 33, 65, 114, 193; critical 10; gender-based understandings of 188, 195, 196; and internalisation of written language 122, 149; learning by 70, 74, 75; phonics method for teaching 52; story 34, 35

recognising 39
Record and recall 4
Rees, M. 12–13
referential language 119, 120, 141
reflection on experience 8, 10, 11
religious education, writing in 136, 137
representation 114, 183; of experience 67, 69, 124–127, 137, 156; pictorial 33, 34; symbolic 7, 8, 66–67, 124, 183
research: acceptance of findings 160–161; accumulation, in physical sciences 160; applicability of findings 160, 161, 162–163; basic 159, 163–164; context and applicability of findings of 160, 161; critical method in 161; demystification of 162; in physical sciences 154, 159–160; as process of discovery and learning 160, 161; rigour in 161; *see also* teaching and research
responding 39
Richards, I.A. 5, 153, 176, 192
Richardson, D. 109
Richmond, J. 163–164
rigour, research 161
risk taking 78
Rose, M. 148
Rosen, C. 55, 62, 63–64
Rosen, H. 3, 6, 51, 83, 113, 178
rote learning 78, 85
routines 39
running commentaries 8, 17, 22–25, 26–27
Ruskin College speech (James Callaghan, 1976) 52–53

Sapir, E. 62, 116, 119, 124, 139, 140, 180, 183
Sartre, J-P. 35
school leaving age 4, 5
Schools Council 6, 113, 114, 138, 154, 155, 194
science 102–106, 110; research methods in 154, 159–160; writing in 77–78, 136, 137
scientific concepts 76, 101
scientific hypotheses 76–77, 106
scientific observation and recording 77–78
Scrutiny (journal) 194
secondary modern schools 4
semantic relationships 68

213

Index

Shakespeare, W., *midsummer nights's dream, A* 196–197
'Shaping at the point of utterance' 115, 143–150
shared social behaviour 169–171
shared values 99
Slobin, D. 32, 80
social dimensions of learning 84
social speech 8, 25, 27, 28
socialised speech 26
sociology 153, 156
spectator role 116, 137, 176, 177, 179, 183, 185, 193, 196, 204; in talk 63, 127, 128–129; in writing 9, 10, 11, 33–34, 114, 116, 117, 130, 132–133, 134
speech 120, 170; conative 141; drawing 30, 31–32; egocentric 25, 26, 27, 28, 166; emotive 141; expressive *see under* expressive language; hierarchy of functions 141; inner 8, 17, 18, 27, 28, 43, 46, 47, 63, 140, 169, 201; monologic *see* monologue; for oneself 25, 27, 43, 63, 168–169; social 8, 25, 27, 28; socialised 26; and writing, relation between 139–141; *see also* talk
Spencer, M.M. 3, 143
spiels 42–43
spontaneity 144, 146, 147
spontaneous concepts 168
Standard English 58–59, 60
Start, K. 65
story reading 34, 35
story writing 29, 30, 32–33, 34–36; built-in associations 36; linguistic conventions 36; structure 35
storytelling 10, 11, 31, 34
subconscious 190, 191
subsidiary awareness 36, 144, 150
Summerfield, G. 178
surveillance, regime of 73, 79, 80
Sweet, H. 58
symbolic representation 7, 8, 66–67, 124, 183
symbolism, discursive and presentational 37
symbols and signs, writing as system of 29, 30

Tajfel, H. 138
talk 8, 9, 11, 18, 39, 65, 114, 193, 203–205; at home 19–25; collaborative 84, 85, 203; cooperative, and learning 51, 62; expressive *see under* expressive language; gender differences in 194; learning by talking 54, 56, 70, 72, 74, 75, 107–108; learning to talk by talking 54, 56; in a participant role 62, 63, 127–128; running commentaries 22–25, 26–27; in a spectator role 63, 127, 128–129; to support activity 22, 24, 25, 26, 27; value of talking in school 51, 54–64
'Talking to learn' 83–100, 203–205
teacher(s): authority of 106–107; as examiner, writing and 136, 137; interaction in the classroom 161–162; as listener 107, 108, 115, 121, 134; managerial role 107; as reader 80, 121, 134; as researchers 159, 161–163
teachers' centres 155, 158
teaching as heuristic 159, 163
teaching and research 153–173; applicability of findings 160, 161, 162–163; notion of 'development' 154, 155, 157, 158, 159, 163, 164; teachers as researchers 159, 161–163
teaching/learning relationship 72–73, 107; trust in 73, 78, 79–80, 85, 106, 107–108
teenage revolution 200
Texts and pretexts (Huxley) 47
Thatcher, M. 65, 74
theoretical concepts 76; mastery of 72, 77
Thought and Language (Vygotsky) 166, 167, 176, 191–192
thought/thinking 18, 19, 114, 169; abstract 168; and expressive language 140; and language 5, 7, 8, 68; verbal 8, 18, 63, 169; *see also* cognition
Times, The (newspaper) 73
Torbe, M. 51, 83
Toulmin, S. 169
transactional language 6, 130, 131; in writing 35, 116, 129–130, 134, 136, 137, 142
trend of reading standards, The report (Start and Wells) 65
trust, in teaching/learning relationship 73, 78, 79–80, 85, 106, 107–108

understanding 85
University of London Institute of Education 114

Valentine, C. 20
value systems 85, 99, 109–110, 129, 204
verbal thought 8, 18, 63, 169
Vinogradova, O. 66
visual memory 67
voice of poetry in the conversation of mankind, The (Oakeshott) 188–189
Volosinov, V. 46–47
Von Kleist, H. 143, 145
Vygotsky, L. 6, 8, 17–18, 19, 26–28, 29, 30, 31, 32, 33, 38, 54, 84, 140, 141, 180, 188; abstract thinking 168; concept development 35, 168; consciousness 166, 167, 169–170, 201; imagination 44–45, 170; inner speech 17, 18, 27, 28, 63, 140, 169, 201; 'speech for oneself' 25, 27, 63, 168–169; word meanings 168; zone of proximal development 171; *Mind in Society* 41, 44, 101, 166, 169, 201; 'Prehistory of the development of written language' 29; *psychology of art, The* 45, 167, 190–191, 192; *Thought and language* 166, 167, 176, 191–192
'Vygotsky's contribution to pedagogical theory' 154, 166–171

Wells, B. 65
Welsh, C. 32, 80
'What is English?' 178–187
Whitehead, F. 178, 184
Wilkes, A. 138
Williams, J. 76, 101
word meaning 168, 192
'Writing to learn and learning to write' 114, 115, 116–134

writing/written language 9, 18, 54, 60, 65, 113–115, 193; abstract thinking and mastery of 168; audience 6, 10, 11, 114, 135–136, 137; Board of Education (1925) on teaching of 56–57; as contemplative act 143, 148; development in young children 29–37; expressive writing 10–11, 72, 76, 77–78, 84, 101, 116–134, 136, 137, 140, 142; function 6, 10, 11, 114, 135, 136, 137, 141–142; gender-based understandings of 188, 194–195; informative writing 77, 142; internalised forms of 122, 134, 144, 149; invention in writing 144, 145–146; and knowledge generation 69, 70; learning by writing 70, 74, 75–76; learning to write by writing 117; operational view of 133–134; participant role in writing 9, 10, 114; poetic writing 116, 130, 131, 134, 136, 137, 139, 142; process of writing 115, 143–150; projective structuring 148; retrospective structuring 148; in science 77–78, 136, 137; spectator role in writing 9, 10, 11, 33–34, 114, 116, 117, 132–133, 134; and speech, relationship between 139–141; spontaneous shaping of 144, 146, 147; story writing *see* story writing; as system of symbols and signs 29, 30; taxonomy of 6, 9, 10–11, 137; transactional writing 35, 116, 129–130, 134, 136, 137, 142; writing as motor skill 29, 30

'Young fluent writers' 29–37

zone of proximal development 171

For Product Safety Concerns and Information please contact our EU representative GPSR@taylorandfrancis.com
Taylor & Francis Verlag GmbH, Kaufingerstraße 24, 80331 München, Germany

www.ingramcontent.com/pod-product-compliance
Lightning Source LLC
Chambersburg PA
CBHW052019290426
44112CB00014B/2298